*Learning to Speak, Learning to Listen*

# LEARNING TO SPEAK, LEARNING TO LISTEN

## How Diversity Works on Campus

SUSAN E. CHASE

*Cornell University Press*

ITHACA AND LONDON

First published 2010 by Cornell University Press
First printing, Cornell Paperbacks, 2010

Printed in the United States of America

Library of Congress Cataloging-in-Publication Data

Chase, Susan E.
    Learning to speak, learning to listen : how diversity works on campus / Susan E. Chase.
        p. cm.
    Includes bibliographical references and index.
    ISBN 978-0-8014-4912-3 (cloth : alk. paper) — ISBN 978-0-8014-7621-1 (pbk. : alk. paper)
    1. Multicultural education—United States—Case studies.   2. Intercultural com-
munication—Study and teaching (Higher)—United States—Case studies.   3. Minorities—Study and teaching (Higher)—United States—Case studies.   4. Discrimination
in higher education—United States—Case studies.   5. College students—United
States—Attitudes—Case studies.   6. Education, Higher—Social aspects—United
States—Case studies.   7. United States—Race relations—Study and teaching
(Higher)—Case studies.   I. Title.

    LC1099.3.C488 2010
    378'.017—dc22

                                                                        2010010964

Cornell University Press strives to use environmentally responsible suppliers and materials to the fullest extent possible in the publishing of its books. Such materials include vegetable-based, low-VOC inks and acid-free papers that are recycled, totally chlorine-free, or partly composed of nonwood fibers. For further information, visit our website at www.cornellpress.cornell.edu.

Cloth printing         10 9 8 7 6 5 4 3 2 1
Paperback printing     10 9 8 7 6 5 4 3 2 1

*for BC, with gratitude*

# Contents

# *Preface*

I became interested in how college students understand diversity when I began teaching sociology courses on race, class, gender, and sexual orientation. Like many college professors, I found that teaching these courses can be difficult because they are about real life situations that evoke strong emotions. Anger, defensiveness, confusion, frustration—and silence—can fill the classroom when diversity issues get addressed. I went to many faculty workshops—and organized some on my own campus—and learned about how to teach these courses. But I craved the opportunity to talk directly with students. And I wanted to do so in a context that was not burdened by my role as a teacher. To me this meant talking with students at other universities.

So, in the mid-1990s I traveled to two universities to conduct intensive group and individual interviews with a wide range of undergraduates about how they learn and think about diversity. One, which I call City University, or CU, is a private university with fewer than three thousand undergraduates, less than 20 percent of whom are students of color. The other is a large public institution with about the same percent of students of color. Although I purposely chose universities that differ from each other, I didn't anticipate how significant their differing environments would be. At CU I found that diversity was "on the table" in a way it wasn't at the large public university. At the latter, students' talk about race, gender, and sexual orientation seemed to be shaped primarily by ideas they had grown up with rather than by ideas circulating at the university. In addition, some students simply were not interested in diversity issues; they didn't see them as part of their education.

At CU the story was different. In both group and individual interviews all of the students had plenty to say, including heterosexual white men who were not involved in student organizations concerned with diversity. Thus I found that students' talk about diversity was at least partially conditioned by what was going on (or not) on their respective campuses.

As I studied the interviews I developed an especially strong interest in CU. What intrigued me was that something seemed to be *working* there. In the midst of conflict and controversy about diversity issues, some students were able to speak and listen across differences of race, gender, and sexual orientation.

Eventually, I decided to do a case study of how CU students engage diversity on campus. The result is this book. It is based primarily on data I collected shortly before, during, and after one semester in the mid-2000s, and it focuses on events during that academic year. Three years later I returned to CU for a brief follow-up study, which I report on in the epilogue.

What I found at CU in the mid-2000s sharpened my sense from the earlier study: *some*times, in *some* contexts, *some* CU students *do* learn to speak and listen across social differences, especially race. In this book I explore what that means through a sociological approach called narrative inquiry. This approach highlights something we usually take for granted: the importance of language —talk, stories, accounts—in everyday life. Throughout the book I argue that there is a relationship between how CU students speak and listen (their narrative practices) and the contexts in which they learn to speak and listen (their narrative environments). That relationship goes both ways—students' learning to speak and listen is shaped by, and it also shapes, those contexts.

The three-part structure of the book embodies this argument, which I lay out in detail in the introduction. Part I documents the contentiousness of diversity in CU's narrative environment. Everyone I talked with at CU agreed that, for better or worse, "diversity is something we talk about here." Conflicting ways of talking about diversity at CU get played out in various contexts on campus, for example, in the student newspaper and during student government meetings. Although many diversity categories are on the table at CU—gender, class, sexual orientation, ability, and nationality—race was the most prominent and contentious during the period of my study.

Part II focuses on individual students' personal narratives about learning to speak and listen across differences. For students whose voices have historically been marginalized in higher education and at CU, that learning includes discovering when and how to speak out about their experiences. For students whose voices have historically been privileged in higher education and at CU, that learning includes "putting oneself in the other's shoes" in ways that alter one's view of the other, oneself, and the social world. Students' personal narratives reflect their individual backgrounds and experiences, but patterns across their narratives show that they are also conditioned by CU's narrative environment.

Part III focuses on a protest by CU students of color against the university's failure to live up to its diversity commitments. This protest is an example of how students can explicitly disrupt a narrative environment. My interviews with faculty and administrators show that the protest affected—at least to a degree—how they took responsibility for the university's commitment to diversity. White students' responses ranged from dismissive to hostile to engaged. White students who supported their peers of color demonstrated what it means to listen, at least in this case: they made cognitive and emotional shifts that undermined conventional understandings of race relations that take white privilege for granted.

Like any case study my findings are specific to CU at a particular moment in time. And yet some readers may find CU students' stories familiar. Still, on another campus, or at CU at another time, a different diversity category might be in the spotlight and might provoke a different playing out of events. But by studying students' narratives and accounts about diversity on this campus at this particular time, I bring to light a social process that is part of daily life on any campus (or in any context for that matter): the two-way relationship between narrative practices and environments.

My study of that social process at CU reveals several things that may be useful to students and educators on other predominantly white campuses: collaboration among student organizations, student affairs offices, and academic programs can encourage speaking and listening across differences; under the right conditions, personal stories can play an important role in students' learning to speak and listen; speaking and listening across differences are intellectual and emotional skills that exemplify the educational process itself; what students are learning is not always visible to others on campus; and the voices of working-class students, *as* working-class students, are particularly difficult to hear, given the structure of many colleges and universities. I discuss these ideas in my Reflections at the end of the book.

Because race is a central topic in this book, readers might wonder how a major event in the life of the nation—the election and presidency of Barack Obama—shapes conversations about race on university campuses. Are we living in a postracial world? Like many sociologists, I observe that far from making race irrelevant, Obama's presidency has made conflicting racial discourses more visible: we hear the pride of African Americans who thought a black man would never be elected president; we hear claims that Obama is white and Kenyan and so should not even "count" as African American; we hear racist hostility on anti-Obama websites and radio talk shows, including the charge that Obama is not even American; and we hear hope for greater dialogue across differences. These racial discourses are at once familiar and reflect shifting narrative landscapes in the United States. These discourses circulate in many venues, including university campuses. But *how* they circulate and *how* specific groups engage them are empirical questions. My study offers a way of exploring these questions, no matter what events shape narrative realities in any particular time and place.

My first thanks go to all of the people at CU who gave me their perspectives on how diversity shapes their lives on campus, who invited me to observe or participate in campus events, and who responded to further questions that arose for me as I studied the interviews and other materials. I especially want to thank the CU students who shared their narratives with me, in both the group and individual interviews. Without the trust and generosity of all of these people at CU, there would be no study, no book. Furthermore, what I have learned from this study about speaking and listening across differences has influenced me personally, as a teacher and as a member of various communities.

Jessie Finch and Misti Sterling, two sociology majors at the University of Tulsa, used their sharp intellectual skills as we worked together on the content analyses. I appreciate their patience, thoroughness, and their hundreds of hours of work. We created innumerable finely detailed Excel files that record each piece of the content analyses. The tables that appear in this book summarize the results and show just a tiny portion of our work. Nonetheless, the content analyses are central to my understanding of CU's narrative environment.

I thank my sociology colleagues, Jean Blocker, Lara Foley, Ron Jepperson, and our departmental assistant, Tina Henley, for cheering me on at every step of this project. Ron made great suggestions for measures to use in the content analyses, and Tina assisted me with countless clerical tasks. Misti Sterling and Kathryn McDonald, another sociology major, served as my trusty transcribers. The University of Tulsa Research Office gave me several faculty research grants, which funded part of the transcribing and part of the work on the content analyses, as well as the purchase of Atlas-ti, a qualitative data analysis software program.

My friend, Cathey Edwards, read drafts of several chapters and gave me supportive, enthusiastic feedback. Ann Blakely, also a friend and my favorite librarian, helped me resolve tricky questions about online materials. Another friend and colleague, Joli Jensen, read every word I have written, demonstrating what it means to listen carefully to what a writer is trying to say. I am deeply grateful for her incisive questions and observations and for our long discussions about the issues themselves. Her faith in my work is a gift.

There are many people at Cornell University Press whom I want to thank. Peter Wissoker for seeing the value in my project. Anonymous reviewers for constructive criticism that helped me strengthen my arguments. Peter J. Potter for being a writer's editor—giving me specific feedback, pushing me to explain my methods and ideas clearly, caring about the writing itself, and understanding the importance of speaking and listening. I also want to thank Rachel Post for prompt, generous assistance with many details. Jack Rummel for respectful copyediting. And Karen Laun for patience with my questions and careful guidance through the production process. It has been a pleasure working with all of them.

My parents, George and Elizabeth Chase, and my family—sister, brothers, siblings-in-law, nieces, and nephews—have been a bedrock of support for me. Finally, my endless gratitude goes to my husband, John, and my daughter, Marie, who have been listening to my stories and sharing theirs with me for years.

# Introduction

At predominantly white City University, forty-five undergraduates of color and a few white allies formed an ad hoc group—and called themselves the Activists.* Fed up with the university's failure to address racial issues on campus, the Activists focused on several key concerns: the weakness of the curriculum's cultural diversity requirement; the difficult classroom climate for students of color; the lack of racial diversity among faculty; the student newspaper's problematic tone and content concerning race; and the student government's disrespectful treatment of racial matters.

The Activists' first and most public action was an unannounced silent rally. Dressed in black, they showed up en masse at a student government meeting where two of the Activists, who were student government representatives, did not answer roll call. At noon, which was partway through the meeting, the Activists stood up and left the meeting. Student government representatives debated whether to adjourn at that point. Those who argued for adjournment wanted to show support for the students of color; those who argued against felt that adjourning would disrespect the students whose business was currently on the floor. Neither argument won: they did not adjourn but they lost a quorum as some representatives left to follow the Activists.

Meanwhile, the Activists marched into the square outside City University's main administrative building, which is always busy at noon. They stood silently in a half circle and revealed their signs: "Can you hear us now?" and "Our voices must be heard." After a short while they walked around the square, and one of the Activists spoke into a microphone: "We demand a voice." Two other students came to the microphone and repeated the same

---

*"City University" and "the Activists" are pseudonyms, as are the names of all CU individuals, groups, programs, and organizations discussed in this book.

phrase. The protesters then marched into the main administrative building and gathered at the Office of Multicultural Affairs. Although they refused to talk to student newspaper reporters, they distributed a flyer that called on CU's administration to address racial issues in keeping with the university's official commitments to diversity.

During a long interview, two students of color who were members of the Activists told me about the silent rally:

*Kia:* There's so many perceptions of students of color on campus. We're the angry emotional outspoken people who always bitch and moan about things. And also we've said what we have to say but people haven't been listening. And so it was our turn to not say anything and to just do it to show how we felt. And we had signs . . . [that said] "Can you hear us now?"

*May:* "Our voices must be heard." Sometimes if we are loud and we do a rally with lots of talking or shouting people take us as . . . "the angry students of color."

*Kia:* And we *were* angry but they didn't hear us. And a lot of people were confused and they even talked about it [later] at a student government meeting. "How come they were silent?" And "Why didn't they say what they wanted?" And again we said, "We really told you and you didn't listen."

Kia and May describe the Activists' public display of silence as a strategy for *showing* that they haven't been heard in the past, a strategy for getting heard *this* time. They withdrew speech as a way of expressing their voice in a context where they have been silenced. Of course, their signs and flyer contained words that got their immediate message across, but Kia and May portray the silent rally—where no speeches were given and where protesters refused to talk to student reporters—as making a new statement: we have told you time and again why we are angry but you have not listened.

Kia and May also present the stereotype of the angry person of color—a racial image with deep roots in American culture—as a mechanism by which their voices have been dismissed in the past.[1] While they reject that "controlling image," they acknowledge that they *are* angry.[2] In addition, they express frustration with their peers' confusion about their silence. Student government representatives later asked why the Activists didn't just *say* what they were angry about. Kia and May view this as another example of people not getting the point: we were silent in order to communicate that we have spoken many times in the past and been ignored. The topic this time is our voice and your refusal to listen.

Did anyone listen this time? Yes and no. One of the Activists' demands was to have their representatives meet with members of the administration —two such meetings were held before the end of the semester. Students and administrators involved in those meetings told me that together they made plans to address the specific racial concerns the students felt had been ignored for a long time. In addition, according to faculty members I spoke with, one central administrator began to address curriculum and classroom climate with the faculty in a way he hadn't before. Another upshot was a mediated meeting between the Activists' reps and the student journalists. Accounts I heard about this meeting from some of the Activists and mediators as well as from the student journalists suggest that the journalists tried to understand the Activists' anger about how race gets presented in the paper but that the journalists remained ambivalent and confused. Nonetheless, they later published an apology for an editorial decision they eventually came to see as exhibiting unconscious racism. I also heard accounts from other groups of CU students: some dismissed the Activists' protest as irrelevant to their lives; others expressed hostility toward the Activists' claims.

What it means to listen to the Activists was demonstrated most clearly by white student allies—members of an informal group called White Students Resisting Racism. These students were already practiced in listening to their peers of color by the time of the silent rally. The Activists asked them to join their group to help them strategize their protest. When I asked the white students about their role as members of the Activists, they said:

*Sarah:* It's a very quiet role. . . .

*Melanie:* For me personally . . . it was really interesting to go to the first couple of meetings [of the Activists] and . . . have a *background* role. Because . . . in all the organizations I'm in . . . I have a pretty vocal role. But then to be a part of *this* and . . . have a more silent role, it's *unusual* for me anyways. So . . . it's been interesting to be part of this group. . . .

*Sarah:* At times it's been really exciting. Especially the first couple meetings, it was just like *exhilarating* . . . because it was like . . . "This is the way it's *supposed* to happen! . . . This is the role I'm *supposed* to be playing, and I'm not supposed to be out there." . . . We were talking about how it felt like a SNCC* meeting the first one we went to [laugh].

Sarah and Melanie describe their role among the Activists as quiet, silent, in the background. Both say this is an unusual role for them to play: they are accustomed to being leaders in their various campus activities. As such, they point to a significant shift they have undergone in their activism during recent events on campus—from being vocal and in the lead to being quiet and in the background. Over time I came to understand their quietness, their stepping back among the Activists, as representing the shift these students have undergone more broadly regarding racial consciousness.

As Sarah and Melanie hint at, that shift involves understanding that some-

*SNCC, the Student Nonviolent Coordinating Committee, played an influential role in the civil rights movement of the 1960s, organizing marches, sit-ins, and freedom rides. African American students created and led this organization, which some white students joined.

times *others*—students of color in this case—are entitled to be at the center, to speak, to tell their stories. This shift is an unfamiliar experience for people—white students in this case—who normally take for granted their entitlement to speak and get heard. Although it is unfamiliar, Sarah describes this new relationship as exhilarating, as the way it's supposed to be, as reminiscent of interracial cooperation during the civil rights movement of the 1960s.

## The Book

Kia and May's account of the silent rally and Sarah and Melanie's account of their role among the Activists capture much of what this book is about. First, it is about the complexity of voices and stories like those of the Activists. These students of color construct CU as infused with institutional racism. Their complaints are familiar—much research has documented racism at predominantly white colleges and universities across the United States.[3] At the same time, these students present themselves as entitled to speak forcefully against racism on campus. Their voice—projected paradoxically in their silence during the rally—is confident and creative. And *that* aspect of their voice and their story—*that* they speak with confidence, creativity, and a sense of their right to get heard—is what interested me. What does that confident voice sound like? Where does that confidence come from? And what difference do their voices and stories make on campus?

Second, the book is about the complexity of the listening exemplified by the white allies. Their account about their quietness in relation to their peers may sound odd. Does being quiet mean being passive? As we shall see, these students construct their listening not as passivity but as an active posture that requires learning to understand race and racism in new ways. What does that active listening look like? How have they learned to listen? And what difference do *their* voices and stories make on campus?

Finally, this book is about the social contexts in which CU students' speaking and listening takes place. What conditions encourage students whose voices are not usually prominent in institutions of higher education to speak out—and encourage privileged students to listen? What circumstances make the Activists' protest possible? What allows for the range of responses to the Activists' protest—the administrators' partial responsiveness, the student journalists' ambivalence, some students' dismissiveness, other students' hostility, *and* the white allies' supportiveness?

I use the words *accounts, stories, voices, speaking,* and *listening* because I address what is going on at CU through a sociological approach called narrative inquiry. This approach zeroes in on the fact that much of our daily lives consists of talk, stories, and accounts of various kinds. Narrative inquiry is grounded in theoretical traditions that treat language as *constituting,* or *constructing,* social reality.[4] As people talk about themselves, others, and the world around them, they do not simply convey information; they also give meaning to actions and events. Indeed, we can see that Kia, May, Sarah, and Melanie's accounts are *about* speech and silence in the events they describe; their accounts are about who said—or didn't say—what to whom, how, and why.

There are several types of narrative inquiry, but the type I use focuses on *narrative reality.* This concept, coined by Jaber Gubrium and James Holstein, refers to features of our everyday lives that we usually take for granted —not only the ubiquity of talk, stories, and accounts of various kinds, but also how they unfold through interaction in specific situations, and how they are consequential for our identities, relationships, and communities.[5]

One aspect of narrative reality consists of our *narrative practices,* what we are doing as we speak (or write). As we talk, tell stories, and give accounts, we are not only talking about things, we are simultaneously constructing our identities, experiences, and social realities in relation to this audience in this time and place. Another aspect of narrative reality consists of our *narrative environments,* the set of circumstances and conditions—the contexts—in which we speak. These contexts are both local and general, both spatial and temporal. They include who I am talking to and where I am speaking (for example, to myself in my journal, to my friends in a dorm room, to the whole campus in a letter to the student newspaper); the understandings that my audience and I bring to this situation because of our backgrounds, life experiences, and the kind of situation it is; and the broader cultural meanings that shape how this topic can be articulated and addressed at this time and place in history.

Perhaps the most important point about the concept of narrative reality is that the relationship between our narrative practices and our narrative environments is reflexive: our narrative practices are at once shaped by *and* shape our narrative environments. This means that narrative reality in any particular case is dynamic and constantly re-created.[6]

I can say all of this more simply. We all know (usually without thinking about it), that what we say and how we say it are influenced by various circumstances, such as who we are talking to, where we are speaking, and what we are trying to accomplish by speaking in this way to this audience in this time and place. We know that when we speak or communicate in any way we are *doing* something—we might be joking, insulting, explaining, entertaining, spinning a tall tale, trying to provoke or avoid a confrontation, any combination of these, or any number of other things. We know that we can't just say *anything*—that what we say and how we say it has to make sense to and be credible to those we converse with, otherwise we get treated as crazy, incompetent, or irrelevant. In this sense, we know that when we speak, we are constructing our identities and our realities for ourselves and others. For instance, in different situations on campus, a student might speak in ways that construct his or her identity as a good friend, a trusted leader, an aspiring journalist, or a fun-loving partygoer.

Furthermore, we know that what we say and how we say it—and how others respond to us—will have consequences for our interactions and relationships, including what others think of us and what we think of them. Finally—and this is the sociological leap—what gets said, where, how, to whom, why, and with what consequences *itself* becomes part of the circumstances that influence what we and others say next and how we and they say it. This is the reflexive interplay between narrative practices and narrative environments.

We know these things but we don't usually stop and think about them. This doesn't mean they are unconscious in a psychological sense. It means that we enact these social processes constantly and at the same time we typically take them for granted as we go about our lives. Social theorists call this the "natural attitude" of daily life, and they call what we take for granted the "seen but unnoticed background expectancies" of our activities.[7]

My study brings these social processes to the foreground. It is about CU students' narrative reality—it is about the reflexive interplay between CU students' narrative practices concerning diversity and CU's narrative environment.

Let me spell this out through the example of the silent rally, which can be understood as a narrative practice within CU's narrative environment. Through the silent rally, the Activists "spoke" with a specific goal in mind (changing the way race is treated on campus); they spoke to specific audiences (student journalists, student government representatives, faculty and administrators, the campus at large); and they spoke in a specific set of contexts and circumstances (the student government meeting they attended and left; the campus's main square; a long series of events on campus that year; and the myriad ways that diversity gets discussed on campus and in American culture).

As a narrative practice, the silent rally did not come out of nowhere. As we shall see in part I, CU's narrative landscape is filled with controversy about diversity topics, especially race. In part, then, the silent rally was made possible by—it was conceivable and intelligible in—CU's narrative environment. On another campus, a silent rally like this might be inconceivable or unintelligible. A broader narrative environment is also relevant here. The Activists didn't invent the idea of a silent rally and neither did anyone else at CU; the strategy of communicating through a public show of silence has a long history in efforts to bring attention to social injustices.[8]

Although the Activists' silent rally was influenced by these features of the narrative environment, it was not *determined* by them. The very concept of narrative practice means that speech (like any action) is conditioned but not determined by its circumstances. Furthermore, the influence goes both ways. The silent rally had consequences for others on campus. It became part of the narrative environment at CU to which others responded in a variety of ways.

And those responses in turn had consequences for the Activists. Again, because the relationship between narrative practices and narrative environments is reflexive, narrative reality is dynamic and constantly re-created. What people say and how it gets heard can be predictable—or surprising, jolting, and disruptive.

While part I explores the contentious character of CU's narrative landscape, parts II and III show that in the midst of conflict and controversy over diversity issues, *some*times, in *some* contexts, *some* CU students *do* learn to speak and listen across social differences, especially race.

I am not arguing that CU and CU students are unique. Research on diversity in higher education shows that many colleges and universities are creating programs, policies, and curricula that facilitate learning across social differences. My work is indebted to and draws on this research. My work also contributes to it. I bring to light what is present but usually goes unnoticed in these studies, even those that describe successful programs and student learning across differences. What is present but typically unnoticed is the narrative reality that is a central feature of social life on any university campus. Successful programs and student learning across differences consist largely of people interacting with each other, creating relationships and communities with each other, *with words, stories, and accounts of various kinds.* I am asking: what is going on at CU—what kinds of narrative practices in what kinds of narrative environments—such that some students are learning to speak and listen across differences? What does it look like (sound like) when students speak and listen in these ways? And under what kinds of narrative conditions does it happen?

My work is also indebted to research on racial discourses in American culture and how they get expressed in everyday talk. In these studies, researchers focus, like I do, on language—words, stories, and accounts—as social action through which people construct their identities and realities. A major finding of this research is that racism is so deeply institutionalized in Western culture that even people with good intentions who don't think of themselves as racist often end up reproducing racism in their talk.[9]

These studies help me to analyze how broad cultural discourses about race infiltrate CU students' narrative practices. At the same time, my book contributes to this body of research by bringing the *local* narrative environment into view. My study shows that university students' talk is conditioned not only by broad cultural discourses but also by the local circumstances of its production—by features of the campus contexts and specific situations in which their talk takes shape.[10]

To put this somewhat differently, when I decided to do a case study of how CU students engage diversity, I didn't begin with a focus on race. Rather, I *found* that race is the most prominent and contentious diversity category at CU. At another university it might have been gender, religion, nationality, sexual orientation, something else, or some combination of these.

Twenty years from now it might be something different at CU. My focus on CU students' narrative reality means I ask *how* race gets constructed as the most prominent and the most contentious, how racial (as well as other diversity) issues unfold through students' interactions in specific situations on campus, and how CU students' engagement with various diversity topics is consequential for their identities, relationships, and education.[11]

Finally, I recognize that the narrative practices of speaking and listening across differences are not unique to universities. Many groups and organizations in the United States and throughout the globe are dedicated to dialogue across social differences as part of their commitment to peace and social justice.[12] But it makes sense to look to the university as a site where this learning to speak and listen *might* happen. The university is, by definition, an institution where education—especially of young people at the cusp of adulthood—takes place. A deeply taken-for-granted aspect of higher education, especially in universities and colleges based in the liberal arts, is that this is a time and place where students learn to open their minds. As I demonstrate that some CU students, sometimes, in some contexts learn to speak and listen across social differences, I will argue that this exemplifies the educational process itself—opening one's mind, thinking critically, and reconsidering familiar ideas.

## The Case Study

CU is a private university with an undergraduate enrollment of fewer than three thousand students, less than 20 percent of whom are students of color. I collected most of the data for my study shortly before, during, and after one semester in the mid-2000s.

I conducted intensive interviews with a wide range of student groups as well as with individual students. And I conducted interviews with faculty, staff, and administrators to get some background on how CU approaches diversity and how the issues play out on campus. (I did forty-nine interviews total; see appendix C.) I also did a limited amount of participant observation. For example, I attended the annual awards ceremony of the Office of Multicultural Affairs, and I participated in a discussion held by a multiracial group of students that had been meeting all year to discuss social justice under the auspices of a campus office. Between interviews I hung out at the student center and in the residence halls where I had a chance to observe students interacting in small groups.

Before I went to CU to conduct the interviews, I read several months worth of the student newspaper and student government minutes, so I was well informed about what was going on. For example, I knew about events that led to the formation of the Activists and about the silent rally, as well as about various perspectives on the Activists' protest.

After I left CU, I wanted to get a wider angle on its narrative environment than I could gather from the interviews alone. And so Jessie Finch, Misti Sterling (sociology majors at my university), and I conducted multiyear content analyses of CU's student newspaper, student government minutes, curriculum, calendar of events, and web site (the last at one point in time). We also conducted identical content analyses (same years, same methods) of the same documents at another university (RU) that is structurally similar to CU (private, less than three thousand undergraduates, less than 20 percent students of color). These comparative content analyses helped me to characterize CU's narrative environment. (Appendix D has details about the content analyses.)

In addition, the student newspaper and student government minutes gave me another source, beyond the interviews, of students' accounts about diversity. The student newspaper and student government are realms in which students exercise substantial control—unlike the curriculum, the events calendar, and the university's web site, which are largely controlled by faculty and administrators.

I found that CU students frequently discussed diversity issues in the newspaper and during student government meetings. For example, in Kia and May's account about the silent rally, Kia quoted student government representatives' questions about the Activists' silence at the student government meeting: "'How come they were silent?' And 'Why didn't they say what they wanted?'" The minutes show that student government representatives did discuss at length the Activists' presence at their meeting and what they should or shouldn't do in response. By comparing various accounts—in different interviews, in the newspaper, in the minutes—I was able to describe events that I had not observed. Furthermore, the amount of talk in students' individual and group interviews about what was written in the newspaper or said during student government meetings suggests that those student-controlled arenas are narratively consequential at CU.

A final source of data for my study consists of numerous documents that various people gave me or that I got from the web site, for example, the official protest document that the Activists sent to CU administrators, a zine published by White Students Resisting Racism after the silent rally, a study comparing CU to peer institutions in terms of its services to students of color, a student's honors thesis about CU's cultural diversity requirement, administrators' speeches, reports about the Faculty Diversity Group on campus, and a history of CU written by a CU alum.

I approached *all* of the various accounts about diversity issues and events as data about CU students' narrative reality—the stories students told me during individual and group interviews; the letters and opinion pieces students wrote in the student newspaper; the debates they had during student government meetings; the accounts faculty, staff, and administrators gave me; the documents I gathered; and my own field notes about the events I observed. In so doing, I was able to bring to light the interplay between students' narrative practices and CU's narrative environment. Taken as a whole, these accounts reveal patterns within CU students' narrative reality.

After the provost gave me permission to do my case study at CU, other administrators helped me identify student groups as well as faculty, staff, and administrators to contact. My aim was to get a wide range of perspectives (see appendix C). I met with twelve groups of students: several student newspaper journalists; several student government representatives; the Southeast Asian Association; the GLBT Student Organization; Students for Firearm Safety and Recreation; the Black Collegians; the Conservative Students; the Women's Coalition; Students for Disability Rights; White Students Resisting Racism; and two informal groups of students in the residence halls who were pulled together for me by their resident advisers.

Dressed casually and armed with snacks, I met with student groups in the location they chose: a quiet room in the student center, their student organization office, a residence hall lounge, or their apartment. Because students in each group already knew each other—either from their activities in their student organization or from living together—I didn't have to work too hard to turn the interviews into group discussions of the type they might ordinarily have with each other. In that sense, these were different from focus group interviews where participants are strangers and the interaction is governed by the interviewers' questions. I got the discussion going with general questions: What issues has your group been dealing with this year? How, if at all, is your group involved in diversity issues? Does productive dialogue about diversity take place on campus? What have been the most contentious diversity issues on campus this year? (See appendix C for the interview guides.) Then I followed students' lead as they talked with me and each other about these topics.

At the end of the group interviews, I asked students to write down background and demographic information about themselves, and I asked for volunteers for individual interviews. By the time I interviewed students individually, I had already talked with them in a group setting and I knew quite a bit about them personally. I guided the twenty-five individual student interviews with these general questions: What were you like in high school? What was the transition to college like for you? What have been your most important learning experiences at CU? And if diversity had not already come up (usually it had by this point): What is your perspective on diversity issues at CU? Again, I followed students' lead as they developed narratives in response to these questions.

My interviews with faculty, staff, and administrators gave me another angle on CU students' narrative reality. With faculty, staff, and administrators, my identity as a professor seemed to make connection easy because I shared with them knowledge about such things as academic freedom, administrative hierarchies, mission statements, the slowness of institutional change, and ratings in *U.S. News and World Report*. I did discover, however, that some faculty thought I had been hired by CU as a consultant. I quickly cleared up that misperception, but it is interesting that it arose. A faculty member explained that I was probably mistaken for a consultant because some of CU's diversity-related programs have been externally funded, and the funding agencies require external evaluations. It wasn't odd at CU to have an outsider come in to ask questions about diversity.

In fact, CU students, faculty, and administrators were already so accustomed to talking about diversity that my interest in studying that did not surprise anyone. Mostly, people seemed to see me as an outsider—but as a knowledgeable outsider. In the course of the interviews, people would sometimes interrupt themselves to ask, "Have you heard about x?" and most of the time I was able to say, "Yes, I read about that in the student newspaper or in the student government minutes or in such and such a document." Because I knew those accounts were contentious, though, I would always add "but I need to hear your take on that."

What about the fact that I am a white, middle-aged woman? I can't know exactly how these aspects of my identity made a difference, but I'm sure they did. At one point in my discussion with the Black Collegians, a student turned to me to explain the slang word she had just used ("tude"). That was the only time someone *verbalized* an assumption that I wouldn't know what she was talking about because of my race, my age, or both. I suspect that students, faculty, and administrators of color talked more or less easily with me about race and racism in large part because these are frequent topics in a variety of contexts at CU. Many people of color at CU are accustomed to talking with white people about race and racism on this predominantly white campus.

Nonetheless, because social identities influence how people perceive and interact with each other, it is likely that people would have talked differently to a researcher of color or of a different nationality, or to a researcher who is younger, older, male, visibly disabled, and so on. In fact, Steven, a student of color and one of two students I interviewed who did not participate in any of the group interviews, told me at the end of our time together that he would not have talked to me at all if I had not approached him by saying "Professor Moore told me that I should I talk to you." He meant that our racial difference had been an issue for him. More than anyone else I met at CU, Steven shaped our interview into a conversation, with him asking me as many questions—mostly about my teaching and how my university approaches diversity—as I asked him. My sense was that he enjoyed our exchange as much as I did.

## Turning Talk into Text

Using the lens of narrative inquiry to study how students engage diversity had consequences for how I turned the interview data into text on the written page.[13] Transcribing interviews is often treated as a technical issue—you just type what people say. But there's another way to look at it. Catherine Riessman argues that the very act of transcribing reveals the researcher's theory of language and so is not just a technical matter.[14] I explained earlier that narrative inquiry is grounded in theory that treats language (talk, stories, and accounts of any kind) as social action, as giving meaning to events and experiences, as constituting social realities in particular ways in particular situations. This theory of language differs from a more commonsensical one that treats words as referential, as containing self-evident content that exists apart from the circumstances and situations in which the words are used. Narrative researchers who embrace a theory of language as social action, and who treat talk, stories, and accounts as the focus of our studies—make careful decisions about how we turn talk into text.

If this sounds odd, the analogy of photography may help, as Elliot Mishler and Catherine Riessman point out.[15] At first thought, a photograph seems to capture an objective reality "out there." It seems like a copy of the scene. Similarly, a transcript seems to be a copy of spoken words. But any photographer knows that in taking a picture (as well as in developing, photo shopping, and framing it) he or she directs the viewer's attention to particular aspects of a scene. Narrative researchers also direct a reader's attention in specific ways when they turn talk into text. They choose a transcription style that highlights the narrative practices they want to study.

Like many narrative researchers, I aim to make visible what people are doing as they narrate their experiences. This means attending to what people say *and* how they say it. I include speech practices such as interruptions, laughter, repetitions, and direct speech (also called reported speech, which means quoting oneself or other people). I also attend to the contexts in which they speak. These contexts include the relationship between me and the individuals I interviewed, the interaction among students in the group interviews, the contentious narrative environment at CU, as well as broad cultural discourses about diversity in American culture. My aim is to understand what a speaker is communicating, to whom, for what purposes, and with what consequences (to the extent that I can determine the latter by attending to different people's accounts about the same issue or event).

Let me show you how transcription style matters. Below is a revised version of the excerpt from my interview with Kia and May, which appears as the first interview excerpt in this chapter. This time I use the transcribing method that I use in the rest of the book. My point is not that this transcription method is objectively better than the other one, but that this one better serves my interpretive interests in this study. For the sake of showing the revisions clearly, I have put in bold the parts of the transcript that I did not include earlier. (See appendix B for specific transcription notations.)

*Susan:* **Can you tell me in your words—**
**Just say more about why it was a silent protest**
*Kia:* There's so many perceptions of students of color on campus
We're the angry emotional outspoken people who always bitch and moan about
    things
And also we've said what we have to say
But people haven't been listening
And so it was our turn to not say anything
And to just do it to show how we felt
And we had signs
*Susan:* **What did your signs say?**
*Kia:* "Can you hear us now?"
*May:* "Our voices must be heard"
Sometimes if we are loud
And we do a rally with lots of talking or shouting
People take us as **the angry or the—**
**"That's how they are"**
**"They're always angry"**
"The angry students of color"
*Kia:* And we *were* angry but they didn't hear us
And a lot of people were confused
And they even talked about it [later] at a student government meeting
"How come they were silent?"
And "Why didn't they say what they wanted?"
And again we said
"We really told you and you didn't listen"
*Susan:* **So you were making a new kind of statement by being silent this time**
*Kia:* **Right.**

This transcript makes visible two things that we cannot see in the earlier transcript. First, by including my questions and comments, this transcript shows that Kia and May's description of the silent rally arose during an interview with me, and specifically in response to my questions. So this transcript gives the reader access to one layer of context—one aspect of the narrative environment (the interview with me)—in which their story arose. It's noteworthy that although the silent rally was an occasion *not* to speak in order to communicate, Kia and May *do* speak to me. And in contrast to the student government reps who didn't understand the silent rally, the last two lines of the transcript show that I *do* get what they are saying. Importantly though, I didn't always get what students said to me during interviews, and in those cases I also include my questions and comments in the transcripts. Not getting something doesn't necessarily mean I was slow or stupid, but it does indicate that I was missing something about the narrative environment. In those cases, what I didn't get became data about CU's narrative environment and thus worthy of interpretation.

Second, instead of using a conventional paragraph format as I did for the transcript earlier in the chapter, I use line breaks to separate speech clauses, which are often but not always subject-verb clauses.[16] This transcription style accentuates the differences between talk and prose writing. In fact, it makes people's speech look like poetry. Some narrative researchers even group lines together in what they call stanzas, which are thematically distinct. I do not present my transcripts in stanza form. But I do use line breaks to make it easier for readers to see that as people talk, they sometimes rephrase their thoughts, repeat themselves, or interrupt themselves to comment on what they are saying. A conventional paragraph format, which imitates prose writing, makes these narrative practices seem superfluous and makes the transcripts difficult to read. After all, people don't write prose with repetitions and interruptions. Or, if they do, that writing is difficult to read. But people *do* speak that way. When line breaks are used, these narrative practices become more visible and they invite interpretation.

For example, in the earlier version of the transcript, I deleted the lines where May repeats the word *angry*. (Deletions are shown by ellipses.) In the new transcript we can see that May uses the word *angry* not just once but three times, and that the second and third times she uses direct speech to put the words in others' mouths. In his studies of how college students use reported speech when talking about race, Richard Buttny states, "Direct speech is a powerful way to hold another accountable, since it more fully reconstructs the particular speech acts of the event purportedly through the person's own words."[17] Buttny also finds that people frequently use reported speech to criticize members of another racial group. Here, by quoting what white students presumably say, May presents white students' perception of students of color as angry, *and* their anger as more than a temporary condition. When May states that white students say "'That's how they are,'" and "'They're always angry,'" she captures her sense of a narrative reality on campus in which white students construct students of color as *inherently* angry, not angry because of certain circumstances. She uses others' statements to communicate her understanding of *how* white students dismiss students of color's speech. Students who are always angry, inherently angry, are unreasonable; they do not deserve to be listened to. May's repetition of "angry" and her use of direct speech communicate clearly that she feels this dismissive perception of students of color is deeply unjust. Similarly, Kia uses reported speech to give evidence of *her* claim: student government members do not get what students of color are saying.

I also pay close attention to students' narrative practices when I present excerpts from students' editorials and letters in the student newspaper, their discussions during student government meetings, and documents they wrote during the public protest. Of course, I keep these texts in their original written format. But in these texts as well, students construct their identities, experiences, and social realities, for specific audiences, for specific purposes, and with specific implications for their interactions, relationships, and communities on campus.

# PART ONE

# City University's Narrative Landscape

# I   Diversity at City University

In the United States, most predominantly white colleges and universities paid little attention to matters of race, gender, and sexual orientation until the 1950s and 1960s. That inattention was disrupted by both internal and external pressures: student and faculty involvement in the civil rights, women's, and gay liberation movements, the passage of federal antidiscrimination laws, and the increase in the number of women and people of color enrolling in higher education.[1]

Now, well into the twenty-first century, "diversity" has become *institutionalized* in higher education.[2] This does not mean that colleges and universities have *achieved* diversity and equity. It means that colleges' and universities' attention to diversity has become expected and routine. In predominantly white institutions, the general direction of change has been toward greater racial and ethnic diversity in the student body,[3] and to a lesser extent, the faculty;[4] a proliferation of student services aimed at retaining and graduating diverse groups of students; the creation of policies on affirmative action, discrimination, harassment, violence, and accommodation (of student with disabilities);[5] and the establishment of courses and programs in women's studies, racial-ethnic studies, disability studies, and GLBT/queer studies.[6]

At the same time, universities have embraced institutional narratives about commitments to diversity, which they do not always live up to in practice. Clarence G. Williams writes, "MIT is typical of many predominantly white institutions in that . . . concepts like diversity, recruitment, and inclusion are often expressed but not always or consistently acted on."[7] In the United States, 74 percent of universities now include statements about their commitment to diversity in their mission statements.[8]

## City University's Diversity History

In many ways, CU's history concerning diversity follows this general pattern for predominantly white universities. The following examples from historical accounts and documents show that, over the years, CU has developed a consistent institutional narrative of commitment to diversity and to a safe, welcoming campus.[9]

In the late 1960s, CU's arts and sciences faculty endorsed the university's first formal statement of intention to recruit a more diverse student body, faculty, and administration. Within a few years, CU created a permanent committee whose purpose was to enhance cultural diversity on campus. The long-range plan of the late 1970s called for increased support for people of color on campus. In the early 1990s, a president-appointed commission on diversity outlined several goals and the financial resources required for reaching them. These goals concerned representation of women and people of color among the university's trustees, administrators, faculty, and staff; racial and geographic (including international) diversity of students; curriculum changes to include the contributions of women and people of color; a commitment to creating conditions that would encourage individuals from different backgrounds to learn from each other; and attention to racism, sexism, and homophobia in the campus climate. In the mid-1990s, after a year of campuswide discussion and debate, CU's board of trustees adopted a cultural diversity policy that, among other things, affirmed a commitment to campuswide education about racism, sexism, and homophobia. In the early 2000s, the first goal of the arts and sciences strategic plan focused on establishing and maintaining a diverse community. That goal included increasing the number of students of color, international students, and faculty of color; making efforts to retain them; increasing the number of CU students studying abroad; and providing funds for proposals to integrate diversity topics into the curriculum.

Several concrete changes have accompanied CU's institutional narrative of commitment to a diverse and safe, welcoming campus. CU's first efforts to recruit students of color began in the early 1970s with the creation of the Office of Minority Students. During the 1970s, the percent of students of color increased from almost none to 3 percent, but retention was an ongoing problem. In the early 1970s, African American students created the Black Collegians, an organization chartered by the student government. The Office of Minority Students went through various transformations but for many years it had little support from the institution in terms of staffing or financial support. In the late 1980s, the director of Multicultural Affairs told a researcher he felt he was colluding with the university's lack of commitment by working in the understaffed and underfunded office. Currently, the Office of Multicultural Affairs is better staffed, but its budget remains near the bottom among ten peer institutions. As mentioned earlier, fewer than 20 percent of CU undergraduates are now students of color. Over the years, various groups of students of color created organizations that were chartered by the student government.

CU's cultural diversity report of the late 1970s noted that the university employed only one or two faculty of color. By the late 1990s about 10 percent of full-time faculty in the college of arts and sciences identified themselves as of color, including international people of color. By the mid-2000s, 15 percent identified themselves as such, two-thirds of whom were U.S. citizens of color. About half of full-time arts and sciences faculty were women.

In the early 1980s, CU students created a student-run women's center. Although students and faculty hoped that the center would get financial support to hire a full-time director, that never happened, and in the early 1990s, the center became the Women's Coalition, a student organization chartered by the student government. The GLB Student Organization was chartered in the mid-1990s, and later added "Transgender" to its name, as has been the trend at universities across the nation. An Office for Disability Support was created in the early 2000s, and it currently has a full-time director and assistant director. Students for Disability Rights was chartered in the mid-2000s. By that time, most professors were routinely including in their syllabi a statement encouraging students with disabilities to self-identify with the Office for Disability Support. Nonetheless, one of the main administrative buildings on campus is still not easily accessible by wheelchair, a point of contention for students with physical disabilities. A student who uses a wheelchair told me, "I have never been in that building in my four years at CU."

Over the last twenty-five years, like many universities, CU has created several interdisciplinary academic programs that focus on the study of race, ethnicity, gender, and world cultures. In the late 1980s, also like many universities, the arts and sciences faculty voted to add a cultural diversity component to the general curriculum. That component required students to take three courses from at least two of three categories: courses that include the contributions and experiences of women and racial/ethnic minorities; courses about other world cultures; and courses that develop cross-cultural skills and personal understanding of other world cultures either through studying abroad or learning a foreign language.

Ten years later, the faculty curriculum committee proposed several changes to the requirement: that class, ability, and sexual orientation be added to the first category; that students be required to take one course from the first category; and that "other world cultures" in the second category be changed to "non-western cultures." Only the first of these proposals was approved by the faculty. Since then, apart from slight changes in wording, the cultural diversity requirement has remained the same. One of the Activists' major complaints was that CU students can fulfill this requirement by studying a European language and European history and can graduate without ever taking a course on race or any other diversity topic *in the United States.*[10]

## City University's Diversity Strength

So far CU's diversity history seems fairly typical of predominantly white universities in the United States. Changes in CU's curriculum, student services, and in the composition of its student body and faculty reflect the general direction of change exhibited by most institutions. But that is not the whole story about diversity at CU. Unlike some predominantly white universities, CU has also developed substantial diversity-related strengths. Most notable are the interconnections among four organizational entities: the Office of Student Affairs, the Office of Multicultural Affairs (housed in the Office of Student Affairs), certain student organizations, and the Faculty Diversity Group. Through their informal collaborative work, these entities constitute a small but critical mass that has succeeded over the years in creating programs and spaces that strongly support students of color, international students, GLBT students, women students, students with disabilities (to a certain extent), as well as white students, straight students, male students, and able-bodied students interested in diversity issues. Of course, students are not only supported by but also contribute to this community.

I will describe each of these organizational entities in some detail because I found that together they play a pivotal role in how diversity gets addressed at CU. Readers need this information in order to understand students' personal narratives and their accounts about events at CU. This "interconnected group," as I will refer to it, appears many times throughout this book. (In addition to these four entities, some individuals such as librarians and staff and faculty in other departments also contributed to the interconnected group's activities.) My finding about the significance of this interconnected group supports one of Williams's "principles and strategies" for institutional change: "Recognize that growing numbers [of students and faculty of color] are only one measure of success; qualitative aspects—culture, human psychology, communication, interaction—need equal if not more attention."[11]

### *Office of Student Affairs (OSA)*

The services and programs of CU's OSA are similar to those of its counterparts on many campuses, except that they are infused with diversity-oriented practices. In the early 2000s, all OSA staff participated in long-term diversity education; those at the level of program director attended ninety hours of workshops over three years. In their accounts about these workshops and about the high quality of the discussions they have had about diversity since then, OSA staff echoed what one director told me: "In my professional experience, those have been unusual conversations." OSA's focus on diversity education extends to workshops provided for students who work as resident advisers in the residence halls and as student leaders in various capacities on campus.

OSA's Office of Student Life provides a house on campus for a handful of African American students and one for GLBT students; it also organizes theme floors in the residence halls on social justice issues.[12] In the mid-2000s, it began offering students the option of male/female roommates when one of the roommates is gay or lesbian and the other is straight. Responding to a recommendation by the GLBT Student Organization, first-year students are now asked, along with other questions about their living preferences, whether they would be comfortable rooming with a GLBT student.

OSA's Service Learning Program offers spring break trips focused on economic and racial issues, as well as community service through a long-term project on homelessness. In the early 1990s, CU began a university–public school partnership with a nearby school, the aims of which are to support children in their goal to prepare for college and to support CU participants in their desire to learn from and contribute to the local community.

In the early 2000s, OSA was instrumental in creating CU's crisis response team. Through this mechanism, CU's administration has responded quickly to hate incidents such as antigay and anti-Semitic graffiti on campus. The administration informs the campus community by e-mail that an incident has occurred and what steps they will take in response.

### Office of Multicultural Affairs (OMA)

Despite a limited budget, OMA has created programs that are widely recognized on campus as providing strong support for students of color, international students, and white students with an interest in racial justice. These include events that are familiar on many campuses, such as celebrations of Martin Luther King Jr. Day and cultural heritage months. But they also include programs that are less common, such as an annual social justice symposium which examines commonalities across various social justice concerns (racism, classism, sexism, heterosexism). OMA hosts an orientation for first-year students of color, as well as one for international students; an annual retreat for students of color, and one for international students; a peer mentor program for students of color and international students; a quarterly newsletter; and an annual ceremony at which academic, service, and leadership awards are given.

And there's more. Each year OMA organizes a multiracial group of students, faculty, and staff who attend the five-day National Conference on Race and Ethnicity in Higher Education (NCORE). After the conference, the group meets regularly and develops programming for the next academic year to further education on campus about race. Projects initiated by NCORE groups over the years include a Race Column in the student newspaper; a monthly public conversation, called My Life, which features students, faculty, staff, and community members from different racial and ethnic groups talking about how their various identities have shaped their lives; an informal group for white students who want to discuss race, racism, and white racial identities; and a local Race Conference (RC).

RC is an annual three-part conference that focuses on race, racism, racial justice, racial identity development, and bridging divides among racial groups on campus. Students must apply, and a multiracial group of about forty students gets selected each year. A multiracial group of facilitators is drawn from faculty, administrators, and students who have attended NCORE or RC in previous years. RC includes a preconference meeting on campus at which students begin building connections across groups, learn the difference between individual prejudice and institutional racism, and take stock of where CU stands in its commitment to diversity. The weekend retreat itself, which takes place off campus, aims to create a safe environment where students can discuss difficult racial topics. A postconference meeting, held back on campus, helps RC participants plan how they will individually and collectively put what they have learned into practice.

When I asked students about instances of productive dialogue about diversity on campus, they talked about RC more than anything else. Both white students and students of color who had attended RC described it as a very powerful learning experience. Even students who had not attended had heard about it. As one student who had not been to RC said, "Every single person that I've talked to that's done it has said that it was the most traumatic but also the best weekend they've ever been through."

### Student Organizations

CU's student government grants charters to student organizations that apply for chartered status, which makes them eligible for student government funding for programming and conference travel. During the chartering process, the student government officially designates certain organizations as "advocacy organizations." These are groups whose purpose is to advance the culture and rights of people who have not had equal access to opportunities and privileges at CU or in the United States generally. They include the Women's Coalition, the GLBT Organization, Students for Disability Rights, Black Collegians, Asian Student Organization, Southeast Asian Association, Latino/a Coalition, Association of African Students, International Student Organization, and Organization for Multiracial Students and Transracial Adoptees. Advocacy organizations are expected to provide support for their members and to offer educational programs for everyone on campus. A standing committee of the student government serves as an advocate within the student government for the advocacy organizations.

Many student organizations at CU—not just the advocacy groups—are chartered and thus are eligible for funds. Student of color organizations and international student organizations use these funds to sponsor many events during traditional cultural heritage months; the GLBT Organization provides programs during National Coming Out Week; and the Women's Coalition organizes events for Women's History Month. These groups are active during the rest of the academic year as well.

At CU there are also informal diversity-oriented student groups that are not chartered by the student government but which forge ties with those that are, either through common membership or common interests. These include White Students Resisting Racism, Men Against Sexism, Multicultural Student Group (which encourages leaders of the student of color and international student organizations to work collaboratively), and Community Commitment (which sponsors a campuswide speaker each fall on a social justice topic as well as an annual Not on Our Campus Rally, which targets multiple forms of discrimination).

### Faculty Diversity Group (FDG)

Since the late 1990s, a group of twenty to twenty-five faculty members from a broad range of disciplines across the university has met regularly to discuss diversity issues. Their discussions often revolve around readings that help them understand what students of *all* colors face in the classroom when race is part of the curriculum (or not) and how faculty can support their learning. Over the years, the group has developed an ethos of support for faculty who teach diversity topics in their classes as well as support for faculty of color on campus. By design, at least one-fourth of FDG's members are faculty of color. The group has limited its numbers and emphasized consistent participation to facilitate trust and conversation in which members are willing to risk challenging themselves. A Jewish faculty member's comments indicate the sense of trust that has developed within FDG: "It's one of the few places I feel comfortable even raising the issue of anti-Semitism on campus. Not that I experience a lot of anti-Semitism, but you don't have to experience it to worry about it. It's one of the only places I've felt comfortable even saying the word and feeling heard and supported and able to talk about it."

In recent years, FDG has developed a reputation on campus as a pressure group, helping to keep diversity on administrative agendas—for example, pushing for rewards for faculty involvement in diversity efforts, pushing for a strong response system to hate incidents (which developed into the crisis response team), and pushing for sustained attention to diversity in faculty recruitment and retention. In the early 2000s, the dean of arts and sciences supported FDG's recommendation that leaders of color in the local community be invited to serve on faculty search committees. He offered to pay honoraria to community leaders who serve on these committees. CU administrators now routinely call on FDG members to facilitate faculty conversations about diversity in the curriculum and classroom, for example, at the annual faculty retreat.

In addition, FDG has functioned as support for funded projects carried out by the group's coordinator, including focus group research on classroom climate at CU; grants for supporting faculty in curriculum transformation (grants were awarded to non-FDG faculty); a seven-week summer workshop on teaching diversity and social justice; and the training of students, staff, and faculty so that they can help educate others on campus about diversity. This last project funded the first NCORE group, which later came under OMA's purview. The coordinator of FDG stated that in his more than twenty years as an educator and consultant in higher education, he has found FDG's collaborative work unusual.

### The Interconnected Group

Although these four entities are organizationally distinct, there are many informal connections among them. For example, OMA provides substantial support to student of color and international student advocacy organizations, and it fosters ties among them. The director of OMA often calls on members of FDG to serve as facilitators at RC or to become part of an NCORE group. Many students in the advocacy groups attend RC and a few of them later become RC facilitators. Some of them attend NCORE. When OSA staff began revising the sexual assault policy, they specifically sought the input of the Women's Coalition and the GLBT Organization. FDG occasionally invites to their meetings students interested in diversity—many of whom belong to advocacy organizations—to hear their perspectives on the curriculum and classroom climate.

Further, this interconnected group constantly reaches out to the broader community at CU. Each year the Office of Student Life educates a new group of resident advisers about diversity, and the Service Learning Program recruits new students for its various trips and projects. Each year OMA seeks applications for RC from students who have not attended before, and applications for NCORE from students, faculty, staff, and administrators who have not attended before. The NCORE group's projects for each academic year include outreach activities. For example, during the academic year of my study, the NCORE group worked with the student newspaper editors to publish the Race Column, and they organized a one-day conference on intersections among various diversity categories. Many staff across campus attended that conference as part of their professional development. FDG's coordinator, as well as a few other FDG members, provide diversity education and conflict resolution for departments and groups across campus, as well as in the community and at other universities.

The informal connections among these four organizational entities are not captured by a name, which underscores the informality of the connections. I refer to these four entities as the "interconnected group" because they function that way.

## City University's Narrative Environment

Descriptions of CU's diversity history and strengths set the stage for my study. But the idea that CU, like any university, can be viewed as a complex narrative environment is at the core of my study. Jaber Gubrium and James Holstein define narrative environments as "contexts within which the work of story construction and storytelling gets done."[13] As people narrate their lives and events in the world around them, they take into account and are accountable to the contexts in which they speak—their audience, the meanings circulating in those contexts, and the anticipated consequences of saying one thing rather than another. A narrative environment can be as small and intimate as a friendship, as large and impersonal as an institution, or as broad and diffuse as a national culture.

Like other institutions, universities can be viewed as complex narrative environments that "provide participants with preferred ways of linking together and composing matters of concern to them."[14] What, then, are the preferred ways that universities provide to students for narrating their lives and social realities on campus? And what are the characteristics of CU's narrative environment when it comes to diversity issues?

### College Is a Time for Learning as Much as You Can

One key narrative that circulates in higher education—especially in universities and colleges based in the liberal arts—is that college is a time when and a place where traditional-age students get exposed to new ideas, open their minds, and learn to think critically about the world around them.[15] Not surprisingly, many CU students I talked with drew on this narrative resource as they told me about their college experiences.

An example is from my interview with Mason, a white student. I met him during a group interview I conducted with members of Students for Firearm Safety and Recreation, a student organization chartered by the student government. A few days later he and I sat down for an individual interview. He described himself as growing up in a conservative, born-again Christian family. When he arrived at CU, he expected to major in management, and he imagined a career at a Fortune 500 company. But he said his first year of college made him "reevaluate everything." He "fell in love with Chinese culture," and now he's wondering whether his career could integrate his interests in business and China. At the same time he joked that "my major's probably going to change a hundred and fifty times from now," reflecting his openness to new ideas as a liberal arts student. Self-reflection and self-transformation were such prominent themes in his personal narrative that I wrote in my field notes that Mason could be a poster child for the liberal arts. The following exchange came after yet another story about seeing things in a new light.

*Susan:* Again you're questioning in a way that you hadn't before
*Mason:* Yeah
*Susan:* What's influencing you to question?
*Mason:* I guess just the environment
I guess just the environment of learning that I've never experienced before
I mean I can think of an example
Like it was the first really nice day on campus
And everyone was outside wearing shorts and T-shirts
And outside studying and reading and going to the library
And I felt as though the environment was so geared towards learning as much as
    you can
And I thought that was great
And so I even picked up a book that I probably would have never read before
And sat down and started reading it
Just because I wanted to be in the community of learning like that
And I would have to say that that would probably be what's bringing about the
    questioning
Just because I know everyone else is going through the exact same thing right now
Like I've even talked to different people about how this is—
The world is a lot different than I thought coming into this place
And I guess I just have to say it's just [pause]
*Susan:* The whole environment
*Mason:* The whole environment.

Mason's story could appear in a brochure or on a website for any liberal arts college across the United States or even across the world. In fact, it *is* represented visually in many universities' website photos of students sitting in the grass under shade trees or amidst flower beds, reading. Admissions staff might tone down or even edit out "the world is a lot different than I thought coming into this place" for fear that parents would be leery of a college education that challenges rather than complements a student's upbringing. But "college is a time for learning as much as you can" is a narrative that is institutionalized in the culture of the liberal arts.[16] It is a "preferred story," to use Gubrium and Holstein's as well as Riessman's term, a narrative promoted by liberal arts institutions in ways they largely take for granted.[17] In addition to admissions staff, college administrators and professors also promote this narrative because it legitimates their work, the expense of tuition, and the endless hours of reading and writing they expect of students.

The familiarity of Mason's story points to "institutionalized rules" that constitute "the student," as John Meyer and his colleagues would say.[18] In slightly different terms, the familiarity of his story points to narrative resources that liberal arts colleges provide to students for "linking together and composing matters of concern to them" as Gubrium and Holstein describe it.[19] Of course, another key narrative circulates in liberal arts colleges as well as in professionally oriented business, nursing, and engineering colleges: a university education should equip students with skills and credentials for professional jobs.[20] Nonetheless, Mason could be a student at virtually any liberal arts institution.

### Diversity Is Out There on the Table

In addition to broad narrative resources, local narrative resources circulate at *specific* institutions. A close look at CU as a local narrative environment reveals that "diversity" is a significant and highly contentious resource for "linking together and composing matters of concern" on campus.[21]

During a group interview with four members of the Faculty Diversity Group, I asked about CU's strengths in terms of diversity issues. Two of them responded in this way:

*Prof Turner:* Diversity is out there on the table
It's under discussion
And that's not always been the case
I mean there was a period of time that getting it out on the table for discussion
Was kind of like
*"Oohhh"* [imitating sarcastic voice]
Rolling of the eyes
*"We got to talk about that"*
And that's not the case anymore
It's not the rolling of the eyes
*"Oh diversity again"*
I mean it's taken as a serious topic of discussion I think pretty much across the
    campus
*Prof Young:* I think so, in many places
*Susan:* Do you mean among faculty?
*Prof Young:* I think campuswide especially this semester.

These two white professors distinguish between the past when the topic of diversity was greeted with sarcasm, and the present when it is being taken much more seriously by people across campus. Professor Young connects that seriousness to events that semester, a reference to the Activists' protest, among other things.

Although these professors are talking about a change for the better over time, I came to understand "diversity is out there on the table" in a different way, as capturing the "big story"—a relatively stable, overarching narrative —about diversity at CU.[22] Everyone I met at CU said, in one way or another, that "diversity is something we talk about here."

Nonetheless, the people I talked with had very different perspectives on that overarching narrative. Like professors Turner and Young, some people described diversity as a matter of serious dialogue on campus, and they pointed, for example, to CU's Race Conference, events put on by student advocacy organizations, some professors' classes, and workshops sponsored by Student Affairs. Some also viewed student activism—such as the Activists' protest—as producing serious dialogue about diversity.

At the same time, some of these same people, along with others, described a certain kind of talk about diversity on campus as lip service, as empty rhetoric without any follow-up in action. These comments were usually directed at the central administration. As one student said, "The president will be giving speeches and he'll mention diversity fifty times." But, she said, his actions (his inaction) contradicted his words. From yet another angle, some students described diversity as a "buzzword" that oversaturates the narrative environment. They portrayed "diversity" as signaling an agenda—someone else's agenda—that they rejected. For example, I heard some students talk dismissively about diversity workshops offered in the residence halls, and I heard some students talk dismissively about the Activists' actions. And some expressed hostility toward what they interpreted as others' diversity agendas.

At CU, then, diversity is out there on the table *contentiously*. Who or what gets defined as diverse, and which actions should be taken about what and by whom, were matters of debate that got addressed in a variety of campus contexts. But while there was contention concerning these matters, the very idea *that* diversity gets talked about, *that* it is an ongoing topic in the life of the university, made sense to every group and individual I met. Everyone I spoke with at CU had ready answers to my questions: What does diversity mean at CU? Who are the major players on campus when it comes to diversity issues? Does productive dialogue about diversity take place at CU? Which diversity issues have produced the most contention on campus this year?

### CU's Diversity Discourse in Various Contexts

"Diversity is out there on the table" is reflected not only in accounts I heard during my interviews with students, faculty, staff, and administrators, but also in a variety of campus contexts. Jessie Finch, Misti Sterling, and I conducted multiyear content analyses of CU's student newspaper, student government minutes, calendar of events, curriculum, and web site, and we did identical content analyses for RU, a university that is structurally similar to CU.

We coded for diversity when an article in the newspaper, an instance of talk in the minutes, an event on the calendar, a course in the schedule, or a web page included explicit diversity content. We coded for race/ethnicity, class, gender, sexual orientation, ability, global/international, religion, and general references to diversity. In table 1.1, "diversity" refers to all eight categories in aggregate. (See appendix D for an explanation of explicit diversity content and for details about the methods of content analysis.)

**Table 1.1.** Content analyses of CU's and RU's documents

| | Student newspaper | Student government minutes | Events calendar | Curriculum | Web site |
|---|---|---|---|---|---|
| | Percent of articles that include diversity | Average number of times per meeting that diversity gets raised | Percent of events that include diversity | Percent of courses that include diversity | Web pages with attention to diversity |
| CU | 31% | 6.2 | 44% | 17% | Extensive |
| RU | 18% | 2.3 | 30% | 10% | Minimal |

Table 1.1 shows that there is a greater amount of discourse about diversity at CU than at RU and that that pattern persists across all five contexts (newspaper, minutes, events, curriculum, and web site). This comparison suggests that two structurally similar universities can produce different narrative landscapes. Diversity is *more* "out there on the table" at CU than at RU.

# 2    *Conflicting Discourses*

> Today I attended a special lunch where several tables of staff, faculty, and
> student leaders were set up to discuss diversity issues on campus. I joined
> a table that included Ida Brown, the African-American director of the
> Office of Multicultural Affairs. . . . At one point Ida asked me what I
> thought about what's going on at CU concerning diversity. Since I have
> just begun my research, I felt really awkward. I wanted to observe rather
> than offer my perspective. But I also didn't want to be "the aloof re-
> searcher," and this, after all, was supposed to be a discussion. So I
> fumbled my way through a reply, saying something along these lines:
> "Compared to my university, it seems like CU has come pretty far in
> making diversity issues part of the ongoing life of the university." Ida
> laughed and then launched into a tirade about the administration's
> failings, faculty and student resistance to taking diversity seriously,
> and how much remains to be done at CU.
>
> —Chase, CU field notes

I wrote these field notes during my research at City University in the mid-
1990s, but it wasn't until after my research at CU in the mid-2000s that
I found a way to interpret the exchange between Ida Brown and me, an exchange that has stayed with me throughout this project.[1] At that moment
my hesitant comment reflected what I had observed that day: the prelunch
speaker integrated diversity topics into his talk about the role of universities
in developing the life of the mind. The administrator who introduced the
speaker mentioned several times the university's ongoing commitment to
diversity. Even the fact that a lunchtime discussion was organized around
diversity topics seemed significant to me. Much later, though, I came to understand my comment as a nascent observation of CU's overarching narrative about diversity: "Diversity is out there on the table."

And eventually I understood that Ida Brown's response to my comment communicated a *specific* narrative about diversity at CU. She was saying something like: "Yes, diversity is out there on the table at CU, but *how* is it out there on the table? What are we really accomplishing? What you're hearing is lip service. What we need is frank dialogue about how the university's structures and culture disadvantage some students and advantage others. We need to change those structures and that culture so that students of color and others who are marginalized on campus can get the education they deserve, and so that students who are accustomed to being at the center learn how their privileges operate in ways that exclude others." Ida Brown was referencing certain meanings and understandings of diversity—specifically, a discourse of social justice. Everyone at CU, however, did not view diversity through the lens of that discourse.

Eventually, then, I understood that diversity is out there on the table at CU, but that it is out there contentiously. And I identified three major discourses about diversity that circulate implicitly at CU, providing distinct, conflicting resources for students' interpretations of diversity issues on campus. A discourse of *social justice* critiques systems of privilege and oppression and highlights the need for social change. A discourse of *abstract inclusion* purports that "we are all the same" and that social differences like race don't matter. And a discourse of *political difference* assumes that universities like CU are bastions of liberal thought and that conservative students are the ones who end up being oppressed.

This chapter explores the characteristics of these three discourses, showing how each is based in broader discursive resources in American culture *and* how each operates in particular ways at CU. To demonstrate my arguments, I present examples from CU's student newspaper and student government deliberations, as well as from my interviews with students, faculty, and staff. I decided to use "discourse" (rather than "narrative") to describe these three sets of meanings and understandings because "discourse" indicates more clearly that these ways of interpreting diversity are in an important sense external to the people who use them.[2] CU students, faculty, and staff did not create these discursive resources—they are all rooted in much broader cultural debates. However, the ways in which people at CU *use* these discursive resources as they go about their everyday lives *creates* narrative reality about diversity on campus. The tensions between these distinct discourses constitute an important part of the narrative environment at CU. Students, faculty, and staff take those tensions into account—and they reproduce and reconfigure those tensions—as they narrate their lives and events on campus.

## Social Justice

Social justice discourse is conspicuous at CU. That is due in large part to the activities of the interconnected group of students, faculty, and staff whom I introduced in chapter 1. I found that *other* students, faculty, and staff recognize the presence of social justice discourse in the narrative landscape, and sometimes even use it, but most don't embrace it. Nonetheless, the prominence of that discourse in many different contexts at CU—such as the student newspaper and student government meetings—makes it a force to contend with.

### Privilege, Oppression, and Social Change

Each year, CU's Office of Multicultural Affairs (OMA) selects a group of students, faculty, and staff to attend the National Conference on Race and Ethnicity in Higher Education (NCORE). And each year, the NCORE group, as they are called, brings back to campus projects they will work on during the next academic year. During the year I focus on in my study, the NCORE group included sixteen people—half white, half of color; half men, half women; half students, half faculty and staff. This group chose for one of their projects writing a regular column on race for CU's student newspaper. For the next two years, they collaborated with the newspaper editors to publish the Race Column. In their inaugural article, they wrote:

> Our major goal this year [in writing the Race Column] is to engage students, staff, and faculty in dialogues about racism and justice. We expect that these dialogues will anger our community because we will be real about the systems of privilege and oppression that we maintain. The dialogues will be educational as well. Ultimately we want to inspire you to join the network of people working to end racism.

These few sentences capture three major characteristics of social justice discourse as it gets expressed both in the society at large and at CU. First is a focus on injustice as a matter of "privilege and oppression." This language suggests that some groups of people, by virtue of their social identities and social locations, accrue social, economic, and political privileges while others are disadvantaged or oppressed by the same mechanisms. In the United States, the latter include people of color, the working class, women, GLBT people, people with disabilities, immigrants from Third World nations, and people who practice non-Christian religions.

Second is a focus on injustice as a matter of "*systems* of privilege and oppression." The word *systems* locates the source of injustice in institutions, organizations, and cultures, rather than in individuals' attitudes or behavior per se. A focus on systems resists the usual assumption that racism is a matter of individual prejudice. According to social justice discourse, systems of privilege and oppression operate regardless of a person's attitude about racial matters, and they produce an individual's privileges or lack thereof. For example, the ways in which white people are socially privileged are systemic and cannot be disavowed. A white student cannot dispossess herself of white skin privilege as she goes about her everyday life, attending class, working, shopping, interacting with her peers, and so on. Only by understanding how deeply injustice is embedded in social systems can we understand how different groups of people suffer from and reap benefits from them. Individual prejudice is harmful, but it reflects broader systems of injustice that operate even when individuals do not harbor prejudice.[3]

And, third, is a focus on social change—"end[ing] racism." According to social justice discourse, once one understands the nature of the problem and its harmful consequences for individuals, groups, and the society as a whole, the next step is changing institutions, organizations, and cultures.

Social justice discourse flourishes in many contexts in the United States. Social movements that have fought and continue to fight for the rights of people of color, women, workers, GLBT people, people with disabilities, immigrants, people of non-Christian faiths, and older people mobilize this discourse. So do some religious groups. And so do a wide range of nonprofit organizations that advocate for the rights of various groups.[4] And, of course, within higher education, academic programs such as women's studies, racial/ethnic studies, GLBT/queer studies, and disability studies are often based in a social justice framework, as are some offices of student services on university campuses.

## Dialogues that Anger Our Community

But while social justice is familiar as a broad cultural discourse, it gets expressed in particular ways at CU.[5] Three aspects of the quotation above reflect those particularities.

First, the goal to "engage students, staff, and faculty in *dialogues*" reflects an emphasis on serious conversation, on speaking and listening. This emphasis is noteworthy because social justice discourse in the society at large often emphasizes that talk alone does not constitute a commitment to social justice: if you're going to talk the talk, you've got to walk the walk. However, in the form it takes at CU (as well as in some other contexts), social justice discourse includes the idea that dialogue itself can be action, a way of walking the walk. What matters is the quality of the conversation.

Second, the expectation that "these dialogues will *anger* our community" reflects an understanding that the majority of people on campus do not embrace social justice discourse, that it is highly contentious and emotionally volatile. The phrase, "because we will be real about the systems of privilege and oppression," suggests that the NCORE group perceives itself as exposing truths that are difficult to hear, truths that anger some people because they challenge cherished ideas. There is also a hint that it takes courage to anger others in the community. Relationships may be at risk. At the same time, though, new relationships can be created when people are educated by dialogue and "inspire[d] to join the network of people working to end racism." The NCORE group uses social justice discourse to challenge other meanings and understandings about diversity on campus.

## The Work

The third particularity reflected in the Race Column quote is the focus on working to end racism. I found that CU students, faculty, and staff who treat diversity as a matter of social justice sometimes use a set of related expressions—"the work," "diversity work," "social justice work," or "race work" —as they describe their activities. For example, when I interviewed Mr. Robert, the African American director of the Office of Multicultural Affairs, he described the faculty and staff he recruits as facilitators for CU's Race Conference as those "who have done race work before." Connie, a white student, used such a term after telling me how she learned to listen to a friend of color: "I really learned that I had to do the work for racial justice not just on an intellectual level but also on a very personal and emotional level." And Marshan, an African American student, used a similar term as she talked about learning to understand her privilege as a student from a middle-class family: "And so that's one thing that I've learned from this diversity work— recognizing my privileges."

I didn't notice these expressions of "the work" during the interviews. But as I listened to the interview tapes, I came to understand these occasional references to "the work" as a significant aspect of social justice discourse at CU. And it wasn't until after I became aware of "the work" in the narratives of people I interviewed at CU that I noticed its expression elsewhere, for example, in descriptions of some of the daylong institutes offered at The Ninth Annual White Privilege Conference in the spring of 2008. Here is the description for "What's in it for us? An Institute for People of Color":

> Working on the elimination of racism often focuses on helping white people understand racial privilege. Although persons of color who have attended past WPCs [White Privilege Conferences] acknowledge that cross-racial collaboration is crucial, they have also found that too little attention is paid to the intellectual, spiritual, physical and emotional toll *the work* takes on persons of color at the conference and beyond. In this institute, we will investigate the consequences of working with white people who are struggling to come to terms with white privilege. [emphasis added]

And here is an excerpt from the description of an institute titled "Understanding White Privilege:"

> This day-long pre-conference session is for participants who want to work with others to sharpen their knowledge and understanding of white privilege

as it affects people personally and institutionally. This day-long institute is designed to:

- Enhance our clarity about the necessity of doing *our personal work* in order to be effective anti-racists and identify strategies to make *that work* most strategic;
- Explore why, as white people, it is in our best interest to do *the hard work* required to understand what it means to be white. [emphasis added][6]

In these descriptions of "the work," as well as in its manifestations at CU, that phrase communicates that social justice discourse requires more than a perspective or an outlook—it requires a commitment that changes one's everyday life. Social justice cannot be accomplished in one-time conversations or events or activities or protests but requires an ongoing commitment to acting on oneself, acting in relation to others, and acting in the world. In *Understanding White Privilege,* Frances Kendall (who offered the second institute above) describes white people's "personal work" as fundamental to a commitment to social change: "Our life task . . . is to examine at increasingly deeper levels what it means for us to be white and then to alter our behavior so that we are better able to change our systems to be just and equitable and ourselves to enter into authentic cross-race relationships."[7]

At CU, I found that "the work" signals a distinct narrative community, one that is cultivated by the interconnected group of people involved in the offices of Student Affairs and Multicultural Affairs, the Faculty Diversity Group, and the student advocacy organizations. As we shall see in later chapters, "the work" shows up in some students' personal narratives and in their accounts about events on campus.

One example of what "the work" looks like at CU, and the importance of dialogue in accomplishing it, was narrated by two staff members in the Office of Student Affairs, one Latino, one white. As they told me about the extensive diversity education their office has undergone—which amounted to ninety hours over three years for program directors—they described these sessions as really "pushing us." Mr. Perez, who is Latino, elaborated:

*Mr. Perez:* I remember one session in particular where we separated into racial caucuses
And staff of color went together
And we talked about things that we had experienced
And when we brought it together as a group
I think it was for a lot of [white] people that felt
"I'm an ally to you"—
*Mr. Jay:* Yeah
*Mr. Perez:* "I thought we were friends
I thought I was your ally"
And when they heard many of us talking about

"Yes we have a good relationship
But I just—
There's something—
Still a barrier there"
That's where I think it was—
That's the pushing you know
The facilitator asking "well why?" on our end
And then towards someone who's white saying
"Why don't you think about these issues that they're talking about?"

Mr. Perez depicts the separate racial caucuses during that workshop as giving staff of color a chance to articulate their common experiences, and he describes the discussion between staff of color and white staff as bringing into the open barriers to full understanding in interracial relationships. Later in our conversation, Mr. Jay described those barriers as "misperceptions about race and power and privilege and difference" that "simmer under the surface" if they are not explicitly named. In the above, Mr. Perez also explains how the facilitator pushed staff of color and white staff to explore those barriers in order to dismantle them. In Mr. Perez's account, the facilitator pressed staff of color to develop their voice, to *explain* to their white colleagues why barriers still exist between them. When he uses direct speech to report what staff of color said to their white peers, he stumbles slightly ("but I just—there's something—") which may suggest that it is difficult to be this direct. According to Mr. Perez's account, the facilitator also pressed the white staff to think about why they don't even know what their colleagues of color are talking about—in other words, the facilitator pressed them to listen more fully.

As I listened to Mr. Perez and Mr. Jay talk about their diversity education as well as many other aspects of campus life, it was clear that they were accustomed to talking together about race at this personal level. It is noteworthy that Mr. Jay—who has worked at other universities—described the conversations staff had during their extensive diversity education (and have had since) as *a*typical in his professional experience.

But the aim of their diversity education did not end with this work on relationships among colleagues. As Mr. Perez continued, he said,

*Mr. Perez:* Then taking that further—
"Well ok, if *we're* dealing with this
What about our relations with our students?
And the students with each other?"

Mr. Perez and Mr. Jay described how they and others in student affairs educate students they work with—resident advisers in the residence halls and student leaders in various organizations across campus—about barriers to and possibilities for cross-racial relationships. Further, by doing that education in cross-racial teams whenever possible, they model for students what that work and those relationships look like.

### What Are You Doing about Diversity Issues on Campus and How Are You Educating Yourself about Social Justice?

From time to time, CU administrators attend student government meetings, giving students a chance to ask them questions. At one meeting, students asked four white senior-level administrators about improvements needed in the residence halls, the possibility of adding a student to CU's board of trustees, and "top-down diversity initiatives." Here is an excerpt from the student government minutes:

*Student Rep #1:* What top-down diversity initiatives are you taking and how are they being implemented?

*Administrator #1:* The issue of diversity has three major aspects. Two are diversity of faculty and diversity of the student body. We actively are committed to trying to find the most diverse pool of finalists possible in hiring faculty. We've slipped up on this from time to time. We currently have several searches going on, so I got the chairs of the departments together, and said that while searches have typically begun in the fall and ended in April, this time we will continue the searches until we have the diverse pool we need. Some could end in December, some could continue on further than normal. In order to have the pool of finalists that we need it could take much longer than a year. Most schools are looking for the same type of diversity we are looking for. By changing our time frame I am hoping for a better result. The admissions office mainly looks at diversity of the student body. The third piece has more to do with attitudes on campus. One of my concerns about social and racial justice is that I've gone to too many meetings where you're preaching to the choir, and the people that are at the meetings all believe in this. Ms. Jones [an African-American woman administrator] and I have worked on taking all of these issues, that are combined under the question of how do we treat each other, to the part of the community that is not necessarily made up of people with a personal incentive or passion on the issue. We need to reach out to the 80 percent of students and staff to whom this isn't an issue. So that the opportunity to rethink racial privilege and other such issues meets the people who wouldn't normally take it onto themselves.

Administrator #1 describes what the college is doing to increase faculty diversity. When he states that "most schools are looking for the same type of [faculty] diversity that we are looking for" he references the institutionalization of this commitment in higher education (as discussed in chapter 1). His attention to faculty diversity does not *necessarily* mobilize social justice discourse—his talk here could just as easily be interpreted as complying with broader institutional constraints. By contrast, his talk about what he and Ms. Jones are doing to engage the 80 percent of people on campus who are not involved in social and racial justice clearly mobilizes social justice discourse. In particular his statement that those people need "the opportunity to rethink racial privilege" evokes that discourse. The minutes continue:

*Student Rep #2:* How is each of you personally educating yourselves about social justice issues?

*Administrator #2:* I think you are looking at, in each of our cases, a person who has committed themselves to a diverse community as expressed in CU's mission statement. . . . I was in college when the Vietnam War and civil rights movement took place, and I was deeply involved in those, and I am committed to these types of issues. . . .

*Administrator #1:* I listen to John Smith [the director of one of CU's academic programs that addresses diversity issues]. That program was created when I was [in another administrative position] and I have spent a good amount of time trying to raise money to support it. . . .

*Administrator #3:* I have spent 18–20 years working with people with disabilities. I listen to students in John Smith's' classes who have pushed me to get involved in investments [sic] in the community . . .

*Administrator #4:* There are many opportunities at CU [for education about social justice]. There are workshops on racism. I've been involved in the [religious] scholars' conversations on racism. Student Affairs is trying to educate themselves as well.

Each administrator responds to Student Rep #2's question in ways that show their facility at deploying at least some aspects of social justice discourse: they speak about movements for social change, groups of people who have experienced injustice in our society, and programs on campus oriented to social justice. Nonetheless, I wouldn't be surprised if this student rep heard Administrator #2 (and possibly Administrator #1) as offering lip service to that discourse because he does not describe how he is *currently educating himself* about social justice. Instead of answering the question, Administrator #2 presents his credentials, in particular his social movement involvement from decades ago. But implicit in the question is the idea that the social justice approach to diversity requires *ongoing personal education or work on oneself.*

Of the four, Administrator #4 speaks most directly about his self-education, and indeed, he was a participant in the ninety hours of diversity education for student affairs program directors. It is possible that the other three administrators are more familiar with social justice discourse in the broader culture and less familiar with "the work" as an integral component of how the interconnected group of faculty, staff, and students deploy that discourse at CU. It is clear that the student rep asks his question from within that distinct narrative community.

## Abstract Inclusion

A discourse of abstract inclusion pervades the narrative landscape at CU. It is pervasive not because a particular group works to keep it on the table, but because it is deeply embedded in American culture. At CU, abstract inclusion gets expressed in ways that would be familiar in many other contexts, but it also functions in ways that reflect CU's narrative environment. Sometimes students mobilize abstract inclusion as an implicit critique of social justice discourse. Sometimes, however, the critique is explicit.

### *We Are All People*

In a letter to the student newspaper, Sandra, a white student, criticized what she saw as a general tone of disappointment and complaint in the opinion section of the paper.

> CU should stop harboring victims. There are victims of teasing, bullying, stigma, criticism, athletes who settle for CU's division status, and everyone has nothing to do but complain about problems that don't exist. . . . Every week the newspaper includes articles by disappointed people complaining of racism, reverse racism, oppression, political correctness, and anything else one can imagine. . . .
>
> We focus more on our differences and we forget our commonalities. We need to realize that we are all people and that we need each other no matter what our superficial differences are. We have the power to choose. As Eleanor Roosevelt said, "No one can make you feel inferior without your consent." Choose not to be a victim.

Sandra's letter captures several characteristics of the discourse of abstract inclusion as it gets expressed in American culture. First, "we are all people" focuses on what everyone has in common—being human. In some philosophical and religious contexts, universal statements like this are used to evoke profound moral and spiritual connections in the midst of significant cultural and social differences. For example, in her defense of the liberal arts in higher education, Martha Nussbaum argues that students need to cultivate "an ability to see themselves not simply as citizens of some local region or group but also, and above all, as human beings bound to all other human beings by ties of recognition and concern."[8] But Nussbaum does not discard social differences like Sandra does. Nussbaum also argues that students need to cultivate "the ability to think what it might be like to be in the shoes of a person different from oneself, to be an intelligent reader of that person's story, and to understand the emotions and wishes and desires that someone so placed might have."[9] In Sandra's letter, by contrast, "we are all people" transforms differences among people into something "superficial" and thus insignificant. Her statement, "we are all people," includes everyone by *abstracting* from their differences. It is not a both/and move, but an either/or move. Sandra's "we are all people" communicates something like: "Some people focus erroneously on differences, but we should focus on what we have in common."

The second characteristic is the idea that a focus on differences separates people in ways that are harmful. In particular, a focus on our differences turns each of us into victims of injustices that exist in our minds rather than in reality and causes us to complain about "problems that don't exist." Those who claim to be victims of some form of inequality in our society are really just allowing others to make them feel inferior.

Third, the solution to this problem is for people who think of themselves as victims to recognize that they have the power to choose not to be victims. According to this perspective, people simply need to change their view of reality and their place within it in order to mobilize their power to choose. Further, because each of us has the power to choose not to be a victim, we are responsible for our own fates. Any inequalities among us are the result of individual choices and inadequacies.

It is noteworthy that Sandra's statements are broadly inclusive in terms of who is presenting themselves as victims. She includes those who complain about racism and those who complain about reverse racism, those who complain about oppression and those who complain about political correctness. She even includes those who are dissatisfied with CU's division status in athletics. Through this diffuse—or abstract—inclusiveness, Sandra indicates that no complaint is distinct. CU students of color who complain about the institution's racist practices are no more or less guilty of enacting an inauthentic identity as victim than athletes who complain about CU's division status.

Thus Sandra's deployment of the discourse of abstract inclusion undermines any claim to a distinctive voice of complaint. By including everyone, Sandra does *not* single out students of color who complain about racism on campus. But her claim that "we are all people" whose social differences are insignificant implicitly dismisses social justice discourse because the latter highlights the importance of different social identities and locations.

It is not surprising that Sandra—and many other CU students—use the discourse of abstract inclusion because variants of this discourse—individualism and color blindness—permeate American culture. And because this discourse is so deeply institutionalized in American culture, CU students draw on it *unselfconsciously and with confidence in its rightness*. Choosing not to be a victim does not require education or difficult dialogues that push us to challenge previously taken-for-granted ideas. All it requires is a cognitive shift that can be accomplished with little effort. One does not need any experience dealing with diversity issues in order to propose with confidence that "we are all people." Anyone can mobilize this discourse of abstract inclusion at any time. If a great American heroine like Eleanor Roosevelt said, "No one can make you feel inferior without your consent," it must be self-evidently true. There is no need to think about what that statement could mean in specific situations.

In American culture at large, the discourse of abstract inclusion often takes shape as "color blindness." Mark Chesler and his colleagues write:

> The widespread but distorted belief that we now live in a color-blind society, or should act as if we do, has emerged as a central way of thinking about race in the United States. . . . In this vein, the dominant culture officially stigmatizes explicit, traditional, or old-fashioned racial prejudice and overt discrimination (though it often tolerates these in informal or private contexts). At the same time it condemns efforts to raise racial issues, label racist values and practices as unjust, or mobilize racial consciousness to challenge institutionalized racism.[10]

Chesler et al. express a widespread critique in the social sciences of the discourse of color blindness. But despite that critique, color blindness continues to be "a central way of thinking about race in the United States." Eduardo Bonilla-Silva goes further to argue that it is "the *dominant* racial ideology" in the post–civil rights era [emphasis added].[11] In either case, the discourse of color blindness is so embedded in our cultural fabric that Americans "know" they are not supposed to think or say that race matters.

Color blindness is reflected in the multicultural education that most American schoolchildren get concerning race: they are taught that overt discrimination is wrong but that it exists mostly in the past, and that current instances of discrimination are infrequent aberrations from the equality that has been achieved. Everyone's difference can now be embraced and celebrated at school during cultural heritage days and in advertisements sporting slogans like "the united colors of Benetton" because race is no longer a problem.[12] Those who continue to complain about racism are causing trouble, living in the past, or looking for a scapegoat for their individual failures. In Sandra's words, they are complaining about "problems that don't exist."[13]

### We Are All Diverse

While "we are all people" is a culturally familiar version of abstract inclusion, "we are all diverse" is a version that students adopted for specific purposes in CU's narrative terrain.

This exchange came near the end of my conversation with three white members of Students for Firearm Safety and Recreation (SFSR), one of CU's student organizations:

*Susan:* What do you guys think should be done differently when it comes to CU's diversity-related policies or approach?
What would you like to see done differently?
*Jackson:* I would say—
Well the whole diversity itself
The definition doesn't just involve race and sexual orientation
Which is pretty much how our campus takes it
*Susan:* What else does it involve?
*Jackson:* It would be just general differences
People who are economically different places
Like as far as social [pause]
*Susan:* Social class?
*Jackson:* Social classes
People with different ideas
Like ours [SFSR's] just aren't considered diverse at all
Are just considered wrong.

Jackson resists the prominence of race and sexual orientation in what he sees as the dominant definition of diversity at CU. When I guessed that he was looking for the term "social class" I supplied it, but that is not what he dwells on. When he states "people with different ideas," he may be indicating that many different kinds of people and ideas should be included in the definition of diversity, but at the very least he means the ideas of *this* group —SFSR—need to be included. His statement that SFSR's ideas "are just considered wrong," refers to the student government debate over SFSR's bid to become a chartered student organization, which would give them access to student government funding.[14]

Student government minutes show some representatives speaking *for* SFSR's proposal to become a chartered student organization (it conforms to the student government constitution; this group is like any other recreational student organization). The minutes also show some representatives speaking *against* their proposal (student fees shouldn't be used so that a small group of students can learn about gun safety; no other organization gets funds to pay for equipment storage off campus). At the next meeting, the proposal was discussed again and approved. Here is an excerpt from the minutes of that second meeting:

*Student Author of Proposal:* I want to start this organization and I have 38 people on an interest list, almost all of them are first years. We meet all the requirements in the by-laws for being a student org. To cover previous concerns, our main purpose is safety. I would like to make sure that everyone understands that at no point will there be firearms on campus.

*Student Rep #3: . . . This is a legitimate and good org that will create more diversity on campus.*

*Student Rep #4:* Also, in many debates on campus, many people would not like money going to support the use of firearms, but we need to put our own wishes to the side. We all pay student fees and they all go to causes we don't necessarily support. *This will bring diversity to campus.* [emphasis added]

How do we understand this diversity-related defense of SFSR's proposal? This defense brings a group that would not be considered diverse according to the social justice approach under the umbrella of diversity discourse. The logic of the defense goes like this: at CU we all know that diversity is valued (at least we *say* it is); SFSR is different from other groups at CU; therefore, we should value and include this group. Within this logic, "diversity" becomes synonymous with "different," thus any group could be considered "diverse." The idea that "we are all diverse" exemplifies abstract inclusion in that anyone and everyone can be viewed as contributing some kind of difference.

The student government minutes show that students routinely defend resolutions for conference funds or for charters for new groups on the grounds that they advance the student government's commitment to diversity. Diversity-related defenses are used to support proposals for groups or activities that could be interpreted as falling within social justice discourse as well as those, like SFSR, that clearly do not. When the resolution to create an endowment to support scholarships for students of color was presented, a representative stated, "We talk a lot about diversity; this is a tangible way to support diversity." Students seeking funds to attend a Residence Hall conference and students requesting funds for an Amnesty International conference pointed out that they would be attending diversity workshops at the conferences. The proposal for a new group on Environmental Spirituality was defended with the statement that "having more religious diversity on campus is important." In these examples, "diversity" *may* function as shorthand for groups and activities that belong to traditional social justice categories, but that shorthand does not *clearly* reflect the social justice approach to diversity.

It is clear, however, that students also use the very same shorthand, the very same defense, to bring groups like SFSR—groups that definitely are not considered diverse according to the social justice approach—within the purview of diversity discourse. A representative speaking in support of a proposal to charter a new student organization for Christian athletes stated, "This is probably the most well run and diversified group in terms of events on campus." And a representative supporting a proposal to use student government funds to purchase and display student art on campus stated, "We talk a lot about representing the underrepresented," implying that student artists are an underrepresented group at CU. In this case, we see a direct appropriation of a term—*underrepresented*—that belongs to social justice discourse. And at the end of the year, the student government president began a summary of the student government's accomplishments that year by talking about its support for diversity. In that context, the president stated that the student government had chartered new groups ranging from a theater group to an animal rights group to SFSR.

These examples show that students deploy a discourse of abstract inclusion —"we are all diverse"—to mobilize resources (organizational charters and student government funds) in a narrative environment where "diversity is out there on the table" as a set of powerful, contentious discourses. Students' use of abstract inclusion shows that that discourse is ready at hand when strategically needed. Anyone can claim at any time that "our group adds diversity" at CU. One does not need any particular education about or experience with the diversity categories embedded in social justice discourse in order to claim that one's group contributes diversity. All one needs to know is that in this narrative context—in these cases, CU's student government deliberations—that claim is effective.

The idea that "we are all diverse" is a particular manifestation of abstract inclusion, one that makes sense in CU's narrative landscape. If social justice discourse was not conspicuous at CU, there would be no need for student government representatives to claim "we are all diverse." Like "we are all people," "we are all diverse" operates in a way that subtly rather than overtly undermines social justice discourse. If *any* group can be considered diverse, then the claims of groups that traditionally have been seen as unjustly excluded and as needing to be included get no particular attention. "We are all diverse" takes away the distinctiveness of their claims. As such, "we are all diverse" functions as an implicit critique of the social justice frame.

### Diversity This, Diversity That

Students sometimes expressed abstract inclusion in tandem with an *explicit* critique of the social justice approach. Here is another excerpt from my interview with Students for Firearm Safety and Recreation:

*Kane:* I think as far as like the general student population
They hear the word *diversity* thrown around a lot
[And] it's probably one of those things that's become nearly meaningless by now
*Jackson:* The word itself is becoming a buzzword pretty much on campus
"Diversity this diversity that."

That anyone can mobilize "diversity" at any time—such as during student government meetings—certainly contributes to these students' perception that CU's narrative terrain is oversaturated with diversity as a "buzz-word." But I found that CU students' complaints about too much diversity talk were usually aimed at social justice discourse and were often grounded in an abstract inclusion approach. This is seen in the following excerpt from my individual interview with Kane:

*Kane:* There's just a lot of people who don't care
Because they're probably just so blasted with all this crap all the time
That they just try to block as much of it out as possible
*Susan:* When you say blasted with all this crap, what—
Which crap is—
*Kane:* Well just like the "oh we should be diverse"
And "we need to accept everything"
And like a lot of that's true
But I mean you hear it so often
I don't know
It's just there's a lot of emphasis on the whole like racial profiling and things like that
That maybe it sort of needs to be there
But in all honesty
It's probably just making things worse
And like—
*Susan:* And how does it make things worse?
*Kane:* Well I don't know
I mean if you have to start like lumping people into different groups
Then automatically you just start having preconceived notions about them
Stereotyping people
And that goes like for the whole society
I mean when you fill out like a job application
It asks you what your gender is
So there's that already
And then there's like "what race are you?"
And that just breaks things down too much
I mean if you're able to do the job
I mean as long as you're qualified
It shouldn't matter what race or gender or what your sexual preference is or what religion you are or anything so
*Susan:* So you would like the idea—
You would prefer a color-blind—
A kind of neutral stance on these things
*Kane:* Yeah I mean—
Just like you're a human and that's about it
It doesn't really matter
I mean I don't know.

Kane's statements exemplify two of the rhetorical moves that Eduardo Bonilla-Silva argues often characterize "color-blind racism." The first is what Bonilla-Silva calls "yes and no, but," which starts with a presentation of different sides of an issue and then takes a stand.[15] Kane does this when he states that "a lot of that's true" and "maybe it sort of needs to be there" (in referring to the emphasis on diversity and race on campus), and then he moves on to say "but in all honesty. . . ." Kane uses "yes and no, but" to signal that he is not racist but that it's difficult to say what he wants to say because someone might *interpret* his words as racist. "In all honesty" indicates that what he says next is the stand he wants to take: the emphasis on diversity and race on campus is "probably just making things worse." This is difficult to say because it is contentious, both in U.S. society in general and at CU in particular. In this passage, Kane says "I don't know" three times, which may reflect his discomfort in this contentious discursive terrain.

When I interrupt and press him to explain, Kane states that "lumping people into different groups" makes things worse by causing people to think about stereotypes about people. This is an explicit critique of the social justice approach to diversity because one of its fundamental premises is that race, gender, sexual orientation, and religion shape people's social identities and social locations. According to social justice discourse, we *need* to view people as members of social groups in order to understand how privilege and oppression operate in our society. Kane is suggesting, however, that the social justice approach to diversity on campus is *itself* the problem. If the people who advocate for social justice would just tone it down—stop "blasting" students "with all this crap all the time"—things would be a lot better. This is where Kane uses a second rhetorical strategy identified by Bonilla-Silva: "projection," or blaming the problem on those who identify racism as a problem in the first place.[16]

Kane draws himself further into color-blind discourse when he says that he's not just talking about CU but also about society at large. His statement —"as long as you're qualified it shouldn't matter what race or gender or what your sexual preference is or what religion you are"—references culturally familiar critiques of affirmative action. At the same time, he implicitly evokes an association of certain groups—like people of color—with *lack* of qualifications, which policies like affirmative action presumably ignore.

Finally, in attempting to articulate what he does espouse, Kane settles for "you're a human and that's about it." In other words, he espouses abstract inclusion.

The lens of abstract inclusion allows Kane to interpret diversity-related events and programs on campus as a constant stream that oversaturates the narrative environment. He claims that this frustrates and irritates many students, and so they "try to block as much of [this crap] out as possible." For them, "diversity" signals events to be avoided. "Diversity" advances a social justice agenda that they reject.[17]

## Political Difference

A third set of meanings and understandings about diversity treats it as a matter of differing political perspectives. Although this discourse circulates in public venues such as CU's student newspaper and student government meetings, it is not as conspicuous on campus as social justice discourse, and it is not as pervasive on campus as the discourse of abstract inclusion. Nonetheless, a discourse of political difference is explicitly promoted by members of a student group called Conservative Students, as well as by other students and a few faculty. As they talk about diversity on campus, they appropriate *and* resist social justice discourse.

### Creating a Strong Conservative Voice on a Very Liberal Campus

In a letter published in the student newspaper, James and Rhonda, two white members of Conservative Students, wrote:

> Some may think the words "CU" and "conservative" create an oxymoron. That could not be more untrue. In fact, there are more conservative students on campus than you might think. Three CU students [names deleted] recently attended the Conservative Political Action Conference in our nation's capital. We listened to prominent speakers and gained valuable resources and important knowledge for creating a strong conservative voice on our very liberal campus. [The letter goes on to describe opportunities available to conservative students: for example, meeting national, state, and local political figures; networking with conservative students in other states; and political internships.]
>
> Our goals are to create an environment that is open to conservative ideas and to educate CU students on these opposing viewpoints. We plan to bring a pro-life group to campus as well as some well-known conservative speakers. We would like students who are conservative and afraid to speak out in class to join us. Being more knowledgeable about the issues will help reduce the anxiety that comes from disagreeing with the entire class.

James and Rhonda's letter expresses several components of political difference discourse. First, it assumes that many universities, like CU, are bastions of liberal thought, and that that is a problem. The problem is that many students are uneducated about conservative ideas and thus are misled by liberal ideas that dominate the classroom. The solution is to "create an environment open to conservative ideas and to educate CU students on these opposing viewpoints." Second, it claims that there are plenty of conservative students on campus but their voices are not heard. Because a liberal view dominates campus discourse, conservative students are afraid to speak out, especially in class. And third, it argues that there are plenty of resources in the world beyond the university that will help them develop a conservative voice on campus. When conservative students become more knowledgeable about conservative viewpoints, they will develop the confidence to speak out about their ideas.

Like social justice and abstract inclusion, the discourse of political difference is grounded in a broader cultural framework. In this case, that broader discourse is one promulgated by conservative thinkers, especially David Horowitz, but it also has roots in the "culture wars" of the 1980s and 1990s.[18] Horowitz critiques the liberal culture that he claims has proliferated in the institution of American higher education over the last two decades. His specific focus is the curriculum. In *Indoctrination U.*, he writes:

> An academic movement for "social justice" has inserted its radical agenda into the very templates of collegiate institutions and academic programs, and into the curricula of secondary schools as well. Pursuit of this goal both requires and justifies indoctrinating students in the ideas that radicals regard as "transformative" and "progressive." Far from being a consensus that supports the pluralistic community of the American social contract, the political correctness of the left is the orthodoxy of one social faction seeking to impose its agenda on all the others—a new and disturbing development in the educational culture.[19]

Horowitz claims that "social justice" is the "banner" of leftist faculty who are imposing their political agenda on college students in the classroom.[20] By calling their actions "indoctrination," Horowitz charges these faculty with failure to *educate* students, failure to teach them to think critically about any idea they encounter, failure to give them intellectual resources that will open their minds. Thus he grounds his critique in the most fundamental cultural script that legitimates the university as an institution: the university is one of the most important sites—if not *the* most important site—for open exchange of ideas in a democratic society. (In chapter 1, we heard Mason express this as "college is a time for learning as much as you can.") Horowitz's specific critique is that politically conservative ideas get silenced in the classroom, in part because most faculty in American universities lean left politically and in part because some left-leaning faculty trample conservative students' ideas when they express them in class.

Horowitz's challenge to this state of affairs has revolved around his attempt to get legislatures and universities to adopt an Academic Bill of Rights, which he created in 2003, and which is "designed to restore intellectual diversity and academic standards" to institutions of higher education.[21] Horowitz's campaign has produced immense controversy in public and academic venues across the United States.[22]

While discourse about the dominance of leftist ideologies in academe gets bandied about on the national scene, it gets expressed in particular ways and has particular meanings at CU. James and Rhonda's description of conservative students as fearful of speaking in class (because that means taking a stance against the majority) echoes a consistent complaint of CU students of color: they often find themselves having to correct classmates' misunderstandings about race, and they feel they are expected to speak for their entire race. Doing so is painful because the majority of students don't know how to listen to what they say, and faculty don't know how to facilitate dialogue about the issues they raise.[23] Whether intentionally or not, James and Rhonda impute to conservative students a social location like that of students of color on campus. Similarly, James and Rhonda's emphasis on a conservative *voice* and *speaking* echoes the emphasis in CU's social justice discourse on dialogue.

### No One's Representing Us

The Conservative Students requested funds from the student government to support their travel to the national-level Conservative Political Action Conference that James and Rhonda mentioned in their letter to the student newspaper. Here is an excerpt from the minutes of the student government meeting during which their proposal for conference funds was discussed.

*Student Rep #5:* This came up a couple of weeks ago in the budget committee, and they have been waiting patiently to get this to the floor. They brought us a bunch of information, and this seemed to be a good conference fund request.

*Student Rep #6:* We have passed such things for the Liberal Students in the past, just as a matter of precedent.

*Student Author of Proposal:* I laid everything out in the resolution, but *I really feel that conservatives have been absent on this campus,* and this conference will give us a bunch of motivation and ideas, and we hope to bring a lot of things back. *To adhere to the diversity policy I feel that we need to support conservative ideals as well* [emphasis added].

The minutes note that the proposal passed without any more discussion, which suggests that it was not controversial. The diversity-related defense of the proposal sounds like the abstract inclusion defense for Students for Firearm Safety and Recreation and other groups mentioned above. But the defense of the Conservative Students' proposal includes another concept— "conservative students have been *absent* on this campus"—which hints at something more than a situation where yet another group needs to be included in the always-expandable list of diverse groups on campus. In the discourse of political difference, that absence becomes the foundation for a much more developed argument than that of abstract inclusion.

Here is the Conservative Students' response to my first question—during my group interview with them—about what issues they've been dealing with this year.

*Evan:* Our biggest fight or push on campus is just to have our conservative ideals
   respected and noticed
Because I think we're always forgotten about
Like that there even is another side
And so we're just trying to promote that and get our ideas and thoughts out in the
   classroom
We are probably the most vocal about it
Because a lot of conservative students on campuses like ours are intimidated
Are afraid to voice their opinions in class
Because there's such a large gap between—
Sometimes it's like 55 to 2 or 3
*Susan:* In the classroom
*Evan:* In the classroom
So it's very intimidating to voice conservative ideals and opinions
That's our biggest issue on campus.

Evan constructs CU's narrative environment, and particularly the classroom, as excluding conservative ideas. By framing conservative ideas as
"another side" that is usually forgotten, he implies that the other, more
prominent side, consists of liberal ideas. While he suggests that the classroom is an intimidating environment for many conservative students, he presents himself (and the three other students present during this interview with
me) as vocal proponents of conservative ideas. They do not have a problem
speaking out about their ideas.
   Dan jumps in here:

*Dan:* [We want] to maintain our presence as a conservative advocacy organization
   around here
In that sense it's a little different than say the Black Collegians or the Southeast
   Asian Association
Because we're not dealing with any sort of racial or ethnic identity
[But] rather an ideological identity
"Hey we're right wing students
We realize we're a minority here
But if you'd like to show up and be a part of something
We meet every Wednesday."

As Dan describes how the Conservative Students try to maintain their presence on campus, he appropriates concepts embedded in CU's social justice
discourse. Most important, he describes the Conservative Students as an "advocacy organization," a term with a specific history and meaning at CU.
   In the mid-1990s, after a year of campuswide discussion and debate, CU's
board of trustees approved a cultural diversity policy which (among other
things) required all organizations on campus to develop their own explicit
cultural diversity policy. During the campuswide discussions, many students

involved in the student government resisted the idea that some groups of students have different needs because those groups have historically been (and continue to be) denied equal opportunity on campus and in the society at large. But once the trustees adopted the cultural diversity policy, the student government had no choice but to comply. The student government created a cultural diversity policy recognizing the importance of advocacy organizations. As explained in chapter 1, advocacy organizations are chartered groups that advance the rights and culture of people who are denied privileges and opportunities because of race, gender, sexual orientation, nationality, political affiliation, disability, or religion—at CU or in the society at large. These statements clearly use social justice discourse.

Although "political affiliation" is included in the list of statuses that can be the basis for an advocacy organization, neither the Conservative Students nor the Liberal Students are deemed advocacy organizations by CU's student government. These organizations cannot be chartered by the student government because they campaign for and spend funds on political candidates. As a nonprofit organization, CU cannot allow student fees, which support the student government budget, to be used for political campaigning. It is legitimate, however, for the student government to fund the Conservative Students' and Liberal Students' conference travel.[24]

Because the Conservative Students is *not* an advocacy organization, Dan's claim that they are a "conservative advocacy organization" is a *narrative* move. By using that term, he implies that conservative students are denied privileges and opportunities on campus simply because they are conservatives.

In addition, Dan claims an "ideological identity" for conservative students, which he presents as different from but analogous to the racial or ethnic identity claimed by students of color. And finally, he describes conservatives as "a minority" at CU, a term with cultural and historical resonances of exclusion and discrimination.

In appropriating social justice concepts, Dan's account at once depends on that discourse *and* resists it. The argument embedded in Dan's and Evan's statements is this: liberals created the social justice definition of diversity; that definition leaves out conservatives; thus the groups (such as students of color, GLBT students, and women students) who claim *they* have historically been excluded end up excluding and oppressing conservative students. This argument makes sense in CU's narrative environment where social justice discourse has a public presence and where advocacy groups have successfully achieved—at least in certain quarters—recognition for their particular needs.[25]

As the Conservative Students continued their conversation with me, they mentioned that recently they had been among a small group of students who had been invited to meet David Horowitz at the state capital. That meeting took place after a press conference on the Academic Bill of Rights that a state senator had introduced to the state legislature. Dan explained that Horowitz's aim "is not so much to get this legislation through state houses and state senates as it is to put a little pressure on universities and institutions themselves to take a sharper look at their own curriculum and hiring and say, 'Hey you know what? This may or may not be an issue. Let's just review it.'" Dan captures well Horowitz's own description of his intentions.[26]

A little later in my group interview with the Conservative Students, Olivia said:

*Olivia:* A lot of liberal speakers will come here [to CU]
But [we have] to go to the capital to see David Horowitz
Or to [a nearby university] to see Ann Coulter
And it's kind of ridiculous that the university spends so much money on all these [other] speakers
And there's no one here for *our* thoughts
So there's all kinds of religions or African Americans
And all bunch of varied speakers for *those* diversity groups
And no one's representing *us.*

Olivia argues that the diversity groups that are usually thought of as *dis-* advantaged on campus are actually the ones that are *advantaged.* She constructs the diversity groups—"all kinds of religions or African Americans"— as having too much power and taking up too much of the university's resources, in this case, for speakers. But further, she specifically equates "diversity groups" with "liberals," and in so doing, she configures the discursive terrain as a political battle between liberals and conservatives. That configuration allows her to imply that inclusion of conservative ideas would require fifty/fifty air time for conservative and liberal speakers and views. Liberal diversity groups are overrepresented on campus, Olivia argues, while "no one's representing *us.*" Along with Evan and Dan, then, Olivia presents conservative students as the ones who are oppressed on campus.

When we hear from these students again in chapter 7, we will hear them develop more fully their critique of social justice discourse, and in particular, their hostility to the Activists' protest.

## Discursive Resources, Discursive Tensions

Because social justice, abstract inclusion, and political difference are discursive *resources,* one does not need to embrace them in order to *use* them. Some administrators, for example, are skilled at using social justice discourse when speaking in certain venues—such as student government meetings— but are perceived as failing to act in accordance with its principles. And using expressions embedded in one discourse—such as "underrepresented group" or "advocacy organization"—to articulate ideas within another discourse shows how it is possible to appropriate a discursive resource for a certain purpose. It is important, then, to view these discourses not only as distinct, relatively stable sets of meanings and understandings about diversity, but also as collectively constituting an important aspect of CU's particular narrative environment. Through the particular ways that CU students (and others) use these conflicting discursive resources, they continuously constitute the narrative landscape as complex, contested terrain.

A nice example of that complexity and contentiousness—and, specifically, of how discursive resources can get used in a variety of ways—is displayed in an article published in the annual farcical issue of the student newspaper. The author of the article, a squirrel, argues that his species, which has resided on campus grounds since before CU existed, has been denied a voice at CU. In particular, squirrels have been denied the right to vote and to run for office in the student government. The squirrel charges the student government with anthropocentrism, a form of discrimination that everyone on campus should work to eliminate. By using expressions such as "denied a voice," "discrimination," and "anthropocentrism," the article makes fun of—rather than embraces—social justice discourse. And by arguing that squirrels should be included in the inexhaustible list of groups considered "diverse," the article makes fun of the discourse of abstract inclusion. Whether readers find this funny or offensive, it clearly draws on CU's discursive resources about diversity *and* reconstitutes them as objects of fun and even derision. It also points to the student government—and the student newspaper itself—as venues where contentiousness among CU's diversity discourses gets played out.

Despite their commonality as discursive resources, the three discourses operate somewhat differently at CU. The social justice approach is self-consciously embraced by a limited number of students, faculty, and staff—the interconnected group—and it is nurtured by their activities. The political difference approach is also self-consciously embraced, but by an even smaller number of people on campus. The Conservative Students work more than others to keep that discourse on the table. These students are supported in their efforts by staff in the Office of Student Affairs whose job is to develop leadership opportunities for all students on campus. And they are supported by faculty—self-identified conservatives *and* liberals—who invite conservative students to explore and express their ideas in public venues such as the newspaper. During presidential campaigns, the student newspaper regularly prints twin columns written by conservative and liberal students about national political issues.

By contrast, the abstract inclusion approach was not self-consciously promoted, embraced, or supported by any particular groups but was articulated unselfconsciously by students who were not necessarily associated with each other in any way. Its expression on campus was more pervasive and more taken for granted than either the social justice or the political difference discourses.

Another aspect of how the three discourses operate differently at CU has to do with their connections to broad cultural discourses. Abstract inclusion draws on individualism and color blindness, discourses that are so institutionalized in our society that CU students' expressions of them sound like clichés. Students' unselfconscious use of abstract inclusion—even when they have no particular knowledge about race, class, gender, disability, or sexual orientation—speaks to its deeply taken-for-granted character. Most young Americans have learned to embrace this discourse—or at least to be familiar with it—from early childhood on. It is reinforced in families, schools, and young people's extracurricular activities. As Bonilla-Silva states, today's young people "are the cohort that has been ingrained from day one with the ideology of color blindness."[27]

Social justice discourse at CU also draws on a broad cultural discourse deeply embedded in American culture, but that broad discourse is contested in the society at large. Social justice discourse belongs to the history of social movements that have long protested the status quo. Whether or not CU students are exposed to social justice discourse in their families, schools, and communities, this discourse assumes that college students need continuous education about the histories and experiences of different social groups and about possibilities for social change.

The discourse of political difference is embedded in a long history of political battles about the nature and purpose of the university.[28] For example, in the "culture wars" of the 1980s and 1990s—the predecessor to the controversy over Horowitz's Academic Bill of Rights—the curriculum became the site of conflict over what should be taught and why. Women's studies, racial-ethnic studies, and similar programs had arisen from a critique of the white, male, Western-focused curriculum as excluding the experiences and contributions of people of color, women, the working class, GLBT people, and people with disabilities. Counter-critiques claimed that the newly inclusive curricula and programs were threatening "the stability of the culture and values that form the basis of U.S. democratic society."[29] The discourse of political difference, as I've described it in this chapter, expands on that counter-critique. Whether or not students encounter the discourse of political difference in high school, this approach to diversity assumes that once students are in college, they need to be educated about the liberal bias in the curriculum.

As they navigate their everyday lives on campus, CU students encounter, produce, and reconfigure tensions among these three discourses about diversity. Sometimes the tension is subtle, as when student government representatives claim that an organization for students who want to practice shooting guns off campus brings diversity to CU. Sometimes the tension is overt, as when the Conservative Students appropriate terms used by social justice advocates, or the NCORE group warns that its Race Column in the student newspaper will anger the community. But sometimes the tension among the various meanings of diversity is explosive, as when the Activists' mounted their protest on campus.

# 3    *Race in CU's Narrative Landscape*

During my interviews with student groups, I usually asked what "diversity" means at CU. But I *didn't* ask that question when I met with two student of color organizations—the Black Collegians and the Southeast Asian Association. Later, as I transcribed and analyzed those two interviews, I realized that my not-conscious omission of that question reflects the place of race in CU's narrative landscape. I didn't ask students of color what diversity means at CU because I shared a tacit understanding with them that their issues, *racial* issues, take center stage in CU's diversity discourse.

Of course, "race" and "diversity" are often treated as synonymous in American society. This can be seen in discussions of the 2003 *Gratz v. Bollinger* U.S. Supreme Court decision, which upheld the use of race in undergraduate admissions procedures but disallowed the University of Michigan's system of allotting points on the basis of applicants' race. In commenting on that decision, University of Michigan president Mary Sue Coleman stated,

> The court has provided two important signals. The first is a green light to pursue diversity in the college classroom. The second is a road map to get us there. We will modify our undergraduate system to comply with today's ruling, but make no mistake: We will find the route that continues our commitment to a richly diverse student body.[1]

In President Coleman's statements, diversity means racial diversity. A similar equation of diversity and race can sometimes be found in social science research. For example, in *Sociology of Higher Education,* the authors of a chapter titled "The Sociology of Diversity" focus almost exclusively on racial and ethnic diversity.[2]

But sometimes in American society "diversity" refers to a longer list of so-

cial categories. For instance, in discussions of the role of universities in educating a diverse workforce in the United States, "diversity" often means race,
gender, ability, and age.[3] And a social science book titled *Diversity on Campus* includes chapters on sexual orientation, gender, class, and race.[4]

At CU, I found that "diversity" was sometimes used to evoke a list of social categories—some combination of race, ethnicity, gender, class, sexual
orientation, ability, nationality, and religion. At the same time, I found that
race was the most prominent and contentious among those categories. This
chapter explores that prominence and contentiousness as a characteristic of
CU's narrative landscape.

## Race as the Most Prominent Diversity Category

Here is the beginning of my interview with six African American women students who are members of CU's Black Collegians, one of the advocacy organizations on campus.

*Susan:* My opening question is sort of a general one—
What sorts of issues have you all been dealing with
Has the Black Collegians been dealing with?
*Tanya:* We in general as an org
We try to deal with just supporting African American students on campus
And kind of educating the campus as to issues of diversity
Particularly surrounding the African American community here at CU
And just trying to make the campus aware of some of the issues we have
That's mainly what we try to focus on doing.

Tanya responds to my general question by outlining the Black Collegian's
overall goals: to support African American students on campus and to educate the broader campus community about issues African Americans face.
These two goals are not particular to this group—every advocacy organization chartered by CU's student government must provide support for its
members and offer education to the campus community. After providing this
general summary—this "abstract" of a narrative, to use William Labov's
term—Tanya and the other Black Collegians launched into an extensive account of their specific activities, problems they face on campus, and the university's failures (and occasional successes) in dealing with those problems.[5]
(I present more of their narrative in chapter 6.)

By contrast, here is the beginning of my interview with three white women
who are members of the Women's Coalition, another chartered advocacy
organization at CU:

*Susan:* What have you all been dealing with this year?
What have your big issues been?

*Hannah:* As an organization?
*Susan:* Yeah
*Camille:* In regards to diversity or just in general?

Camille distinguishes between the Women's Coalition's issues "in regards to diversity" and their issues "in general," a distinction the Black Collegians did not make. Tanya's statement above—"educating the campus as to issues of diversity particularly surrounding the African American community here at CU"—presents the Black Collegian's issues *as* diversity issues. Members of the Southeast Asian Association, another student of color advocacy organization, also presented their issues as diversity issues. But for the white women in the Women's Coalition, it is not so clear how "women's issues" are "diversity issues."

The Women's Coalition went on to tell me about their role in revising CU's sexual assault policy, their events on the topic of sexual violence, and their extensive organizing for women's history month. The latter included programs on body image and eating disorders as well as celebrations of women's contributions to CU. Then I asked:

*Susan:* What do people mean here at CU when they talk about diversity issues?
When you hear that word what are they talking about?
What are *you* talking about?
*Camille:* To me it feels like diversity is synonymous with race relations
I mean that's just what the overpowering theme I feel is at CU
Because it's been an issue and it still is an issue
And I think that gender issues are more—
"Well that's a gender issue
That's not really diverse necessarily"
Especially because you know you look at the campus
And even though you see 60 percent women
A lot of people still don't see the issues between any sort of gender problems
And even like ablebodiedness—
Well it has been coming up because we have a new student org on campus
Which is helping getting these buildings wheelchair accessible
But I think that race seems to be a huge theme on campus
Which is good
It needs to be addressed definitely
*Felicia:* I'll totally agree to that
But in addition I think that sexual orientation is big too
*Camille:* Yes
*Felicia:* Just because recently we've had hate crimes towards GLBT [people]
Yeah I'd say that race is probably the number one diversity issue that is talked about
Unless something happens like this hate crime
Then that issue of diversity is looked at.

Camille and Felicia construct race as the most prominent diversity topic on campus, sexual orientation as next (as a result of recent incidents, which come up again later in this chapter), and disability as recently gaining import on campus. Camille points to the awkwardness of calling gender issues diversity issues because women compose a majority of students on campus. In so doing, she implies that "diversity" makes better sense when referencing a numerical minority. At the same time, she is troubled by what she sees as a disregard for "gender problems." When these students described a sexual assault that took place on campus the year before, they complained that the university's response addressed the violence but not its gendered character. That incident, however, led to revisions of the sexual assault policy, a process that student affairs administrators invited the Women's Coalition to participate in. The students told me they felt gratified by their participation—the administrators listened to them and gender got addressed in the new policy.

The tone of the Women's Coalition's account is not one of complaint. They feel they have strong support on campus, especially among women's studies faculty and student affairs staff. They are reporting (not complaining) that race is at the forefront of diversity discourse at CU, and they deem it appropriate that sexual orientation should be addressed when homophobia becomes evident on campus.

The GLBT Student Organization is another chartered student advocacy group. When I asked three white student members of that group what diversity means at CU, they said:

*Rose:* It's pretty much focused on racial diversity and then gender issues too
But people don't talk about classism very much—
*Nathan:* No they don't—
*Rose:* Even though almost everybody here is—
*Nathan:* Upper middle at least upper middle . . .
And there's a big problem with ableness not being a big priority for campus
Because so much of our campus isn't handicapped accessible and hasn't been for a long time . . .
Lately there's been a lot more people being a lot more outspoken about that issue
But diversity here tends to mean race
*Susan:* And so sexual orientation is sort of further on down?
*Rose:* I'd actually say it's probably second or third
*Nathan:* Well I think it's second but there's just a big gap.

Rose and Nathan's account is similar in several ways to that of the Women's Coalition. First, they work to sort out the place of various diversity categories—race, gender, class, ability, sexual orientation—in campus discourse. Second, they put race at the forefront of that discourse. Third, they see sexual orientation as less prominent but still important. And fourth, their tone is one of reporting not complaining.

Importantly, these GLBT students generally feel supported on campus. They told me that student affairs administrators invited them (along with the Women's Coalition) to help revise the sexual assault policy and that the administrators listened to their ideas about how to ensure that the policy was not heterocentric. They reported their satisfaction with staff in the Office of Student Life who worked with them to create the option of male/female roommates when one of the roommates is gay or lesbian and the other is straight. Furthermore, Student Life followed their recommendation that first-year students be asked, along with other questions about their living preferences, whether they would be comfortable rooming with a GLBT student. These students were also pleased with the administration's prompt and strong response to recent antigay incidents on campus (which the Women's Coalition described above as "hate crimes"—more on this shortly).

The GLBT students did, however, have two complaints about how sexual orientation issues have played out on campus. One is that the administration did not uphold its earlier ban on military recruiters on campus (the ban protested the military's discriminatory "don't ask, don't tell" policy) but caved to pressure related to the Solomon Amendment. That amendment is a federal law which allows the U.S. Defense Department to deny federal funding to universities and colleges if they refuse military recruitment on campus. The other complaint is that there is less programming on campus for dialogue about heterosexism and homophobia than there is for dialogue about racism.

*Rose:* Something that we want to do next year is to try to bring more discussion
    in . . .
Where people have a place where they can safely discuss homophobia
And not be accused of being antigay
Or where they could say
"You know what?
I *do* have that stereotype"
And admit it and confront it and have a discussion like that
Because there are conferences for race and ethnicity issues but there aren't for
    GLBT issues
*Nathan:* We'd like to see something similar to what we do with RC (Race Conference)
But centered around sexuality . . .
*Rose:* Safe zone training [is good]
But it's definitely not equivalent to going off for a weekend and really dealing
    with it.

Neither Rose nor Nathan has been to CU's RC, but they know about it, as do many other students who have not been, especially those involved in other advocacy organizations such as the Women's Coalition and Students for Disability Rights. But whether they have attended or not, both students of color and white students in the advocacy groups view RC as the site of the most productive dialogue about diversity at CU.[6] Here we get a hint of how an institutionalized practice—the annual RC—shapes the narrative landscape at CU. Treating RC as the gold standard for serious conversation about diversity, Rose and Nathan construct the kind of dialogue they want to have at CU about sexual orientation: it needs to be a "safe" place for discussion of internalized homophobia (they mean for both straight and GLBT students), and it needs to take place over an extended period of time, such as a weekend.

My field notes also speak to the prominence of race in diversity discourse at CU, especially in relation to sexual orientation:

> I'm surprised that students who are very involved in advocacy organizations are not necessarily most active in the area you might think they would be. So for example, Melanie, who is white and who has come out to herself and friends as a lesbian, doesn't find the GLBT Organization particularly helpful to her. She is much more exercised about racial issues. She has been to RC and she belongs to WSRR (White Students Resisting Racism). Alan, who is white and out on campus as gay, is peripherally involved in the GLBT Organization. He is very interested in racial issues and their intersection with sexuality issues. But he seems to find more support for and conversation about that intersection within groups of color. He talked about this especially vis à vis NCORE and the RC retreat he had attended. Like Melanie, he is a member of WSRR. Similarly, three staff members I spoke with are out gay men (two of color, one white): when I talked with them they spoke much more about race than sexual orientation.

My surprise reflects my assumption that if white students who identify as GLBT are going to be active around diversity matters, they will choose the GLBT Organization as their primary source of support and activity. I assumed that student involvement is motivated by social identity and social location, that students would be most active in the area(s) where they belong to the less-privileged group(s). For Melanie and Alan, my sense was that their greater interest in race than sexual orientation was less about problems with the GLBT Organization and more about the *pull* of race-related activities and groups. In other words, their interest in race was shaped by the strength of CU's race-related programs (such as RC and NCORE) as well as the prominence of race in CU's narrative terrain.[7]

## Race as the Most Difficult Diversity Conversation

The prominence of race was so pervasive that I asked Mr. Robert, the director of the Office of Multicultural Affairs (OMA), about it. Although it makes sense that OMA would highlight race in its programming, I wondered why *intersections* among diversity categories were not more prominent in CU's diversity discourse. My curiosity was grounded in the fact that much sociological theory and research emphasizes the importance of intersectionality in understanding people's lives.[8] First, though, I asked Mr. Robert about the Race Conference.

*Susan:* I've heard a lot about RC and NCORE
And RC especially seems to be an incredibly powerful experience for students
Can you tell me what your goals are there?
*Mr. Robert:* Ok, to provide a safe environment where our students can talk about race
Many of our students haven't really talked about race in any in depth
In intentional deliberate cross-cultural cross-racial kinds of ways
So to provide that space
To educate our student participants on racial identity, racism, and racial justice
To build bridges between different student populations
And then to ultimately positively impact the community, the larger community.

In outlining RC's goals, Mr. Robert clearly embraces social justice discourse, including a focus on dialogue and social change ("to positively impact the community"). As we shall see in chapter 4, Mr. Robert's description of RC's goals reverberates in students' accounts of what happens there.

As he continued, Mr. Robert told me that many students return to RC for a second, third, and even a fourth time.[9] White students, he said, return for a variety of reasons, sometimes to listen more, sometimes to talk more, sometimes because they want "to be more open and less resistant," and sometimes to work on specific problems that have come up in student organizations. Students of color return to talk about racial justice rather than racial prejudice "which is what most people think racism means." Here Mr. Robert implies that RC teaches students to resist color-blind discourse (which allows for the idea that prejudice is an occasional problem) and to embrace social justice discourse instead. Students of color, he said, are also compelled by ideas about racial identity development because those ideas help them "to explain their own existence *and* why their peers of color might experience things, see things, and desire to be in the community differently from themselves." The concept of racial identity development suggests that the meanings one assigns to one's racial identity are not fixed but can change over time, as one reconsiders one's relation to various others in the social world.[10]

Mr. Robert explained that he recruits facilitators for RC from faculty and staff "who have done race work before," for example, through their involvement in the Faculty Diversity Group or the Office of Student Affairs' diversity education. And he recruits student facilitators for RC from those who have been part of an NCORE group and/or have attended RC before. At this point, I brought up the prominence of race:

*Susan:* I'm guessing that some people sometimes question putting race at the center
Is that true?
*Mr. Robert:* Yes yes they do
You mean for RC?
*Susan:* Yeah hm hmm
*Mr. Robert:* They do
We explain it that we have to start somewhere
That we can't tackle all the issues
That race is an issue that cuts across the other issues
And there seems to be on this particular campus a dis-ease around the conversation
   of race . . .
When I arrived [at CU] I found it very odd that people could talk about sexual ori-
   entation but not about race
In my experience in my assumptions about higher education
I have found that sexual orientation is a more difficult conversation to have
But not here . . .
Often times when you talk about gender for instance or sexual orientation
Race—because it's the most difficult to talk about—
Is the topic that you spend the least amount of time on
We talk about sexual orientation as if all gay people are white
And you can certainly do that with gender
Unless you go directly at race
I have found that on this campus
You can miss race
Because people will revert back to old familiar conversations
And those topics need to be had as well
But if you don't hit it head on here
You can completely miss race.

Mr. Robert indicates that at RC he and others *make* race prominent as a conscious strategy in CU's particular narrative environment. He compares CU's narrative environment to that of other universities he is familiar with, where sexual orientation is the most difficult conversation. He portrays CU's narrative environment as one where the topic of race is elusive, easily slips away, and must be nailed down—approached directly and conscientiously. He argues that focusing on race is a necessary strategy in a narrative terrain where race is the most difficult conversation.

During my interview with four white members of White Students Resisting Racism (WSRR), an informal group at CU that is not chartered by the student government, Melanie and Mark described an interaction at one RC that shows how race can get lost in "old familiar conversations." Their description came at the end of WSRR's critique of color blindness, which Sarah said is difficult to resist because "we've been hearing that that's the way you're supposed to deal with race since we were five years old."[11] Melanie introduced the following as "one of the first in-depth discussions that we had" at the first RC she attended.

*Melanie:* An African American student was talking about the interaction that would take place a lot of times when he would pass white women on campus
And he would get *the head turn*
*Mark:* It's just so consistent
*Melanie:* Yeah or he called it *the cough*
Women would walk by him and cough
And then Connie [a member of WSRR who was not present during this interview]
Made the point
She said
"I know from the discussion that we're having here
I know that a lot of the white students are struggling with just admitting that they're racist
And it's ok to say that you're racist
You're white
We're within a really oppressive system
Where if you're white you're racist"
So I think just for white students to admit that they are racist is really—
They get really defensive when that conversation comes up
It's really hard for that to get admitted . . .
*Mark:* And what came up was gender
I remember a white woman saying
"Well women are fearful of that interaction because of sexism"
And I think that was a really important point to bring up
But at the same time [there's the question of]
Whether or not there would be the same reaction depending on a white man or a black man
But she was sort of like
"Well because I have this experience then I'm not going to listen to your experience
And I'm going to tell you that this is what it actually was
When you don't experience it that way
When you're trying to tell me that it happens so absolutely consistently so many times
Time and time and time again"
I think that for her to say
"Well this is really an issue of gender it's not race" was not listening to his experiences
Which I think is really legitimate to see as racism.

According to Mark, race got lost in the white woman's response to the African American student's account about how white women interact with him in public places. Mark implies that when the white woman claimed "this is really an issue of gender it's not race," she reverted to what Mr. Robert calls "an old familiar conversation" about gender.

Melanie recounts through reported speech Connie's attempt to keep race on the table—Connie's explanation that within a racist system, white people *are* racist in the sense that they inevitably absorb racist perceptions of people of color, an explanation that draws on social justice discourse.[12] When Melanie describes white students' defensiveness regarding Connie's explanation, we hear her pointing to their attachment to abstract inclusion. The latter discourse allows the white woman to say "it's gender not race," to claim that women are equally afraid of all strange men no matter what color they are, that race doesn't matter in this situation.

Mark also portrays the white woman as *refusing* to listen. His use of reported speech for what she clearly did *not* say is a powerful rhetorical strategy for emphasizing that her stance—it's gender not race—is not only an argument but a refusal of dialogue. His focus on what the white woman was *communicating* to the African American man references the importance of dialogue in CU's social justice discourse. Further, he claims that her refusal to listen amounts to racism, by which he seems to mean an exercise of her white racial privilege. This is not a situation, Mark implies, where the African American man and the white woman simply have different perspectives on which they can agree to disagree. According to Mark, the white woman refuses to hear that the African American man's story is about a persistent pattern of how white women interact with him, and that that persistence is sufficient evidence that race is operating in those interactions. Her refusal to listen replays an "old familiar conversation" in which gender trumps race and race gets lost.

Melanie and Mark also provide an image of what listening would look like in this situation. Listening would include acknowledging the African American man's experience: that white women consistently turn their heads or cough or otherwise express discomfort when they pass him. Listening would include acknowledging that racism operates in white women's greater fear of black male than white male strangers. Listening would include acknowledging that reverting to the old familiar conversation of "it's gender not race" is an exercise of white racial privilege.

While Mr. Robert and others (such as students of color and students in WSRR) worked at moving race to the forefront so that it would not get lost, they certainly did not ignore intersections among various diversity categories. For example, one of the NCORE group's projects during the academic year I focus on in this book was a daylong conference on campus about "major intersections." I heard reports about this conference from several people who told me that it focused on ability, nationality, sexual orientation, gender, class, and religion, and that in each case the question was "what changes when race is included in the conversation?" In other words, the conference explored intersections between race and several other diversity categories in ways that didn't allow race to get lost.[13]

Furthermore, when I talked with students in the advocacy organizations, intersections usually came up in one way or another. Here, for example, I am talking with four white women members of Students for Disability Rights (SDR), a recently chartered advocacy organization.

*Susan:* Are there other orgs that you guys partner with in any ways or—
*Natalie:* We haven't thus far
And at least one of my goals for next year—
Assuming that I'm re-elected to the executive board of SDR [laugh]—
Is to partner with student of color orgs
To draw links between the two diversity issues
Because a lot of times people in the disability advocacy community really tend to ignore racism as an issue
Even within the disability community in big quotations
There's just so many different communities within the larger disability community
And vice versa within the student of color—
Or just African American or any racial minority community
They also don't really necessarily have support systems for people with disabilities in that community
So it would be nice to form kind of a partnership there.

Natalie imagines a partnership where neither ability nor race would get lost. She suggests that working with student of color organizations on disability issues would involve addressing racism in the disability community at CU and in the larger disability community. And that it would involve attending to disability issues within student of color organizations at CU as well as the lack of support systems for people of color with disabilities in communities of color more generally. Her interest in this particular partnership or intersection—disability and race, rather than disability and gender or disability and sexual orientation—may be influenced by the prominence of race in CU's narrative landscape.

And sometimes social justice advocates who do "racial justice work" at CU moved other diversity categories to the forefront while keeping intersections on the table. This is seen in the way an informal men's group, Men Against Sexism, described themselves. In an opinion piece in the student newspaper, fourteen men presented their goals and invited anyone on campus (including women) to join them:

We hope to learn from our various experiences of gender how it affects our identities, relationships, and communities. We want to investigate how gender shapes our privileges and our experiences of oppression in terms of race, sexuality, ability, religion, class, and age. . . . We believe that understanding the source of men's violence is not just a matter of self-reflection or raised consciousness. We believe it also requires political responsibility and a serious commitment to resisting cultural and institutional arrangements that reproduce gender inequality.

The authors of this article bring gender to the forefront, and they conceive of gender as intersecting with other diversity categories in various ways. Their focus on privilege, oppression, and institutional arrangements signals their use of social justice discourse. This group of men includes ten students, two professors, and two administrators; four men of color and ten white men. Three are gay men who are out on campus. Seven have been heavily involved with racial justice activities on campus, through RC, NCORE, OMA, WSRR, or the Faculty Diversity Group.

### Race as the Most Contentious Diversity Issue

Students' accounts of campus events confirm both directly and indirectly Mr. Robert's observation that race is a more difficult conversation than sexual orientation at CU. Whether they are white or of color, whether they are involved in advocacy organizations or not—CU students view race as contentious in a way that sexual orientation is not.

An indirect confirmation is evident in the GLBT Organization's discussion of responses to recent antigay speech incidents on campus.* On several different occasions, antigay epithets appeared on campus sidewalks near some residence halls.

*Nathan:* And that actually happened right around the time that the protests were
   going on at the state capital about the marriage amendment
And so it probably didn't have anything to do really with people on this campus
It's more like just part of a political thing I think—
*Susan:* Now what do you mean it didn't have anything to do with people on this
   campus?

My interruption shows my surprise that Nathan formulated the antigay incidents on campus as *not* aimed at GLBT students. My surprise reveals that,

---

*I heard CU students refer to these and similar incidents as "hate speech incidents," "hate crimes," and "hate speech crimes." I use the term *antigay incident* because I don't know whether the incidents were legally deemed "hate incidents." Like most universities, CU has policies on hate incidents and hate crimes. At CU, "hate incidents" include graffiti in public spaces that target individuals on the basis of race, ability, or sexual orientation. CU's student handbook points out that some hate incidents may be defined as hate crimes under federal, state, or city ordinances.

at that moment, I didn't get how sexual orientation fits into CU's narrative environment.

*Nathan:* Not like specifically targeting students necessarily
But just more like making the political statement
Because it's not just something that's been going on at CU
It's a nationwide thing
*Susan:* Right
*Nathan:* It's more like a political message than saying like "CU students"
I mean it still affects CU students obviously.

By placing the campus incidents in the broader context of the marriage amendment debate at the state capital and across the nation, Nathan explains what he meant. He acknowledges that CU students are affected by such incidents, but he indicates that GLBT students have not felt personally threatened by them.

That feeling may be related to what these students described next—the outpouring of support for GLBT people from CU's administration, faculty, and students in the wake of the antigay incidents on campus. They told me that the administration, after consulting with the crisis response team, sent e-mails to the entire campus condemning the incidents and promising an investigation. They described a public rally on campus, attended by one hundred people (a good turnout in their view), at which both straight and openly gay administrators, faculty, and students spoke against homophobia. And they described a T-shirt campaign—"Gay? Fine by Me"—to which several campus groups contributed funds (the religious life office, student government, student newspaper, among others), and which produced a lobby full of three hundred people waiting to pick up their T-shirts. After recounting these events, Rose summed up:

*Rose:* And so [CU administrators] were really supportive
And they deal with it really well
And then I think that students respond really well
There's always lots and lots of letters that get put in our student newspaper by students
As well as occasionally professors
And then everybody else is talking about it
And word gets around
And people really show support.

Rose's shift from the past tense in the first sentence to the continuous present tense for the rest of her account communicates her sense that the support GLBT students receive is not limited to the response to the recent incidents but is more general, perhaps more institutionalized. Her construction of CU as a supportive environment for GLBT people corroborates Mr. Robert's statement that sexual orientation is not the most difficult diversity conversation at CU. Similarly, students in other groups, including Students for Disability Rights and Students for Firearm Safety and Recreation, as well as two groups of students I met with in the residence halls criticized the antigay incidents, and they spoke positively about the administration's prompt response and the rally.

While GLBT students generally feel supported at CU, students of color generally feel supported only in certain venues—most notably OMA. This is part of what the Activists' were protesting during the silent rally—the unaffirming campus climate. During my interview with three student government officers, a major topic was the student government's unsupportive stance regarding racial matters. In the following excerpt from that interview, Ramita, a student of color from a South Asian country, and Asha, a South Asian American student, are responding to my question about whether productive dialogue about diversity takes place during student government meetings.

*Ramita:* If you ask anyone in student government the definition of diversity
They'll probably say
"The differences between me and everyone else in this room"
Rather than the kind of diversity that *we're* talking about
That needs to be talked about on this campus
In terms of racial diversity ethnic diversity ability age whatever it may be
But accessibility is one issue that's recently become important
Student government feels like it's doing something great when it funds
    accessibility . . .
[But] until you understand the dynamics of racism
You're not going to be able to discuss and talk about it intelligently
And most of the people in [student government] don't have the ability to talk about
    it or understand it or grasp it
*Asha:* It's always a student of color issue that seems to be the hardest to discuss
Because so many people are uneducated about race
And then you have sexism ability sexual orientation
And these issues over here which are much easier to talk about . . .
*Ramita:* In student government if you vote against something for accessibility
You're seen as a bad person
If you vote against something for GLBT issues
You'll be seen as a bad person
But for some reason it doesn't apply with the race issue
*Asha:* Yeah
*Ramita:* They feel like they can double question those issues for some reason.

Ramita begins by critiquing other student government representatives' definition of diversity—"the differences between me and everyone else in this room"—a definition that exemplifies the discourse of abstract inclusion. Ramita espouses the social justice definition of diversity, which focuses on race, ethnicity, ability, age, accessibility, and sexual orientation as categories of privilege and oppression. However, Ramita and Asha point out that when those diversity categories *do* come up during student government deliberations, race gets less supportive treatment than the others. (My qualitative content analyses of student government minutes, which I discuss later in this chapter, support their statement.) Ramita and Asha's tone is one of intense frustration as they complain that their white peers find it easier to challenge resolutions that deal with matters important to students of color. They locate the problem in their peers' lack of education about race and racism, an explanation embedded in social justice discourse. Their account echoes Mr. Robert's statement that race is the most difficult diversity conversation at CU.

It is noteworthy, however, that Ramita and Asha's frustration does not lead them to abandon other social justice issues. During the year of my study, Ramita introduced several major resolutions to the student government concerning accessibility and sexual orientation. One resolution got CU's administration to change a traditional graduation practice: instead of able-bodied students walking up a set of stairs on one side of the platform to receive their diplomas while students with physical disabilities used a ramp on the other side, all students now approach the platform from the same side. Another resolution asked CU's administration to reconfirm its ban on military recruitment on campus because of the military's "don't ask, don't tell" policy. As mentioned before, CU's administration rejected that resolution. Ramita also worked with the president of Students for Disability Rights to write to the *Washington Post* on behalf of CU's student government, to critique a cartoon they interpreted as ridiculing people with disabilities.

During my interview with six white journalists for the student newspaper, they compared the uncontentiousness of sexual orientation to the contentiousness of race on campus.

*Susan:* When diversity is talked about at CU
Which forms of diversity are being talked about?
*Sophie:* Generally race
*Nick:* Maybe if I could even add to that question
It's *how* they're being talked about, too, is an interesting thing
And yeah it's mostly race
And mostly it isn't all that positive
*Grace:* Mostly it's with anger . . .
[They discuss the NCORE group's article about anger in the student newspaper]
*Nick:* And at the same time there's a lot of talk about GLBT issues
These last couple weeks and months
Because there's been some hate speech crimes

*Grace:* That was a really good rally for that
*Nick:* And that was dealt with a lot differently it seems
I think that it was a very supportive environment
*Jessie:* Yeah reaction to that was very different.

These students simultaneously put race at the forefront of diversity discourse at CU and point to the contentious character of campus conversation about race. According to their account, the contentiousness resides in part in the anger with which race gets addressed. (Although it is not clear in this excerpt, Grace is talking about students of color's anger—more on this in chapter 7.) Contentiousness, they suggest, is also expressed in responses to racial incidents. Nick points out that the administration's reaction to the antigay incidents was very supportive, and Jessie compares that to the administration's hesitant reaction to issues that students of color raised during the year.

## Race as the Most Prominent and Contentious Category in the Content Analyses

The content analyses that Jessie Finch, Misti Sterling, and I conducted of various texts offer another perspective on the prominence and contentiousness of race in CU's narrative landscape. Table 3.1 shows the results of the quantitative content analyses for CU, and table 3.2 for RU. As explained in the introduction, RU is structurally similar to CU: both are predominantly white, private universities with undergraduate student enrollments of less than three thousand. The comparison between CU and RU provides evidence that universities' narrative environments may exhibit both similarities and differences.

As we look at tables 3.1 and 3.2, we need to remember that for every type of document, CU exhibits a greater amount of diversity discourse than RU (see table 1.1 in chapter 1). We also need to keep in mind that tables 3.1 and 3.2 are summaries of the more detailed tables, D.1 and D.2, respectively, in appendix D. Tables D.1 and D.2 show, for example, that although race is the most prominent category in the student government minutes at both universities, at CU race appears in the student government minutes an average of twice per meeting, while at RU race appears in the minutes an average of less than once per meeting.

Table 3.1 shows that at CU race is the most prominent diversity category in the student newspaper, events calendar, and student government minutes. This corroborates what CU students told me: race is the most prominent diversity topic on campus.

It is striking that the curriculum is the area where CU and RU are most alike. The prominence of global (or international) as a diversity category in the curriculum at both universities may be explained by the national and

**Table 3.1.** Most prominent categories in CU's documents

|  | Student newspaper | Events calendar | Curriculum | Student government minutes |
|---|---|---|---|---|
| Most prominent diversity category | Race | Race | Global | Race |
| 2nd most prominent diversity category | Gender | Global | Gender | General |
| 3rd most prominent diversity category | Sexual orientation | Religion | General and race (tie) | Global |

**Table 3.2.** Most prominent categories in RU's documents

|  | Student newspaper | Events calendar | Curriculum | Student government minutes |
|---|---|---|---|---|
| Most prominent diversity category | Gender | Global | Global | Race |
| 2nd most prominent diversity category | Global | Gender | Gender | Gender and global (tie) |
| 3rd most prominent diversity category | Sexual orientation | Race | Race | Class |

global push in higher education to internationalize the curriculum and to institutionalize that focus. The detailed tables in appendix D show that global issues appear more than twice as often in CU's curriculum than either gender or race, and that in RU's curriculum global issues appear almost twice as often as gender and race. Although they are distant seconds and thirds, the fact that gender and race are the next most prominent diversity categories at both universities may reflect at least a nascent institutionalization of women's studies and race and ethnic studies in higher education curricula. These curricular similarities between CU and RU may also exemplify what John Meyer and other sociologists see as the homogenization of higher education curricula both nationally and internationally.[14] Remember that "institutionalization" means that (some) inclusion of global, gender, and racial issues has become expected and routine in higher education curricula.

At CU, however, the prominence of global issues combined with the relative paucity of racial issues in the curriculum helps to explain the frustration the Activists expressed about CU's cultural diversity requirement during their protest. CU's bulletin describes the cultural diversity requirement as central to the university's mission to educate world citizens. Students are supposed to learn about historical and contemporary injustices as well as practical skills for interacting fairly and compassionately in various settings with people whose social positions differ from theirs. But as many students and faculty told me, the requirement itself is organized such that students can graduate from CU without taking any courses addressing historical or contemporary injustices or power differences among people.[15] Furthermore, students can fulfill the requirement without studying any form of diversity or injustice in the United States. They can fulfill it by taking courses in a European language and studying abroad in Europe. This critique of the cultural diversity requirement is pivotal to the Activists' protest at CU, the events of which are highlighted in part III.

### Student Newspaper

But *how* do various diversity issues get discussed in these documents? A qualitative analysis of CU's student newspaper during the year when the Activists' protest took place reveals that race is not only more prominent but also more contentious in that context than other diversity categories. Among the articles, editorials, opinion pieces, and letters coded for race that year, several specific events and issues generated substantial coverage and controversy over time: the overrepresentation of students of color in the university's promotional materials (some people defended this while others felt it misleads prospective students of color); two students of color's public criticism of a professor's course (some people were upset about the *public* nature of the students' complaint; some read their complaint as the tip of the iceberg concerning problems with the cultural diversity requirement); an African American student's MLK day speech, which called on students of color and white students to take responsibility in different ways for addressing race (a white student charged the author of this article with reverse racism; some letter writers defended the original speech); and how well CU as an institution is doing in addressing race (some claimed that CU produces more talk than action; others claimed that CU is further ahead than most institutions).

Not every piece coded for race evoked controversy. Read as a whole, the articles written by the NCORE group and published in the Race Column during the year exhibit an educational strategy of providing information and historical background to debunk stereotypes about people of color and to encourage informed dialogue about race and racism. Topics in the Race Column ranged from on-campus issues (misperceptions about student of color scholarships; events sponsored by African students; the disjunction between white students' and students of color's perspectives on race; the conference on intersections among various social justice issues; how to understand the anger of students of color); to broader social issues (immigration; racial profiling in the post 9/11 world; the Hmong people as forgotten U.S. allies in the Vietnam War; facts about HIV/AIDS; racial segregation in the city where CU is located). In addition, the newspaper includes a few articles about events organized around dialogue across racial boundaries, such as one about a panel discussion during which six seniors (of various races) talked about how their racial identities have shaped their lives.

As shown in table 3.1, gender is the second most prominent diversity category in CU's student newspaper (and, in fact, it is a close second, as table D.1 in appendix D shows). But among articles coded for gender during that year, few issues galvanized attention over time and few were contentious. This may help explain how gender could be the second most prominent category in *quantitative* terms in the student newspaper but not be *perceived* by students as a prominent diversity topic on campus. (In addition, although gender is second to global in the curriculum, it does not appear in the top three categories in the events calendar and the student government minutes.)

Nonetheless, the range of gender-related topics in the newspaper is extensive: CU's newly revised sexual assault policy; women in the university's leadership; the new group on campus of profeminist men working against sexism; events for eating disorders week; challenges faced by student moms on campus; a critique of sexism at an on-campus party; and a number of articles addressing issues of women and gender in society. The latter include gender relations in local strip clubs, the city's annual Take Back the Night rally, the city's celebration of women-owned businesses for women's history month, a critique of a sexist TV show, and praise for films and plays that deal with gender. But apart from an exchange of letters about how eating disorders week was presented in the paper, there is little debate or dialogue in the newspaper about these gender topics. When discussing gender, most articles, opinion pieces, and letters use an educational tone.

Among the items coded for sexual orientation—the third most prominent diversity category in CU's student newspaper—one issue got extensive play: the student government's resolution (and the administration's rejection of that resolution) to ban military recruiters on campus because of the military's "don't ask, don't tell" policy. There are more arguments for the ban than against it, but even those against it do not express antigay sentiments; rather, their arguments revolve around the university's need to protect its federal funding. Another topic that galvanizes attention is the antigay incidents on campus. But there is no controversy here: articles, editorials, and letters on this topic are unanimously opposed to and appalled by such actions. Several items address changes in residential life—the reinstatement of a GLBT house and the new option of male/female roommates when one person is straight and the other GLBT. Here, too, there is no controversy—these pieces are reports not arguments. The way issues of sexual orientation appear in the student newspaper corroborates the GLBT students' accounts in their interviews with me that, overall, CU provides a supportive environment for them.

Given that the student newspaper is the only document in table 3.1 in which sexual orientation appears among the top three categories (and there, in third place), how can I explain CU students' construction of sexual orientation as the second most prominent diversity topic on campus? A couple of factors may be relevant here. Like the student newspaper articles on race (and unlike those on gender), those on sexual orientation galvanized attention over time, giving them a sense of prominence. Like issues of race (and unlike those of gender), issues of sexual orientation, such as the hate incidents discussed above, were visible on campus in ways that aren't captured fully in the content analyses. For example, the GLBT rally, the "Gay? Fine by Me" T-shirt campaign, and the administration's all-campus e-mails about the antigay incidents also gave them a sense of prominence. In addition, although sexual orientation did not appear among the top three categories in the student government minutes, the discussion of the resolution to ban military recruiters from campus was extensive and took place over several meetings, giving it prominence in *qualitative* if not *quantitative* terms in that context.

### Student Government

Many instances of talk coded for various diversity categories in the student government minutes consist of routine announcements of events sponsored by student organizations. For example, talk coded as "global"—the third most prominent diversity category in the minutes—includes announcements for events to be held by the International Student Organization, the African Student Organization, and Amnesty International, as well as events hosted by other organizations for World Aids Month. Talk coded as "global" also includes mentions of opportunities for study and service learning abroad, conference funding requests for international student groups, approval of a charter for a group concerned with political freedom in Tibet, and an uncontroversial resolution encouraging the university to get more fair trade coffee on campus. The only *discussion* coded as "global" was about a resolution requesting funds to support relief after a natural disaster in Southeast Asia, a proposal that did not pass because the student government by-laws prohibit donations to external organizations, in this case, UNICEF.

"General" is the second most prominent category in the minutes. This includes any mention of the words *diversity* or *social justice* in contexts where specific diversity categories are *not* mentioned. For example, I coded as "general" several excerpts from the minutes that I discussed in chapter 2, such as talk about Students for Firearm Safety and Recreation bringing diversity to campus, and the students' questions, "What top-down diversity initiatives are you taking . . . ?" and "How are each of you personally educating yourselves about social justice issues?" In addition, I coded as "general" any mentions of the university's cultural diversity policy, the university's cultural diversity curriculum requirement, and student organizations' diversity policies.

Race, of course, is the most prominent category in the minutes. Many instances of talk coded for "race" consist of routine announcements for events sponsored by student of color organizations. Talk coded for "race" also includes a resolution for a new advocacy organization for multiracial students, and a resolution against the city's criminalization of homelessness, which some students said targets racial minorities (that resolution was also coded for "class").

However, we see the *contentiousness* of race in three issues that garnered substantial attention across several meetings. One was a resolution to use funds from the student government's capital improvement account to support an endowment for scholarships for students of color, which would be administered by the university. (The endowment had already been set up by another office on campus, and CU was soliciting donations from alumni of color.) That resolution was rejected by the student government's budget committee and its political affairs committee (which deals with the by-laws and constitution), while several other resolutions for funds from the same account were approved, including funds for dormitory furniture, a recording studio, and accessible chairs for the library (funds ranged from two thousand to ten thousand dollars for these items). The author of the scholarship endowment resolution resubmitted it, this time proposing to use student government funds that remained unused at the end of the academic year (somewhere between seven thousand and twelve thousand dollars). The student government approved that resolution. Much of the discussion of the second resolution was about by-law and budget technicalities, but in the following excerpt from the minutes other issues arose.

*Student Rep #1 [man of color]:* This is a great way for us to support diversity. . . . The more money that we give upfront, the easier it will be for the university to solicit donations from alumni.*
*Student Rep #2 and Author of Proposal [white man]:* Call to question.
Debate does not end. [Discussion of budget technicalities related to the proposal.]
*Student government officer [woman of color]:* [Clarifies budget technicalities] I think this is the best way that we actually support diversity. We have only paid for the improvements for accessibility, we have never given money to the cause of students of color.
*Student Rep #3 [white man]:* People are capital so this is putting money into diversity that is a capital improvement.

*Because I know who these students are, I identify their race and gender in this excerpt. In the excerpts from student government minutes that I presented in chapter 2, I am less sure of who the students are and so I did not include their race and gender.

*Others:* [More discussion of technicalities. The student government officer explains that this will not affect any student organization budgets; it's about funds *not* used at the end of the year, and it's only for *this* year.]

*Student Rep #4 [white man]:* This seems like we're buying diversity. I don't think we need to buy diversity. We should not have to give people money to come here.

*Student Author of Proposal [white man]:* We do want students of color here. This is one of many steps that need to be taken. Also keep in mind that we want money that is going to roll over that in the past people have argued that we could spend on great things the next year, but it never gets spent, so let's just spend it on this great thing.

*Student Guest [not a student rep]:* Who will tell students that their money went to help other people pay for their tuition?

*Student Rep #5 [woman of color]:* I move to limit speaker time to one minute
Speaker time is limited.

*Student Rep #6 [woman of color]:* Call to question
Debate ends
Voting: 14–5 motion passes

The passage of this resolution shows that it had substantial support within the student government, including the support of white men. Indeed the author of the proposal was a white male student. When the student government officer states that the student government has only "paid for improvements for accessibility, we have never given money to the cause of students of color," she is talking about expenditures for special projects rather than conference funds or student organization budgets. It is noteworthy that she compares the scholarship endowment to improvements for accessibility and that she doesn't mention expenditures for the recording studio and dormitory furniture, among other things. She is saying that when it comes to funding *diversity*-related special projects, the student government has spent money on accessibility, but not on anything related to race.

Student Rep #4's objection is grounded in the discourse of abstract inclusion. His idea that an endowment for scholarships for students of color is "buying diversity," and that "we should not have to give people money to come here" suggests that all students should be treated the same and ignores the fact that universities "buy" different students with many different scholarships and financial aid. The Student Guest's rhetorical question—"who will tell students that their money went to help other people pay for their tuition?"—evokes the language of reverse racism. He suggests, implicitly, that through their student fees, the mostly white student body will be paying the tuition of some students of color, and that that is unfair.[16] Student Rep #2, the author of the proposal, references social justice discourse when he argues that "this is one of many steps that need to be taken" in order to encourage students of color to enroll at CU. He implies that college opportunities are unequal for white high school students and high school students of color and that CU's commitment to recruiting students of color requires "many steps," one of which should be scholarships. Student Reps #5 and #6—two women of color—successfully limit the discussion and move it to a vote.

By contrast, here is the brief discussion of the resolution to use capital improvement funds to purchase chairs for the library for people with physical disabilities.

*Student Rep #7 and Author of Proposal [white man]:* I wrote this last semester . . . Basically I asked the directors of the library what their needs were. These chairs will allow microfiche to be accessible to all students. Those were the main reasons for this capital improvement.

*Student government officer [woman of color]:* I would encourage everyone to vote for this. . . . We want to make everywhere on campus accessible.

*Student Rep #8 [white man]:* Where will these chairs be?

*Student Rep #7 and Author of Proposal [white man]:* The initial area where students can see microfiche and microfilm in the front lobby of the library.

*Student Rep #9 [white man]:* For clarification, does this include the back lab?

*Student Rep #7 and Author of Proposal [white man]:* No.

Called to question.

Vote on motion.

Passes unanimously.

Unlike the scholarship endowment resolution, this resolution evoked only informational questions, and it passed unanimously.

The second contentious race-related issue has to do with the character of discussion itself during student government deliberations. Because my data consist of meeting minutes, I do not have access to tone of voice, facial expressions, and behavioral cues such as interrupting, talking, or reading the newspaper while others speak. Nonetheless, throughout the year, the minutes include sustained attention to the topic of how students relate to each other during meetings. Students' construction of this topic as racialized is seen in both implicit and explicit references to silencing and disrespectful treatment of students of color.

Here is an excerpt from a long speech that Elaine, a student of color, delivered during the open forum part of a meeting. The minutes indicate that she had written this speech in advance of delivering it.

I would like to address the student government on an issue that has come up for me again and again and has me very angry and uneasy. [She describes her life-long desire to be part of student government, her deep respect for its members, and her current disappointment about the negative character of discussion during student government meetings.] Now as I stand here before you, I only see the negative feelings you have for one another. I see a group of people who all they do is come up with ways to bring their personal problems into meetings rather than representing the student body. . . . I have struggled to come up with the best way to handle a situation such as this; I have come to the conclusion that the best way to address this topic is to be as direct and straightforward as possible. I want this to stop *now*. I don't mean let's work on it and bring it up at the next meeting. I mean now. I am not targeting certain people; I am targeting student government as a whole.

Elaine speaks to the student government as a body and does not mention race, which indicates that she is using the discourse of abstract inclusion. But the minutes show that three of the four students who publicly thank her for her speech are students of color. The fourth is a white student involved in White Students Resisting Racism. And minutes for the next meeting of the committee whose job is to support the advocacy organizations show that Elaine's speech hit a chord and that members of that committee perceive race as an underlying issue: "The issue . . . is disrespect. When students of color speak, they are automatically shut down."[17]

The topic of disrespect during meetings was so pervasive that Joe, a white male officer of the student government, whose job was to lead the meetings, proposed the creation of a new committee to write a code of conduct that would encourage respect and to develop ideas that would facilitate greater openness during meetings. During discussion of this proposed committee, one representative stated, "If we are going to use this committee to increase openness, we need to make sure that there are non-student-government students involved, as well as students of color." Joe responded, "Any committee that I appoint won't be just of my favorite white heterosexual males." From what I know about Joe in other contexts (for example, his articles in the student newspaper), it is fair to guess that he was speaking seriously rather than sarcastically.

Indeed, woven throughout the minutes are references to the need for better representation of the voices of students of color in student government. Here are a few examples from different meetings:

*Student government officer [woman of color]:* I just went to RC and as reps it is important for us to represent all of our constituents not just our white constituents. The image that people have of student government is that we are racist and sexist as an org.

*Student government officer [white man]:* I remember sitting in [a residence hall lounge] at a student government roundtable discussion and hearing the frustrated complaints of mostly women and students of color regarding the student government system, voices that cannot continue to be lost through systematic means.

*Student Rep #10 [woman of color, after a motion to approve her as a new repre-*

*sentative]:* I decided to step in to be a rep because student government needs the voice of students of color in their meetings.

*Student Rep #11 [woman of color, after a motion to approve her as a new representative]:* I am a first-year student, and I will do my best to make sure that the concerns and struggles of students of color will be heard.

*Student Rep #12 [woman of color, after a challenge to her nomination to chair the budget committee]:* We need to stop just representing the majority on campus.

The third contentious issue concerns the student government's response to the large group of students of color—the Activists—who attended a student government meeting, sitting silently, dressed in black, and who left partway through the meeting to carry out their silent rally in the university's main square. At the time, of course, student government members did not know what these students were up to. During student government meetings after the silent rally, some representatives argued that the student government needed to write a public response to the Activists, including an apology for not specifically making time for the Activists to speak at the meeting, and acknowledging students of color's long-term discontent with the student government. Other representatives argued that no apology was necessary, that the Activists should have simply said what they had to say during the regularly appointed time for open discussion. Some pointed out that the Activists' silence was itself part of the message they were communicating—that students of color *have* spoken in the past but have not been heard. In the long run, nine representatives (rather than the student government as a body) published a letter to the Activists in the student newspaper. The majority of representatives did not sign it. Here is an excerpt from that letter:

> We understand that by not pausing to address you during the meeting you attended, we furthered the point your silent rally was making: student government (and others on campus) do not hear students of color's voices. We apologize for failing you in our responsibilities as your representatives. . . . We commend your courage in standing up for these issues as well as your success in getting the attention of the campus as a whole. . . . We hope you see this letter as a first step toward our better understanding and representation of your voice.

While the minutes show that the majority of the student government did not think the Activists' silent presence at their meeting required special attention on their part, the minutes show that the student government *did* offer support for the GLBT rally. Staff advisers to the student government announced the rally in advance and students encouraged each other to attend. The student government also unanimously passed a resolution to help fund the "Gay? Fine by Me" T-shirt campaign.

Of course, the GLBT rally and the Activists' silent rally differed greatly in their origins and intents. The GLBT rally was a response to several specific antigay incidents on campus, was authorized by CU's administration, and its speakers included administrators as well as faculty and students. By contrast, the Activists' silent rally originated in long-term frustration about a range of race-related concerns, was not authorized by anyone but themselves, was a surprise to the campus as a whole, and its aims were to make visible the weakness of the curriculum on diversity issues and the lack of support for students of color by the administration, student government, and student newspaper. The message of the GLBT rally was "the university as a whole supports GLBT people." The message of the Activists' rally was "we have not been supported by the university as a whole; we have raised our voices many times but we have still not been heard." It was much easier, then, for the student government to support the GLBT rally than to support the Activists' actions.

## Race in CU's Narrative Environment

My interviews with student groups and the content analyses corroborate each other. Each source of data confirms that race is the most prominent and the most contentious diversity topic at CU.[18] Each confirms that "when people talk about diversity at CU they are most often talking about race," *and* that race is where the most tension and volatility lie. The perspective that Mr. Robert offers puts a particular spin on this social phenomenon. Along with others in the interconnected group, he works to *move* race to the forefront and works to *keep* it there as a conscious strategy in a narrative environment where race can easily be marginalized or ignored. That marginalization can be seen in students' use of the discourse of abstract inclusion. That discourse gets mobilized in the story about the white woman's insistence that "it's gender not race" that operates in women's fear of black men. It also gets mobilized in the implicit argument that scholarships for students of color constitute reverse racism and that such scholarships "buy diversity." The tension surrounding race at CU lies at the intersection of conscious efforts to put race at the forefront of diversity discourse and resistance (conscious or not) to those efforts. It seems likely that these social processes reinforce each other.

Structural factors may also play a role in the prominence of race in CU's diversity discourse. While CU has an administrative office devoted specifically to students of color—OMA—there is no specific office for GLBT students or women students. There is an office for disability services, but it is much newer than OMA, and it has fewer staff. In addition, there are numerous student of color organizations, but only one GLBT-related student organization, one disability-related student organization, and two gender-related student organizations. Furthermore, the strongest interdisciplinary faculty group—the Faculty Diversity Group—makes race its priority while including other social justice topics.

But while structural factors may help to explain the prominence of race, they don't, in themselves, produce the *contentiousness* of race. The latter has to do with *how students develop their voices and converse with each other within CU's narrative landscape.* Those are the topics of parts II and III.

# PART TWO

# Students' Personal Narratives

# 4    *Learning to Speak*

A t the end of my group interviews with CU students, I asked for volunteers for in-depth individual interviews. During the individual interviews, I asked what they were like in high school and what their interests were then. I asked how they ended up at CU, what their transition to college was like, other transitions they've gone through during their college career, and what their most positive learning experiences have been. As they recounted their college experiences, nearly all of the students discussed diversity issues at length.[1]

When I asked what the transition was like during the first weeks and months of college, students spoke about this as a "critical biographical moment."[2] They spoke about being either happy or distressed about leaving home, dealing with the responsibility of independence, adjusting to new academic expectations, developing new interests, dealing with roommates, and making new friends. These are issues one would expect traditional-age students to be concerned about at nearly any residential college or university.

For some, the transition to college was relatively smooth. For example, Camille talked about being "excited to be done with high school," being "ambitious" in terms of joining a lot of organizations, and finding the academic load "definitely doable." It was difficult, she said, when she and her high school boyfriend broke up during her first semester, but she viewed that as "just something that happens" to many people when they go to college.

For others, the transition to college was not so easy. One student, for instance, told me that she was date raped during her first semester. That experience, she said, "didn't actually affect me very much when it happened" but several weeks later "that's when the trauma came." She confided in a faculty member who was able to help her get the support she needed. Another student had trouble dealing with the greater accessibility of drugs and alcohol in college. He said "the peer pressure is amazingly higher in college than it is in high school because in college it's 'so what, who cares, every-body's doing it.'" After a month of heavy drinking, he realized that "'this is not what I want to do, this is not where I want to go.'"

As the students who were sophomores, juniors, and seniors recounted transitions they have gone through since their first year and what they have learned during their college years, they inevitably talked about changes in their sense of self.

*Marshan:* I've changed a lot because of City University
Obviously everyone changes in college.

It is obvious to Marshan that everyone changes in college because that is part of a key narrative that circulates in higher education and particularly in liberal arts colleges: college is a time and place where traditional-age students open their minds and begin to think critically about the world around them. By the time teenagers go to college, they know that the next four years are supposed to be a time when they will grow up, expand their horizons, and make serious decisions about their future. They know that they will—or at least should—become adults with a sense of themselves as independent, open-minded people with credentials in their specific fields.[3]

Not surprisingly, CU students drew easily on this narrative of self-development during college. No one told me that they had not changed at all during college. But the narratives of students involved in the advocacy organizations—students of color, GLBT students, women students, students with disabilities, as well as white students in White Students Resisting Racism—included a distinct theme. These students developed the theme of *voice*, of learning to speak publicly about social justice issues. And among these students, that theme was most prominent in the narratives of students of color.

In this chapter I take a close look at the personal narratives of Kia, who is Hmong American, and Rachelle, who is African American.[4] I chose these two students' narratives because they are so different—each develops a very specific story about the development of her voice, about learning to speak publicly about racial issues at CU.

By the time I sat down with Kia and Rachelle for their individual interviews, I had already met and talked with them in the context of a group interview. I knew Kia from my interview with the Southeast Asian Association, and I knew Rachelle from my interview with the Black Collegians. Both had also already provided me with background information about themselves, their families, high schools, and their activities at CU. Kia and Rachelle were active in their respective student of color organizations and both were involved in the Multicultural Student Group (which encourages leaders of the student of color and international student organizations to work collaboratively). Both were among the leaders of the Activists.

As I present Kia's and Rachelle's stories, I focus on their narrative practices, what they are *doing* as they speak, and the ways in which they construct their accounts about themselves, others, and the world around them.[5] Their narrative practices take shape within particular interactional contexts (intensive interviews with me) as well as within the local narrative environment (the tensions and complexities of CU's narrative landscape). Kia's and Rachelle's narratives about how they are learning to speak about racial issues are skillful constructions that define their identities and social realities and that make sense of the biographical details of their lives. Despite significant differences between their narratives, several similarities reveal how CU's narrative environment facilitates their engagement with diversity.[6]

Catherine Riessman's ideas about narrative analysis have strongly influenced how I approach the interview material, especially in this and the next chapter. Rather than beginning by parsing interviews into thematic content *across* interviews (the method used by most qualitative researchers), I focus *first* on the integrity of and themes *within* each speaker's narrative. Only after developing a strong understanding of individuals' narratives do I analyze patterns across them.[7]

## Kia: Developing a Voice of Quiet Authority

Kia is a humanities major whose parents are Hmong immigrants. Her mother did not finish high school, her father has a GED, and both work as manual laborers. She is one of several siblings. When I asked about her high school years, Kia told me that she began high school in a small town where she was the only Hmong student in most of her classes. As she looked back at this time in her life, she described herself as "whitewashed." She recounted a conversation with one of her brothers about how both of them assumed they would marry white people someday, a thought she now interprets as "internalized racism."[8] She also assumed that she would go to college, "because my white peers were going to do that, and I really identified with them and their experiences." Jean Kim, who studies Asian American identity development, states that Asian Americans who grow up in predominantly white environments may experience "Active White Identification." "Such Asian Americans consider themselves to be very similar to their White peers and do not consciously acknowledge any differences between themselves and Whites. They do not want to be seen as an Asian person and do all they can to minimize and eliminate their Asian selves."[9]

Despite her identification with white peers and her assumption that she would go to college like her peers, Kia did not know how to make that happen. And no one in her family knew how to help her. She knew some students of color who were involved in a program that encouraged preparation for college but she didn't think that program was for her.

During high school, Kia moved with her family to a large city where she attended a multiracial high school that had a substantial Hmong population. In that new context she was "shocked to realize that Hmong people didn't have to be pigeonholed," for example, that Hmong students could play sports other than volleyball or could be honored by the school for their volunteer activities. She enjoyed "just walking down the hall and hearing Hmong spoken," and she described these new experiences as "helping me find what it meant for me to be Hmong." By the time she was a senior, some of the Hmong students with whom she was taking AP courses were enrolled in Upward Bound or similar programs designed to prepare low-income students for college.[10] But she was not. Again, it didn't occur to her that these programs could be for her.

When January of her senior year rolled around, Kia still had not applied to any colleges. It was an accident, she said, that she ended up at City University. Somehow (she didn't say how) she found out that CU had a writing scholarship which she applied for and was awarded, even before applying at CU.

*Kia:* And I really applied [to CU] because the application was free as well
And it ended up being I didn't apply anywhere else
And if CU didn't take me
I was not going to go to college
I was probably going to go to a community college or technical college
But CU accepted me
So that's why I say it was an accident really.

While Kia narrates being Hmong as an important part of her identity during her later high school years, she does not explicitly mention social class, even though it is clear from her stories that class has shaped her life experiences. Like many working-class students of color across the United States, Kia lacked knowledge about how to research and apply to college, knowledge that constitutes middle-class cultural capital. Consequently, she describes ending up at CU as "an accident." In other words, she suggests that circumstances (rather than an informed decision-making process) happened to move her in that direction.[11]

When recounting what college was like during her first weeks and months at CU, Kia describes herself as lonely, isolated, and "really quiet." She lived at home—which was what her parents expected and which she did throughout her college career—and so she found it difficult to make friends and become involved on campus. And because no one in her immediate family—including two older brothers—had gone to college, there was no one at home with whom to share her new experiences.

Prior to arriving at CU, Kia had received a letter about student of color orientation from the Office of Multicultural Affairs (OMA). But she didn't go, explaining, "I didn't know *to* go. . . . It may have just been me not paying attention to those words 'student of color orientation.'" She said she knew about OMA but "I didn't think it was for me." A Hmong student told her about the student of color retreat that takes place in September, and she signed up to go, but she ended up not going to that either. While events for "students of color" didn't interest Kia, she really missed speaking Hmong, or "Hmonglish," on CU's predominantly white campus, and so she sought out the Southeast Asian Association (SAA). "When I found the Hmong people on campus, it was just right away a connection." The president of SAA encouraged her to become more involved, but her commuter status made it difficult for her to participate in more than a few of their activities during her first year at CU.

Kia said the most powerful learning experience her first year was the first seminar she took on the topic of rape. Taking that course was another "accident," she said, because few seminars were still open by the time she enrolled at CU. The course included a service learning option—volunteer work at a rape crisis center—and Kia described that as "changing my life." Because she was living at home, she had to explain to her parents what she was doing and why she sometimes needed to go to the hospital in the middle of the night to support a rape victim.

*Kia:* There's no word in Hmong for rape or advocacy you know
So I had to explain all these things to them that I was doing and getting involved
   in . . .
My mom [and I] we would usually talk in whispers
And my mom probably then relayed it on to my dad
*Susan:* And did she appreciate what you were learning?
*Kia:* She did she did
She didn't say it
They never say it
But I know by her body language
By how she was talking to me
And what she was saying that she knew how important what I was doing was
For me in general and for just the work
Because no one [in the Hmong community] really does work like that
Or if they do they can't really talk about it
Because the community as big as it is it is pretty small too.

This passage is filled with themes of voice, silence, language, and authoritative speaking. Kia presents herself as figuring out how to explain to her parents "rape" and "advocacy," concepts that do not exist in their native language. As such, she constructs herself as speaking knowledgeably in relation to her parents. Although she does not say why she and her mother spoke in whispers—perhaps because her younger siblings were around—her mention of the whispering signals the extremely sensitive nature of the topic, both at home and in the Hmong community at large. Despite that sensitivity though, Kia presents her conversation with her mother—and her mother's subsequent conveying of the story to her father—as successful. Although her mother doesn't say so, she communicates through body language her appreciation of the importance of Kia's advocacy work, both for Kia and the Hmong community.

On a more implicit level, this passage resonates with the overall theme of Kia's narrative: she is learning to speak with a quiet voice of authority about important social justice issues. Here, and throughout her narrative, Kia presents herself as developing a voice that quietly but confidently breaks through silences. Notice, as well, that Kia uses the expression "the work." As I explained in chapter 2, CU students, faculty, and staff who treat diversity as a matter of social justice sometimes use "the work" and similar expressions to communicate that social change requires an ongoing commitment. Indeed, Kia continued to volunteer at the rape crisis center for two more years.

Kia's connection to CU changed dramatically her sophomore year. Another Hmong student encouraged her to run for office in the Southeast Asian Association, which she did, and won, and through that position she learned about other organizations on campus for students of color and about how the student government works. "SAA was my stepping stone to working in the CU community in general." Also during the fall of her sophomore year, Kia went to CU's Race Conference (RC). As Mr. Robert explained in chapter 3, the goal of RC is to facilitate cross-racial dialogue and education for both white students and students of color about race, racism, and racial justice. RC turned out to be a transformative experience for Kia:

*Kia:* There was a session that we did that was called "crossing the line"
And so it was a line drawn on the floor
I think it was masking tape
And everybody was on one side
And questions would be asked like
"If you're a sophomore, cross the line"
So it started really general really applicable to everyone
Then it came
"If you've ever been called fat"
"If you are Jewish"
"If you're—"
So then it really got to the identity issue
And the last piece of it was
"Cross over the line if you're African American or Hmong or Asian"
But not at the same time you know specifically the group
And when that happened
When the groups were called over
They were then allowed to tell their story or to talk about their experiences

And that was *huge* for some reason
I mean the other years that we've done it it was just like another event
But that first year for me so much happened.

Kia sets up this experience as an extremely powerful event for her. The level of detail—the masking tape line, the progression from general categories to racial identities, the use of direct speech—indicates that she remembers it well. She also distinguishes her experience of "crossing the line" this year from later years at RC. She continues:

*Kia:* When the Hmong group crossed over
We talked about our families
And our parents' experience with the [Vietnam] War and coming over [to the
   United States]
And issues about the gangs
Being considered gangs
And all this *pain*
And it was a lot of crying
And that session took a really long time
I think it was like two hours
And usually those things are like thirty minutes
So that first RC just blew my mind
And like we were able to just *talk*
And they had to listen because there wasn't anything going on
It was just us talking right now.

By using "we," "our," and "us," Kia indicates that the Hmong students told a "collective story," both in the sense that they spoke with each other and in the sense that their families have had similar experiences with the Vietnam War and immigration to the United States.[12]

Kia emphasizes the emotional power of the story as well as of the telling. Her focus on that emotional intensity suggests that the Hmong students experienced their storytelling with their peers in this setting as breaking through a silence about their families' history. The emotional enormity of the story speaks to a change brought about through the very act of telling. I sensed that for Kia the change was connected to the newness of being part of a group of Hmong students speaking about their families' experiences to a non-Hmong audience.

*Susan:* Was it the first time where you were telling the story of your family and
   your life to an audience that wasn't just Hmong?
I mean there were other students of color and white people [there]
Was that part of what was powerful?
*Kia:* I think so

I think there was that
And also in my freshman seminar
There was a kid from [another state] . . .
Who didn't know about Hmong people . . .
He didn't know what "Hmong" was
And so I was *surprised*
And I think that contributed to what happened at RC
I was like you know "there are people who don't know"
And I was "yeah we have to let them know."

For Kia, finding out about others' ignorance about Hmong people lent urgency to the need to tell the collective story, to speak out at RC. She wanted to inform other students about her community's history and she wanted to debunk stereotypes about Hmong youth and gangs. Although Kia describes the story and the telling as painful, she also communicates that the telling empowered her and her Hmong peers—it gave them a voice. Her narration of this experience at RC expresses her transformation from being lonely and isolated on campus to being part of a group of Hmong students and a community at CU in which she develops a public voice.

It is interesting that Kia emphasizes the telling of this story—the Hmong students' empowered voice—rather than the other students' responses. Her statement (in the previous excerpt), "they had to listen because there wasn't anything going on it was just us talking right now," suggests that the exercise was set up in a way that did not allow for anyone else's story at that moment. Others were a captive audience. But "they had to listen" also hints that there is no guarantee that others *heard* the Hmong students' story. And, in fact, Kia reported later that a white student had said about this event, "'I don't understand why people are crying.'" Kia's response to that was "'ooookaayyyy,'" indicating that it was hard for *her* to understand why the white student didn't get it.

The next year, Kia was invited to help facilitate at RC. "The name *facilitator* gave me a sense of, you know, some authority, so I really wanted to watch what I was saying and how I said things." As she moved into the facilitator role, she gained a sense of speaking authoritatively, but something else shifted for Kia as well.

*Kia:* And I think I realized from [RC] the importance and validation
Of my own experiences and experiences of people of color
But then also "oh my gosh, here's a white student too"
And what—how do they feel?
And what do they feel about whiteness or that identity?"
And especially because not all white people claim that
So that experience really wanted me to open myself up
And start thinking about the white student
And what they were going through as well.

Kia presents RC as influencing her in two ways. First, she realized the importance of her experiences and those of other people of color. Notice that the need to *learn* this speaks to the institutionalized devaluation of those experiences in our society at large as well as in some contexts at CU. Notice also that here Kia identifies with "people of color," a term she did not treat as applicable to herself as a new first-year student (in her earlier narrative). Part of what she has learned through RC, then, is to see herself not only as Hmong, but also as a person of color. This racial identity has become possible for Kia within the distinct narrative niche facilitated by the interconnected group at CU, and RC is one of its most powerful activities.

Second, Kia has learned to be interested in *white* students' experiences of race. Although social justice discourse usually treats the voice of the other as the less privileged group in any situation, Kia clearly treats white students here as "other," as experiencing race in ways she needs to understand. Thus she presents herself as learning not only to speak but also to listen. Her unusual phrase (unusual in English anyway)—"that experience really wanted me to open myself up"—is difficult to interpret. It might suggest that she experienced RC itself as strongly inviting or making it possible for her to listen to white students in a way it was not possible for her do before or to do elsewhere.

From this point on in her narrative, Kia highlights events and occasions in which she speaks in some public arena or another in ways that show she is developing an authoritative voice as a leader on campus. One story is about gender and respect in the Hmong community.

*Kia:* I was giving a speech at a breakfast for prospective students
And I was sitting next to a Hmong family
And the father was sitting next to me and his wife and then the prospective student and the sister
And I really wanted to converse with the student but she really didn't say anything
And it kind of reminded me of me at that time
So I was mostly talking to her parents mostly her dad.
And I gave my speech and then I came back [to the table]
And I had to leave to go to work
And he [the father] shook my hand
Like he offered it first
I was just like "*wow* that was a *first*!"
*Susan:* That's unusual [my tone is one of seeking clarification]
*Kia:* To me
*Susan:* Was it a sign of respect?
*Kia:* Yeah I think definitely
I mean other men who have given me their hand to shake have been younger
But this is a Hmong man about my dad's age
But he did that
And I was just "wow" you know

*Susan:* How'd you feel about that?
*Kia:* I felt—
I really was conscious of it
And I felt good
But I also was like [Kia quotes her own internal dialogue]
"I hope you do that with other Hmong women as well
Or like with your daughter
How you teach your daughter."

By pointing out that the Hmong girl, the prospective student, reminded Kia of herself several years earlier, Kia emphasizes how much she has changed during college. No longer silent, Kia presents herself as easily conversing with the Hmong parents and as comfortably giving a public speech during this event. But the focal point of this story is Kia's interpretation of the father's handshake. Her focus on his gender and age speaks to hierarchies of deference and respect in the Hmong community. Although her account suggests that she experienced the handshake as a sign of his respect for *her*, she does not dwell on that. Rather, she treats as equally important the question of how the father treats other Hmong women, including his daughter. By focusing on the broader implications of this interaction, Kia indicates that developing a confident authoritative voice that earns others' respect is not an end in itself but serves a collective purpose.

When I remarked to Kia that she has become a leader on campus, has earned others respect, and has been publicly recognized for her contributions at OMA's annual awards ceremony, she said:

*Kia:* I've had to fight for that [respect]
Especially among my white peers
When I was working with them
I really had to fight for that
Or they really underestimated me
And I know how that feels
And so when people give me that leverage
I'm really conscious of it
And I do use it.

It is not clear yet what Kia means by "using" the leverage that comes with respect and leadership. But it is clear that Kia narrates the development of her authoritative voice on campus as involving conflict with white peers. While programs such as RC (which are designed to facilitate cross-racial dialogue) have helped Kia learn to speak authoritatively about racial issues, environments where white students are in the majority (which is most environments at CU) are a different story. She has had to fight, she says, to gain her white peers' respect.

When I asked for an example, Kia talked about an incident that occurred the year before when she was chair of the budget committee of the student government. That position is powerful because the budget committee makes decisions about allocating funds, decisions that the chair then presents to the full student government for a vote. The Black Collegians had presented to Kia's committee a request for conference funds. Kia voted in favor of their request but the rest of the budget committee voted against it. In the following, Kia recounts what she did when the Black Collegians appealed the budget committee's negative decision and the appeal came to the floor of a student government meeting.

*Kia:* And you know I really really thought about it
I was like [quoting her internal dialogue]
"Do I stand by the budget committee and the decision that the committee made?
Or do I stand by the Black Collegians and do I go with my feelings and my heart?"
And the question I asked myself was like
"After this how—I mean whatever I did at this meeting—
How was I going to live with myself
With whatever decision I made?"
And so I decided then to speak as the budget committee chair
And then to speak as Kia, as a person of color.

Kia recounts this experience as a moral dilemma in which she was called to take public action with integrity, in a way she could live with later. In her account she acknowledges *both* her responsibility as chair to present the committee's denial of the request *and* her allegiance to the Black Collegians whose request she felt was worthy. She resolved the dilemma by publicly honoring both sides, in other words, both aspects of her identity—as committee chair and as a person of color. Notice that she specifically embraces the identity, "person of color," here, once again referencing her shift to a racial identity that includes being Hmong *and* being part of a broader community of color at CU.

In this passage we also see what Kia means by being conscious of the leverage she has when she takes on a leadership role (in this case, budget committee chair) and how she "uses that to my advantage." By doing something unexpected and unconventional—speaking not only as committee chair but *also* as a person of color, she uses her leadership position to speak on behalf of the needs of other students of color.

*Kia:* And I got a lot of flak for that
*Susan:* From student government?
*Kia:* Yeah from people in student government and people in the committee
And it's still there to this day
I was in the committee again [this year] but not as the chair

And [when] we were setting up guidelines for the group
It was said that
"Oh yeah any decisions made by the budget committee
The chair must go along with that decision."

The budget committee minutes confirm Kia's account; minutes for two different meetings state "the chair will defend the committee's decision," and "the chair will always state the committee's opinion." Although those statements are not explicitly about race, Kia presents this controversy as racially inflected. She narrates the budget committee's denial of the Black Collegian's conference fund request, her public defense of their request, and the flak she got for doing so, as race related. Her account exhibits the contentiousness of race in student government deliberations.

At the same time, though, Kia indicates that the stance she took had an upside as well:

*Kia:* And then so in the committee this year
A lot of people did listen to what I had to say
Cause they felt I had the experience or whatever
And just in general in student government when I spoke
Or the decisions I made influenced how other people made their decisions
*Susan:* You could feel your influence
*Kia:* Yeah yeah.

Kia presents herself as having learned to speak authoritatively, as speaking publicly in ways that influence others. Interestingly, she does not specify whether the people on the committee and the people in student government who *have* listened to her this year are white students, students of color, or both. I suspect she means both since she introduced this story by saying she has had to fight white peers' tendency to underestimate her. One of the points of the story, then, is that her public action during the student government meeting earned her the respect of at least some white students—at the very least their begrudging respect that she *will* use her leadership and authoritative voice to defend what she thinks is right.

Although the quietness of her authoritative voice is not apparent in the story above, Kia told me that her peers of color selected her to be one of the five representatives of the Activists to meet with CU administrators (see chapter 6) because of her "quiet authority": "I listen more to what people have to say I guess, but when I do say something, it *matters*."

Overall, Kia's narrative is about developing a confident public voice; it is about learning to speak with quiet authority about the social justice issues she cares about. But within that narrative, there are several specific patterns. First, she emphasizes her consciousness of her authoritative voice, which suggests she does not take it for granted. That consciousness may come from its newness, or it may indicate her sense that her leadership is tentative rather than certain, at least among white peers. Or it may point to her understanding that had circumstances been different—if, for example, she had gone to a university that does not have programs that foster student of color leadership—she might not have developed the same public voice. Second, her narrative shows a transition to an expanded racial identity that includes not only being Hmong but also being a person of color. In contrast to the story early in her narrative about events for "students of color" not seeming to apply to her, in her later stories she embraces an identity as a "person of color." Developing this broader racial identity makes sense in an environment where any particular group of students of color is small and where OMA specifically encourages that identification through programming for all students of color. Third, she focuses on using her authoritative voice for a collective good. Kia hopes the Hmong father of the prospective student translates his respect for Kia into respect for Hmong girls and women in general. And she uses her leverage as a student government leader to advocate on behalf of other students of color whom she feels have been treated unfairly. Indeed, at one point she stated that "the choices that I make now can't be individualistic—I'm always thinking it's for the broader community or for the future generations." Fourth, Kia's stories about developing an authoritative voice within her family and within the Hmong community focus on gender, while her stories about developing an authoritative voice at CU focus on race. This divergence speaks to her differing experience of these two contexts. While she experiences gender as the most compelling social justice issue within the Hmong community, she experiences race as the most pressing social justice issue at CU.

### Rachelle: Learning to Speak So That Others Will Listen

Rachelle, an African American, is a business major. Both of her parents finished high school and have working-class occupations. Rachelle grew up in an all-black urban neighborhood where "everyone on the block pretty much knows everybody" and where "you could always find something to do, someone to play with, somewhere to go," such as the YMCA down the street or the park on the corner. She described herself at this time in her life as "pretty unaware of life outside [the city]." It wasn't until much later that she understood how much her single mother had struggled; all she knew at the time was that "we ate everyday and we ate good." Her family was very religious—she was raised in a Pentecostal church and she described her family, especially her grandmother's generation, as very conservative on social issues such as sexual orientation. During her childhood, she said, the major form of racism she was aware of was prejudice concerning "good hair" and "light skin" in her African American community.

When Rachelle was a sophomore in high school, she was recruited by A Better Chance, an organization that places academically strong students of color in high schools across the country where they have access to "expanded educational and leadership opportunities."[13] Rachelle moved hundreds of miles from home to live in a group house with a dozen other African American and Latina girls from across the country and to attend high school with upper-middle-class white students. Although Rachelle knew this was "a good opportunity," it took her a year to get involved in her new school because "I really didn't allow myself to participate or get to know anything other than what I already knew, 'cause I thought I knew everything already." She described the activities offered by her new environment as scheduled and monitored, a far cry from the spontaneity she was used to where neighborhood friends played with each other on the block. The white students, she said, asked annoying questions about whether she or her friends back home belonged to a gang. And she was shocked to find that some of her new classmates were "going around the world" for spring break and "getting cars that cost ridiculous amounts of money" for their sixteenth birthdays. When she went to a classmate's home for the first time, she was "astounded, 'cause I had never seen a house that size except on TV." Nonetheless, by the time she graduated from high school, the girls of color she lived with had become a strong support network for each other, she was participating in extracurricular activities, and she had other friends to hang out with, "mostly white, some Asian, a few black."

Rachelle's high school adviser helped her through the process of applying for college, and she was accepted at all three universities she applied to. She chose CU because of a certain academic program and because it offered her the best scholarship package.

Rachelle described her first year at college as difficult, but the difficulty was not about being in a predominantly white environment since she had already made that shift in high school. Rather, the difficulty had to do with the academic challenge, which she felt high school had not prepared her for. The independence was also a problem: "There's no one to answer to, like I'm the person that I answer to." She did go to the student of color orientation and the student of color retreat, which she enjoyed, but the main thing she got out of the latter was a boyfriend with whom she secluded herself for most of the year. "I was young and stupid and you feel like the first person you hook up with is the one you're going to be with."

After Rachelle and her boyfriend broke up at the beginning of her sophomore year, she "really connected" with Dianna, one of the leaders of the Black Collegians, and she "dove head first" into that organization. Just as the Southeast Asian Association led Kia to much greater engagement with other organizations and activities on campus, so did the Black Collegians for Rachelle. Interestingly, when I asked at this point about transitions she's gone through since then, she spoke first about sexual orientation rather than race.

*Susan:* So things have changed for you since you dove into the Black Collegians
   and all that your sophomore year
Can you talk about transitions that you've gone through in these last two years?
*Rachelle:* I'm so much more open-minded these days about everything
Like I was saying I come from a . . . Pentecostal background
And homosexuality was not talked about in my house because it was just taboo
So I grew up with those thoughts with those ideas about the whole GLBT commu-
   nity
And so it took a lot of conversation
A lot of learning to even begin for me to talk about those issues
So I mean not only did I become more aware about my own race and my own
   struggles
But other peoples' struggles and lifestyles and things like that
Because I didn't talk about those things
Like it was *not ok* for me to talk about those things
So I'd say over the past two years I've just become a more open-minded person.

Rachelle grounds her earlier close-mindedness about GLBT people in her
religious upbringing. She does not specifically describe her Pentecostal de-
nomination's take on sexual orientation but seems to assume that I would
know that it treats homosexuality as immoral. Instead, what Rachelle emphasizes is the taboo nature of *talk* about homosexuality. She suggests, then,
that her transition from being closed- to open-minded about sexual orientation has revolved around overcoming *that* taboo.

*Susan:* And how did that happen?
*Rachelle:* Well two of my friends—Paul and Greg [who are gay men]
We all just have cross-dialogue
Not about specific like detailed situations
But just about the things they've gone through and things like that . . .
So they just telling me their lifestyle and just being able—
Just hanging out with them and things like that
I mean just *that*
Really hanging out with people who are gay was enlightening for me
Because I would have never done that
Like it would have been like "*oh my goodness!*"

Rachelle describes how she became open-minded as a matter of having
two gay friends with whom she hangs out and talks about "things they've
gone through." Although she is not specific about what they talk about, her
use of the word *enlightening* implies that she has learned about their lives as
gay men. Her statement that before she came to CU she would not have even
hung out with gay people suggests that her religious education included the
idea that gay people can contaminate straight people, that exposure itself

can cause harm. Rather than causing harm, however, Rachelle presents exposure to and conversation with gay men—who are "other" to her—as opening her mind.

*Rachelle:* And so now it's just like it's who they are
And I have to accept them for who they are
And it's not right for me to judge because I don't have the power to judge anyone
That's between them and whoever it is they believe and things like that
It's not for me to say
So I just kind of had to learn that
And then like I said, Dianna, she kind of had the same viewpoints that I did before
And so just talking to her about how she overcame her closed-mindedness helped me as well
I mean I don't have to approve or anything
But just to know that judging is not my right, so
*Susan:* Do you still have—
What you just said
You don't have to approve
Is there in your religion is there still a sense of that's not right?
*Rachelle:* I mean I'm always going to believe that
I mean that's something I can't change
Like the way my relationship with my creator or whatever
That doesn't—
That's just something I don't feel is right
But that's just for my own personal belief.

Rachelle develops a stance of accepting her gay friends and acknowledging that she does not have a right to judge them, while still embracing her religious belief that homosexuality is wrong. She notes the influence of conversation with her African American friend, Dianna, who shares Rachelle's religious beliefs and who has already made a transition to greater open-mindedness. In my field notes, I wrote about this part of Rachelle's narrative:

I remember feeling here that this was a closed issue for Rachelle, that there was nothing more to say about it, that she's come as far as she is going to (at least for now), and that her religious beliefs are solid and unchangeable on this topic. She's moved in terms of her open-mindedness about talking about sexual orientation, befriending GLBT people, and "accepting them for who they are," but she won't or can't move on her religious beliefs. Perhaps it makes sense that sexual orientation is a dead end topic for Rachelle at this point because her religious beliefs conflict directly with social justice discourse at CU. That discourse includes sexual orientation as one among several social justice issues, and indeed as a much less problematic social justice issue than race.

Because I sensed that Rachelle had said all she could say, I followed up on her statement above that she has also "become more aware about my own race and my own struggles."

*Susan:* And you said you've also learned things about race over these last two years
Can you talk about what you've learned?
*Rachelle:* That I don't know everything
I mean just because I am a black woman doesn't mean I know everything about
  what a black woman goes through
And I don't have the answers for everything
There are times when I'm sitting in class
And I could be the only black woman or black person at all in the classroom
And questions will come up about black people or African American race or cul-
  ture
And it's almost as if I'm supposed to answer those questions
And I can't speak on behalf of the whole black community
I can speak on my experiences my background
How I grew up, my family, my family interaction
That's all I can speak from
And I mean I *knew* that
But there were times like my freshman sophomore year
I would try to answer those questions
Like "well I know this because this this and this"
But the more I took sociology classes
And the more conversations I had with the black people on this campus
The more I realized our backgrounds are completely different
And what you went through may be completely different than what I went through
So I can't say "well we do it this way"
I can say "well *I* did it this way"
And so I learned that just in the conversations I've had in class and on this campus
And with other white people and with other black people too.

Rachelle begins by saying she has learned that she doesn't know every-thing about black women and that she can only speak about her own expe-riences. And yet, halfway through this excerpt, she states, "I mean I *knew* that but there were times . . . I would try to answer those questions." This caveat signals that something else is going on, and that something seems to have to do with racial dynamics in the classroom context: "It's almost as if I'm supposed to answer those questions." Although she is vague about where the pressure comes from—professors? students? herself? all three?—the pres-sure to speak on behalf of all black women or the entire black community is a common refrain in research on students of color in predominantly white classrooms.[14] Thus she constructs what she has learned as not only *that* she doesn't know everything, but also *how* to speak in the classroom about racial issues. In this passage we hear for the first time the most prominent theme in Rachelle's narrative: she has no trouble *speaking* in public settings, but she is learning to speak *differently*.

There are two more significant aspects of this passage. First, Rachelle simultaneously identifies with the black community *and* sees herself as a distinct individual within that community. And second, Rachelle emphasizes conversation. Her story here is about conversations about race in the classroom as well as about conversations in other contexts that have taught her to see that her experiences as an African American woman are connected to but not the same as other black women's experiences.

Like Kia, Rachelle talks about RC as emotionally powerful and as pivotal in the development of her voice. But while Kia focuses on RC as empowering her and other Hmong students to speak out about their families' histories, Rachelle begins by describing RC as frustrating. She told me that when she shared a painful story about her cousin being "gunned down by police over some nothingness," white students asked questions like "why was he there?" Given this unsupportive response, Rachelle complained that RC is more for white students than students of color: students of color are expected to tell their personal—and often painful—stories for the sake of white students' racial education, for example, to help them understand the reality of police brutality in African American communities.[15] She said that she and other students of color have shared this complaint with Mr. Robert, OMA's director, and that "he has challenged us as students of color 'to *make* RC for you, find a way to make it for you so that you also get something out of it.'" This is one of several instances where Rachelle describes an influential conversation with Mr. Robert, whom she and many other students of color consider an important mentor.

Rachelle indicates that that conversation made a difference because "this year RC was really good . . . we scratched the surface of some *real* cross-dialogue." When I asked for specifics, she described an exercise—the fishbowl—in which three white students and three students of color sit facing each other in a circle and take turns talking.[16]

*Rachelle:* There was a point where it was [two African American women] and myself and three white women in the fishbowl
And they basically told us that they were intimidated by us
And it's not because of anything we say or anything we've done
It's just when they see us all together it's an automatic guard that they throw up
Like they don't want to say anything wrong
They don't want to look wrong
And so my question to them was
"Why? Where does that come from?
Is that our problem or is that your problem?"
And the fact that she couldn't answer that question was really poignant for me

Because I'm like "obviously it's not my problem that you've thrown this guard up
Because like you said it's nothing I said to you
It's nothing I did to you
It's just something that happens because of the image you see
So whose problem is that really?"
And so that was really like big for me
Because I'm like
"I know that there are times that I can be really moody
And it might show on my face
Because I'm really bad about hiding emotion
And so I wear it on my sleeve"
And I'm working on that
So if she had said something like
Well I had a frown or I snapped at her or something like that
Then I could have understood
And been like "oh maybe I was a little rough around the edge that day"
But the fact that she couldn't tell me anything just lets me know
That because of who I am and what I look like is what makes her throw her guard
   up
And not part of my personality or my characteristics that made her throw her
   guard up
And so that was really big for me.

As Rachelle begins this story, she sets up the scene as a "we" and "they" situation, where "we" are three African American women students and "they" are three white women students. She describes what the white students said (that they are intimidated, guarded, and self-conscious about their actions and speech around the women of color), but she shifts to direct speech for her own voice. This linguistic device highlights the significance for her of the question of whose responsibility it is that the white students are intimidated: "Is that our problem or is that your problem?" Twice Rachelle describes this interaction as "really big for me," perhaps because she feels she got an honest answer to that question. She learned that the problem is not students of color's actions, and specifically not her actions or characteristics, but *others' image of her*. She doesn't say so directly, but she implies that the image "of who I am and what I look like" consists of the stereotype of the loud, angry black woman.[17] She also uses direct speech to indicate how she reiterated the answer for her white peers: "Obviously it's not my problem."

Although it is clear that Rachelle identifies herself as part of "we"—her black women peers—she shifts to the first person singular partway through this story, expressing (as she did earlier) her simultaneous identification with African American women as a group and her sense of herself as a distinct individual within that group. Indeed, after beginning with a dialogue between "us" and "them," she shifts to a conversation between one of the white students and herself about a specific interaction between them. This shift communicates Rachelle's concern about the development of *her* voice in particular. While African American women in general are subject to the "controlling image" of the angry black woman,[18] Rachelle constructs *herself in particular* as needing to resist certain characteristics in *herself*—her moodiness; her inability to hide her emotions; her tendency to snap (a word she used frequently)—that allow others to easily stereotype her that way. Given her personality, Rachelle needs to know when a problematic cross-racial interaction is her fault and when it is not. Here again we see the central theme in Rachelle's narrative—she is learning *how* to use her voice to speak about racial issues. As she states here, "I'm working on that."

When I asked Rachelle whether there is anything else she wanted to talk about in terms of transitions she's gone through, she said:

*Rachelle:* I've definitely become more mature in the work that I'm doing here
  at CU
Just because like I said I have an attitude
Like I really do have an attitude
But I'm working on that so much.

Once again, Rachelle critiques herself *and* describes herself as working to improve herself. She presents this not only as an issue of self-development but also as a means to further "the work that I'm doing here at CU." Like others who embrace social justice discourse at CU, Rachelle uses "the work" to reference her ongoing commitment to social change. She describes herself as learning to speak in ways that help her to be a more effective agent of social change.

Rachelle continued with a story about a recent incident during which she resisted snapping. She had given a speech (which was later published in the student newspaper) at a commemoration for Martin Luther King Jr. In the speech, she charged CU with failing to live up to its diversity commitments, as evidenced by the lack of racial diversity among the faculty and by the fact that many students of color feel comfortable on campus only when participating in student of color organizations or in OMA-sponsored events. She urged all members of the campus community to work toward social change, outlining specific tasks for different groups. She asked white students to recognize their privilege and to learn about race and racism, but not to rely on students of color to be their teachers. And she asked students of color to recognize that they are not the only ones who face obstacles and not to sit back and expect others to do the hard work of social change for them.

In a critique published in the student newspaper of Rachelle's speech, Carrie, a white student, accused Rachelle of reverse racism. Carrie argued that everyone should live by the same principles and that white students and students of color should not be asked to do different things.

*Rachelle:* Carrie Jones called me a reverse racist in the school paper
That normally would have caused me to find her and talk to her one-on-one
But instead of doing that I channeled that energy into a response article
*Susan:* And did you publish that?
*Rachelle:* Yep I had [that] published through the [student newspaper]
And it wasn't anything nasty or towards her
It was just more so to help her understand that if she had been at the program
    where my speech was given
She would have understood where I was coming from . . .
In no way was it calling out white students
But it was calling out everyone to do their part
And as a student of color and as a white student we can't possibly do the same
    things
We have to meet each other in the middle by doing our different things to get
    there. . . .
And so in writing that article versus snapping on her
It helped everyone on campus . . .
And she even was like "that's true"
*Susan:* She talked to you about it?
*Rachelle:* She didn't talk to me personally . . .
But this one woman that we both know talked to her
And then the woman came back and told me that Carrie after reading my response
She understood where she had made some mistakes
And should have been at the charge
And will probably be there next year
I wouldn't hold my breath
But . . . that could have went in a totally different direction had I snapped at her
Because she could have just really closed up at that point
And then of course I would have been perpetuating every stereotype about a
    black woman
Which I used to do
That used to be me
And that's why I say I've grown up a lot
Because I'm not as flip as I used to be.

Rachelle presents this story as an example of how she is learning to speak publicly about race in a way that invites others to listen rather than in a way that closes off conversation. Although she is angry when Carrie accuses her of reverse racism—a charge that is often used to discredit social justice discourse,[19] she resists the impulse to confront her personally. Instead, she works with two peers in the Black Collegians to publish a response dispelling the accusation. They take Carrie to task for using the discourse of color blindness, for assuming that white students and students of color have the same experiences at CU and thus need to do the same work for racial equality.

This exchange displays how the contentiousness of race at CU gets played out in the student newspaper. It also shows how that contentiousness is sometimes based in the conflict between the discourse of abstract inclusion (Carrie's idea that everyone should live by the same principles) and the discourse of social justice (Rachelle and her peers' insistence that race relations on campus will improve if white students and students of color do their different parts to bring about social change).

At first I was puzzled by Rachelle's comment in this account—and her peers' comment in their newspaper response—about Carrie's absence from the commemoration where Rachelle delivered her speech. As I read Rachelle's speech in the newspaper, her points seemed perfectly clear; I didn't feel I needed to be at the event itself to understand what she was saying. Indeed, a white professor who is a member of the Faculty Diversity Group published a criticism of Carrie's color-blind discourse but said nothing about the need to have been at the commemoration to understand what Rachelle was saying.

Over time, though, I came to understand Rachelle and her peers' remark about Carrie's absence as making sense in relation to a problem that remains unarticulated here: one of the students of color's major complaints about race relations on campus is that white students do not attend their educational events. Students of color told me many times—and the problem was expressed in other newspaper articles and letters—that white students who begin to develop an interest in race continuously ask to be educated but fail to show up when students of color offer educational events. In this situation, then, Rachelle and her peers are angry in part because a white student presumes to understand what Rachelle is talking about even though she hadn't gone to the commemoration to listen in the first place. This subtext to the public dialogue in the newspaper references the volatility of race relations on campus.

Rachelle frames this story—she begins and ends it—as a story about how she has learned to resist her impulse to lash out and instead to channel her energy into a constructive response through which her voice can be heard. That response is collective (she wrote the response with two peers) and it is public rather than private (it was published in the newspaper, a venue where public conversation about race takes place at CU). By contrasting her impulse to snap in a private one-on-one situation to using her voice more constructively in a public venue, Rachelle presents her self-work as part of the work she is doing at CU on racial issues.

Rachelle also includes in her account evidence that her strategy paid off—Carrie told someone who reported back to Rachelle that she (Carrie) had been mistaken and would show up next time. Rachelle's statement "I wouldn't hold my breath" communicates her skepticism. And yet Rachelle expresses confidence that her strategy was better than snapping, which she feels would have closed down the possibility of dialogue, and equally problematic, would have perpetuated the stereotype of the angry black woman.

The overarching theme in Rachelle's narrative is that she is learning to use her voice to speak publicly about race in ways that will further rather than preclude racial dialogue and social change. At the same time, there are several specific themes throughout Rachelle's narrative. First, she constantly moves back and forth between "we" and "I"; she presents herself *both* as strongly connected to the African American community on campus (particularly to black women) *and* as a distinct individual within that community. Second, Rachelle is self-critical, beginning with her description of her disinterest in activities at her new high school because "I thought I knew everything already," and culminating in her persistent focus on her need to resist her tendency to lash out at others when she is angry. Third, Rachelle connects her work on herself to "the work" she does on racial issues. She is motivated to resist her tendency to snap so that she can speak more wisely and effectively about race on campus. Fourth, throughout her narrative, Rachelle emphasizes conversation. She highlights various conversations as influencing her learning: conversations with gay friends, conversations with her friend Dianna, and conversations with Mr. Robert. When I asked how she has learned not to snap, she mentioned conversations with "the positive black women here on campus who . . . have learned to use their attitudes for better so to speak . . . [and who have] learned to vent behind closed doors." In addition, Rachelle treats conversation itself as a goal of her work. Her entire narrative about learning to speak more wisely and effectively is grounded in her commitment to cross-racial dialogue as a means of bringing about social change, a commitment embedded in CU's social justice discourse.

Finally, there is a disjunction within Rachelle's narrative between her talk about race and her talk about sexual orientation, both of which are widely recognized at CU as social justice issues. Rachelle presents conversations with her gay friends and others as breaking through the taboo on talk about sexual orientation and as influencing her to resist judging her gay friends. But her religious beliefs make further movement—and further conversation—unlikely. Although she presents herself as having become more open-minded about sexual orientation, she does not speak out about that issue on campus. Rachelle is most exercised by racial issues at CU, and it is in relation to those issues that she learns to speak out for social change.

## Narrative Patterns

My analysis of Kia's and Rachelle's personal narratives reveals the particularity of each. Kia highlights her transition from being lonely, isolated, and silent to developing a quiet, respected voice of authority on campus. By contrast, Rachelle presents herself as never having trouble speaking but as learning over time to resist her tendency to speak rashly so that she can speak more wisely and effectively than she has in the past.

At the same time, there are several commonalities across Kia's and Rachelle's narratives. Most generally, both of them embrace social justice discourse and treat race as the issue that concerns them most, reflecting the prominence and contentiousness of race at CU. In addition, RC figures prominently in both narratives. RC is a site where they have learned to use their voices to speak about race. Kia emphasizes the very act of speaking; Rachelle emphasizes speaking in ways that make conversation possible. Remember that Kia's and Rachelle's accounts about RC are not about spontaneous interactions but about exercises—crossing the line and fishbowl—that are facilitated by OMA's director as well as faculty and students who have done "race work" before. Yet the fact that Kia and Rachelle experience RC differently, along with Kia's statement that "crossing the line" was not as powerful for her during subsequent RCs, conveys that RC's impact cannot be orchestrated or predetermined. Nonetheless, Kia's and Rachelle's accounts suggest that RC provides *conditions* in which it is *sometimes possible* for students of color to tell their stories and for white students to hear them.

In addition, both Kia and Rachelle speak of "the work"—an expression that signals their membership in a narrative community committed to social justice at CU. Similarly, their use of the term *students of color* (in addition to their particular racial identities as Hmong American and African American) reflects their participation in that narrative community. The center of that community is OMA, which organizes RC among many other programs, and which supports the student of color groups. For Kia it was the Southeast Asian Association and for Rachelle it was the Black Collegians through which they found kindred spirits as well as vehicles for broader connection and involvement at CU. For both Kia and Rachelle, learning how to speak is not just about self-development but also about "the work"—making a contribution to racial dialogue and social change at CU. As they speak about that contribution, they also tap into a cultural discourse developed by leaders of color in the United States about individuals using their skills and accomplishments to serve the community as a whole.[20]

In addition, both Kia and Rachelle include the voice of an "other" in their narratives. Kia recounts how she suddenly realized that *white* students' stories about *their* racial identities and learning were important to racial dialogue at RC and elsewhere. Rachelle recounts how various conversations helped her to become more accepting and less judgmental about gay men. Although listening to the voice of the other is not a prominent theme in their narratives, it is present.

Three more commonalities consist of absences in Kia's and Rachelle's narratives. Both grew up in working-class families and both talk (directly or indirectly) about social class when narrating their precollege years. But neither mentions social class when recounting how they have learned to use their voices on campus. Their limited talk about social class—in comparison to their extensive talk about race—may be shaped by both local and national narrative landscapes. Social class is present but by no means prominent in

CU's social justice discourse. As table 3.1 shows (see chapter 3), social class does not appear among the top three diversity categories in CU's student newspaper, student government minutes, calendar of events, or curriculum. Moreover, it is submerged in many institutional contexts in the United States.[21]

Similarly, gender issues are noticeably absent from their narratives about social justice issues on campus. Kia highlights gender when talking about her work within the Hmong community, and Rachelle mentions several times that her black women friends are a major source of conversation, influence, and support. But neither is exercised by gender issues on campus. Local and national narrative environments may be factors here as well. CU has two active women's organizations—the Women's Coalition and a local branch of the Feminist Majority Leadership Alliance. In addition, gender is the second most prominent diversity category in the student newspaper and in the curriculum (see table 3.1). But white women students who are interested in social justice at CU tend to be drawn to the women's studies program and the women's organizations, while women of color are more likely to be drawn to OMA and student of color organizations. This divide may reflect historical differences between white women's and women of color's concerns and activism in the United States.[22]

The other notable absence in their narratives is the classroom as a learning environment. Although Kia mentions a few classes as good learning experiences (especially the first seminar on rape), she narrates her learning about how to speak authoritatively in public spaces as taking place *outside* the classroom. The contexts in which she has learned to use her authoritative voice include her family, her service learning at the rape crisis center, the Southeast Asian Association, RC, and student government.[23] But in the classroom, Kia told me, she usually finds herself wishing she isn't the only one noticing how race is or isn't being addressed. In her education classes, for example, she said the focus is on getting white students who grew up in white, suburban, middle-class neighborhoods to understand inner city schools with large populations of students of color. But "when they're talking about those kids, those kids are me, they're my siblings, my friends." Kia implies that in the university classroom, her high school experience as a Hmong student in an inner city school gets translated into her "otherness" rather than an occasion for her to speak authoritatively and as a strong resource for others in the class.

Rachelle mentions the classroom as a context where she has felt pressured to speak on behalf of her race, but she also mentions sociology classes as helping her to learn that her experiences as an African American woman differ from other black women's experiences. Other than that, the classroom is absent from Rachelle's narrative as well. She has learned from conversations with OMA's director and with African American women peers how to speak effectively about race. The contexts in which she has used her public voice include RC, the student newspaper, and events such as the MLK commemoration. The disjunction within Kia's and Rachelle's narratives between the classroom (where we expect learning to take place) and extracurricular environments (where learning often takes place) corroborates a finding well documented in the literature on higher education: the importance of peers and extracurricular activities as learning environments on campus.[24]

In short, even while Kia's and Rachelle's narratives are deeply infused with the biographical details of their lives, the commonalities across their narratives indicate that both of them draw on resources embedded in CU's narrative landscape. Most importantly, Kia's and Rachelle's narratives demonstrate that CU's narrative environment has provided conditions in which these two working-class women of color have learned how to speak publicly about the racial issues they care so much about.

# 5 Learning to Listen

During the individual interviews, as CU students told me about transitions they have gone through and what they are learning at college, some of them brought "the voice of the other" into their narratives. "The voice of the other" means the perspectives of people who differ from the narrator in terms of identities, life experiences, and social locations—especially as those are shaped by race, ethnicity, gender, sexual orientation, class, and ability.

Some students narrated the influence of the other's voice in a general sense. Here, for example, is Mason, a white student, talking about his first seminar on leadership, which was co-taught by an African American woman and a white gay man who is out on campus.

*Mason:* I thought [that first seminar] was a really good experience
Because not only did I hear about different diversity-related issues from an African
    American woman
It was also talked about from a gay male
And I thought—
I mean that was—
That was really interesting
And I guess I never really put myself in their position
Where they took us through different stories and scenarios
Where they made us feel as though like we were them type of deal
And the different oppressions they felt and stuff like that.

Mason speaks in general terms about the impact of his professors' openness about their experiences related to race and sexual orientation, presumably in the context of the course material on leadership. He suggests that listening to his professors' stories allowed him to put himself in their shoes, to feel—at least momentarily—what it is like to live their lives.

Similarly, Marshan, an African American, spoke in general terms about learning that people who identify as biracial or multiracial sometimes face a distinct set of issues. She has realized that some students—like a friend who is a Korean adoptee of white parents—feel they don't belong in traditional student of color organizations. At Mr. Robert's urging, Marshan helped start a new organization for students who want to explore their bi- or multiracial identities.

And Nathan—a white gay man who is out on campus—talked in general terms about learning to understand the perspectives of students of color. He does not see himself as an expert on sexual orientation and has never taken a course on sexuality. But he said that whenever an issue concerning sexual orientation comes up in student government meetings—even if the issue has nothing to do with him—others look at him and expect him to speak. This experience, he said, has helped him understand what students of color may feel when they are one of a few people of color in a classroom or meeting.

Some students, by contrast, recounted specific experiences as epiphanies, as turning points in their understanding of certain diversity issues and of people whose social characteristics differ from theirs. In this chapter I present several narratives in which CU students tell about these epiphanies, these memorable experiences of hearing the voice of the other for the first time. Each narrative is particular, of course, shaped by the individual's background, identity, life experience, and social location. At the same time, each student's narrative practices are shaped by their interaction with me as an interviewer as well as by CU's complex narrative landscape. At the end of the chapter I focus on common themes across their narratives that help us understand how CU undergraduates learn to listen to the voice of the other.

## The Liberal Arts Story and the Voice of the Other

Madison is a social science major who grew up in a suburban, white, middle-class home. She has a physical disability and uses a wheelchair most of the time. I met Madison during my group interview with Students for Disability Rights. The following is from the very beginning of my individual interview with her.

*Susan:* Can you tell me what you were like in high school and what your interests were?
*Madison:* I just feel like I've changed so much since then
I don't even know if I can really explain how I was
I don't think I had a lot of worldly interests when I was in high school
I was more into my friends and my social life and getting into college and that was it
I didn't think about diversity issues or politics or worldviews or anything like that

My world has really expanded though ever since I got here
And that's where I've really grown as a person.

By comparing the personal concerns that occupied her in high school to the worldly concerns that interest her now, Madison emphasizes how much she has changed during college. Like Mason (in chapter 1), who talked about college as a time for "learning as much as you can," Madison draws on a preferred cultural narrative that defines a major goal of higher education and particularly of liberal arts colleges: college is a time and place where traditional-age students open their minds and learn to think critically about the world around them. Liberal arts administrators and faculty hope students graduate from college with stories like Madison's, with a sense of themselves as transformed through broadened worldviews.

When recalling her transition to college, Madison said it took a long time to learn to navigate a new physical environment in her wheelchair and that finding new friends was pivotal to her successful adjustment. By her sophomore year she was active in residence hall governance, and during her junior year, she got involved in Students for Disability Rights.

*Susan:* Have there been any other kinds of transitions for you during your college
　　years?
*Madison:* Overall I've grown so much as a person
I don't feel like I am the same person that I was in high school at all
And all in good ways
*Susan:* And what if you can articulate
What is the person you are now?
When you say "I'm a completely different person—"
*Madison:* You ask hard questions
*Susan:* [Laugh]
*Madison:* I care more about other people
I care more about the world
I care more about social justice about policy issues
I care more about people just having their own rights as citizens of the world
More active in terms of people not being discriminated against no matter what
　　their diversity is
I've come out of my little [suburban] bubble
I mean I really was sheltered there
And I've become much more aware
So it's been an awareness awakening.

In response to my questions, Madison reiterates the comparison between her earlier sheltered self and her current worldly self, but she also adds something new. She has become a person who cares about other people and in particular about their rights and experiences of discrimination. She presents her interest in these social justice issues and in people who differ from herself as central to her self-development.

Madison expanded on this theme later in the interview after describing her hometown as including little diversity in terms of race, ethnicity, and sexual orientation, and CU as having "a *little* more diversity in terms of color, and a *lot* more people who are just out there saying 'hey I'm gay, I'm transsexual, bisexual.'"

*Madison:* So at CU I had more exposure
Because in [my hometown] you don't get that
*Susan:* And with the exposure was there sort of growth in terms of thoughts and ideas?
*Madison:* Thoughts and ideas definitely
Thinking about "what's life like for these people?"
Not just knowing who they are and understanding them and accepting them
But really getting a peek into their life . . .
Especially with my friends who are gay
I have quite a few gay friends
When I turned twenty-one I started going to the gay clubs downtown
And just really seeing how it's a completely different culture
And how difficult it is for them
I mean they are so disliked by so many people in this world
And the only thing they have to depend on really is each other
And when the hate crimes started happening here
I attended the rally and everything
And one of my good friends spoke at that
And he made a speech about how he felt comfortable here
And he didn't have to lie about who he was
And I just started to really open my eyes and think
"Wow, I *can't imagine* having to be somewhere where I had to pretend I was someone that I wasn't."

Madison presents herself as moving beyond merely accepting her gay friends to gaining a deeper understanding of what life is like for them. By accompanying her friends to gay clubs, she has caught a glimpse of their culture, which she suggests is necessary for gay people's survival in a hostile world. Madison refers to the same antigay incidents on campus that the Women's Coalition, GLBT students, and the student journalists discussed in chapter 3.

Madison also tells of hearing a gay friend speak at the campus rally that was organized to support GLBT people in the wake of the antigay incidents. She describes listening to him as an epiphanal moment during which she realized how different his life experiences are from hers. In this story, Madison captures how opening her mind is tied directly to listening to the voice of the other, the voice of a person whom she defines as different from herself and whose struggles differ from hers. As she learns that her gay friend sometimes has to pretend he is someone he is not, Madison learns about *herself* that she has *not* had that struggle, one she can't even imagine. In this story, she expresses compassion; she shows that she has become a person who cares about someone whose social identity and life experiences differ from hers.

## Epiphanies and the Voice of the Other

Madison expressed explicitly the liberal arts story about opening her mind. For most CU students, however, that story was an implicit theme running through their narratives. Nonetheless, like Madison, many CU students told stories about an epiphany where they heard the voice of the other for the first time. In the following I explore four of those stories.

I met Hannah during my group interview with the Women's Coalition. She is a humanities major who grew up in an urban environment in a white, middle- to upper-middle class home. During our individual interview, Hannah said that her transition to college included overcoming the intimidation she felt in classrooms where others seemed so much more knowledgeable than herself. She described her involvement in the Women's Coalition as teaching her what it means to be an effective leader on campus.

As a first-year student, Hannah was drawn to classes about women's issues, where she learned how deeply sexism and male privilege are embedded in American society and culture. She described these as issues that are "so close to me and something that I could think about on a personal level." Over time she began to understand that "if there's male privilege, then there are other forms of privilege as well," and that "issues of racism are *just* as complicated as issues of sexism." However, race, racism, and white privilege remained intellectual concepts to her until one classroom experience.

*Hannah:* A student was talking about his experience as a black male
And how women especially would fear him
You know crossing the street at night or locking their car doors
And talking about that . . .
And I had to think
"Well am I more afraid when I see black men than if I see—"
And kind of having that personal—
And realizing that
"Wow, I could have been a person who locked the door when he walked by" . . .
I mean I just sort of realized that that's not something that I want to just do unconsciously
And I want to be really conscious of my feelings and why I'm feeling this way
And why do I feel more threatened by him than—

Because a stranger is a stranger
And it doesn't mean that you sort of embrace everyone
I mean you can still feel threatened by strangers
But why do I feel more threatened by a black person than I would a white person?
And you know being conscious of those feelings.

Hannah presents this moment in the classroom as one in which she really hears—for the first time—the voice of an African American man talking about an experience of everyday racism. Further, she hears his story as directed at *her,* as implicating her as a white woman. As such, it is as much a story about learning about herself as it is a story about learning about him. She wants to be a white woman who is conscious of her racial feelings, who understands why she feels and acts the way she does, and who resists her own nonconscious racism.[1] While acknowledging that women have reason to feel threatened by male strangers, Hannah maintains her focus on race rather than reframing her fear of strange men at night as only a gender issue. (In chapter 3 we heard WSRR students tell a story about a white woman who refused to see the racial component in a similar situation.) Hannah emphasizes that she is learning that she, as a white woman, harbors nonconscious racism.

I met Sydney during my group interview with the GLBT Organization. She is a social science major who grew up in a very small town in a white, middle-class family. Her transition to college included struggling with much higher academic expectations than she was used to in high school and learning to be responsible for herself since her parents were no longer there to guide her. She has been involved in the resident hall government as well as the student government, and she is active in the Asian Student Organization and the GLBT Organization.

In the following account from our individual interview, Sydney is talking about a GLBT conference on another campus that she attended with other members of CU's GLBT Organization. At the conference she participated in a workshop on the Kinsey scale of human sexuality in which attendants were asked to stand—literally—on a line that represented the continuum from heterosexual to varying degrees of bisexuality to gay or lesbian. Sydney said she was the only one standing at the far end of the line representing heterosexuality.

*Sydney:* I've been exposed somewhat to the GLBT community because my sister is
   a lesbian
But it is really different to be picked up and put in the middle of a lot of kinds of
   people that you don't usually see in massive numbers
And the Kinsey scale workshop was the big one
Where I was like
"Wow I'm—"

Because we've got to think that usually that is going to be the position that other
  people who are different for some reason are going to be in . . .
So it just really brought it to my attention
Because I don't think you can just theoretically think of that
Because usually I'm not in the minority at all.

Sydney presents this workshop as giving her, as a heterosexual, the chance
to experience what many GLBT people experience everyday—a sense of herself as "other," as different from the majority. She suggests that this event
was powerful for her because it wasn't "just theoretical" and it wasn't simply a matter of being exposed to the GLBT community through a lesbian sister. She constructs *this* event as distinct because it gave her direct insight into
the experience of others. It is significant that Sydney had already, by virtue
of her membership in the GLBT Organization (and the Asian Student Organization), placed herself in a position to hear others' voices, yet she presents
that proximity as less powerful than *being* in a similar situation. The latter
gave her a concrete experience that allowed her to learn what life is like for
those who differ from her.

Steven is a social science major who grew up in a suburb in a family that
straddled the working and middle classes. He called his family "multiracial,"
explaining that he and his siblings are South Asians who were adopted by
white parents. Steven's transition to college included his growing awareness
of his racial identity, which he hadn't thought much about in high school. He
has been involved in the Asian Student Organization, student government,
Multicultural Student Group, the NCORE group, and the Activists.

In the following excerpt from our individual interview, Steven describes
how he came to understand that other diversity issues are connected to the
racial issues he has devoted much of his energy to on campus.

*Steven:* When I broke up with my girlfriend she said
"The way you view the world as a male you talk down to me"
And I couldn't
I couldn't
*I just didn't understand*
When I was at organizational meetings she said that sometimes I would value the
  men in the room more than the women
*And I just couldn't understand*
And if anything I was in denial . . .
And then I took a class on gender equality a feminist class . . .
And that really opened my eyes like
"*Oh my god!*"
There's one thing I really do value about social justice is that
If you're fighting for some endangered species of tree out there
And this person's fighting for gender equality

And one person's fighting for race
Eventually they all come together
There's that midsection where social equality comes together
And it's a struggle
I struggle with it daily [laugh]
And I think that helps me realize how difficult it would be
To want to change the way you perceive the world as a white person
Because as a male it can be very exhausting [laugh].

Steven recounts his inability to understand his ex-girlfriend's accusations of sexism, and he credits a feminist class on gender equality as opening his eyes to the problem. By directly quoting what his ex-girlfriend said to him, he indicates that he now understands what she meant, he can now hear her voice.[2] By using repetition and an emphatic tone and terms, he highlights his earlier failure to understand and the shock of having his eyes opened.

But there is another "other" in Steven's account—white people who are trying to change how they view the world. He connects the exhausting work he has done as a man trying to hear women's voices to the work white people do when they try to hear the voices of people of color. Thus he constructs himself as a person who is learning to see the interconnectedness of all struggles for equality.

I met Ramita during my group interview with members of the student government. She is a social science major and an international student of color who grew up in an upper-middle-class family in a large South Asian city. During the individual interview, she described her early college days as lonely until a student orientation leader took her under her wing. After that Ramita dove into many opportunities for service work in the community. Her campus involvements include the Asian Student Organization, Students for Disability Rights, and the student government. Her stories about what she has learned in college include gaining an understanding of race in the U.S. context, learning to see herself as a leader, and learning to define herself as an advocate for social justice. Over time she has gained the confidence to speak up about diversity issues in the classroom as well as in her many service and organizational activities.

In the following, Ramita relates a major insight she had after she and another international student talked about social categories and social inequalities in their home countries.

*Ramita:* I was talking with another international student
Who's from the Republic of Georgia . . .
And she was like
"Well in my culture we have poor people in that corner who we have certain labels for
And there are those rich people in the other corner who we have labels for

And that's how we deal with those inequalities in our society"
And I'm like
"But if someone from one corner or the other from the Republic of Georgia comes
    to CU
You're not going to treat them differently because they're part of that corner
You need to treat them because of who they are
Or I *hope* you'd treat them as who they are
What experiences they have to offer
And you might actually end up liking someone who's [from a different social status
    back home]—"
But just talking with her about that made me think about my own issues
Because in [my country] social class is very important
And I feel like the differences just get evened out here [in the United States]
Like if a student from wherever whichever part of [my country]
Whatever class background came to America
It would be totally fine [for me to have] a conversation with them
Because they are at the same school as me
So I regard them as equal to me
But then I started thinking about when I go back home
What a hypocrite I am
Because then I'm suddenly again categorizing people you know
Because it's not something you consciously do
But until you start questioning it you're not going to think about it
And so because of that conversation with [the student from the Republic of
    Georgia]
I started questioning my own issues
I may be a social justice advocate *here*
But what am I doing back home?
I'm driving around in my car
And going to more expensive stores or whatever
And how can I live with those two—?
You know here I'm like
"Oh homeless people need a home"
Whereas at home there are *way* more homeless people than over here
And what am I doing for them?

Ramita emphasizes the jolt she felt after a conversation with another international student: she realized that her sense of self as a social justice advocate was based on her actions at CU and in the United States. In CU's context, she can easily treat as irrelevant the class inequalities that shape the social system at home and that would shape her interactions with a person of another class there. Her realization that she would treat any student from her home country as an equal if they came to CU—no matter what their class status at home—led her to realize that she has never thought about challenging class inequalities at home. Until this moment, she has taken those inequalities for granted as just the way things are. She indicates that the next step in her development as an advocate has to include attending to social categories and inequalities at home. By calling this "my own issue," she implies that it is more difficult to attend to the voice of the other who is closest to oneself, in this case, homeless people she has encountered in her everyday life in her home country. Like Hannah, Ramita points to the ways that nonconscious, taken-for-granted assumptions about people who differ from her have operated in her everyday life.

## My Voice and the Voice of the Other

In a few students' personal narratives, the voice of the other was central—to the point that they integrated that voice into their stories about developing *their* voice. We get a hint of this in Ramita's narrative when she shifts from becoming conscious of homeless people at home to asking, "What am I doing for them?" In defining herself as a social justice advocate, she takes responsibility not only for hearing the voice of the other, but also for speaking and acting in ways that effect social change.

The integration of a student's voice and the voice of the other was most prominent in the narratives of students involved in White Students Resisting Racism, the informal group that meets regularly to discuss white privilege, their everyday encounters with racism, and how they can support their peers of color. Here I focus on one WSRR member's narrative to show how she integrates the voice of the other into her stories about developing her voice.

Melanie is a business major whose middle-class family lived in a small, mostly white town during her middle and high school years. There were few students of color in her high school class. Melanie described herself as a band nerd during high school; she appreciated that the band director encouraged her and other girls to play nontraditional instruments such as the snare drum. She applied to several colleges in the city where CU is located and ended up going to CU because it gave her the best scholarship.

When I asked what the transition to college was like for her, Melanie talked about how her life revolved around the women's volleyball team during her first year. She said, "We separated ourselves and we spent the majority of our time together." In retrospect, she said, she realized that she knew little about what else was happening on campus that year.

*Melanie:* There were a couple cases of really homophobic incidents [my first year]
And I didn't even hear about them
So I think I was like really shut off as a freshman
I just didn't really concern myself with other people's issues
And at the same time I was grappling with my own sexuality issues

Like who I was
Finding out later that I'm lesbian [laugh]
So I think a lot of my freshman year was sort of really centered on myself
And figuring out who I was as a person.

Melanie portrays herself during her first year as self-preoccupied. Ironically, the example she gives of "other people's issues" that she didn't even hear about was homophobic incidents on campus. Those incidents affected people like her (other GLBT students), but she suggests they did not affect her personally, at least not at that time. Although Melanie enjoyed her involvement with the volleyball team, she presents herself as alone in grappling with her sexuality.

As she continued, Melanie said that in high school she didn't have a chance to think about her sexuality because her family, high school friends, and home town were very homophobic. She was "constantly bombarded with 'that's wrong, that's a *sin*.'"

*Melanie:* So coming to college I was finally having an opportunity to think for myself for once . . .
So I think in college and along with CU's diversity policy and so on and so on—
We tend to be known as a pretty supportive campus for GLBT students—
And upon hearing that I was like
"Oh that's cool"
Because there's a week on campus Coming Out Week
Where GLBT students will chalk things on the sidewalk
Like "Gay Pride"
"Gay is Fun" whatever
And I'm seeing this stuff and I'm like
"Oh ok well that's cool" you know
But then I'm getting these messages from some of my teammates
Who are like "*eeeeeww that's weird*" you know
So I don't know
I was—
Freshman year was very uncomfortable
It was just very unsettling
I didn't know what to do
*Susan:* About that?
About sexuality?
*Melanie:* Yeah about the whole sexuality issue
And I really didn't figure that out until my junior year [laugh]
So it took a little while.

In contrast to her home environment where she learned that lesbianism is wrong and sinful, Melanie presents college as a time and place where she could "think for myself." This phrase taps into the discourse of liberal arts education as providing students opportunities for opening their minds. In this case, opening her mind had to do with understanding her sexuality in new ways.

Like many other CU students (see chapter 3), Melanie describes CU as providing a supportive environment for GLBT students. And yet she presents herself as observing from afar the GLBT chalkings and activities. And despite CU's general support for GLBT students, Melanie describes her primary reference group during her freshman year—her volleyball teammates—as homophobic. She indicates that this juxtaposition was unsettling and made her freshman year uncomfortable. Later she told me that she first came out to two hall directors and that she now has close GLBT friends.

When I asked Melanie about transitions she's gone through since her freshman year, she focused not on issues of sexuality but on how she has developed new understandings about race. She has been an RA in the residence halls for two years, and in that context she participated in diversity education each year. In retrospect, though, she described that diversity education as "very surface," as "not challenging you to *really* think about these things." She said RA's were instructed "to just be aware that your white privilege might be affecting a student of color's decision to come talk to you or not, because they don't know where you're at."

At the beginning of her sophomore year, a friend and fellow RA encouraged Melanie to apply to go to the annual Race Conference, but it conflicted with a volleyball tournament so she didn't go. She did go to RC her junior year, however, and that experience made her realize how superficial the RA training had been. When I asked whether there were particularly memorable moments at RC, she talked about the fishbowl exercise in which three white students and three students of color sit in the center of a larger circle consisting of the other participants. (In chapter 4 Rachelle talked about the fishbowl at RC a different year.) The facilitator asks a question and the students in the fishbowl respond while others in the larger circle listen. Melanie was in the larger circle.

*Melanie:* A lot of the students of color just had at some of the white students
I mean *wow*
Like just all of these emotions were coming out
And all of these feelings and experiences that they had had with these particular
    white students
They were just being really open about it
And it just totally hit me
I was like *wow*
I did not know that it was that bad
I had no idea that students of color felt that way about a lot of the white students
    that they run into

This one woman Kim
She just—
Oh god—
She's African American
And it just
Oh god—
It just broke my heart to see those emotions coming out of her
Because I had no idea
*Susan:* It was hurt and anger?
*Melanie:* Yeah just a lot of hurt and anger
And I'd just never seen that
Like you know because of who she is and her physical appearance she gets treated
    differently
And I'd always known that
But I never knew to what extent it actually hurt students of color before
And so that particular exercise was really life-changing.

In describing what she observed in the fishbowl, Melanie focuses on the voices of students of color, particularly Kim's. She presents that voice as intensely emotional. Indeed she highlights the emotions Kim and the other students of color expressed rather than the specific experiences they were talking about. Her use of the term "had at" (in the first line) portrays an explosion of emotions long held back. When I ask, Melanie confirms that those emotions were hurt and anger, but her account emphasizes hurt more than anger.

Melanie does not indicate how the white students in the fishbowl responded, but she does indicate her own response. Her repetition of "wow," "oh god," and "I had no idea" communicate how emotionally powerful this experience was for her. She distinguishes between *knowing* that students of color get treated differently because of their race and *hearing* the hurt they express as they talk about getting treated differently. Melanie describes hearing her peers' stories of pain as a life-changing experience, as an epiphany.

*Melanie:* After that I was crying the rest of the conference
It was just so hard for me
And it was just like so emotionally and mentally traumatizing
*Susan:* What were the tears about?
*Melanie:* That's such a good question
I'm still having a hard time thinking about that
And also getting into this year I did RC again
And I don't know
I'm not someone to cry
I'm not a crier
So like this was—
Both of these conferences were very difficult for me

Because I think just seeing and hearing the hurt come out of these individual people
I think that's what was really hard for me
I think just sitting there and listening to someone just hurt because of what I had
  done
I guess
I think
I think that's what was really hard for me
The fact that I could have said something
I could have done something
But I didn't
And that I caused a lot of hurt for someone
*Susan:* It changes your sense of who you are
*Melanie:* Yeah and it really—
I don't know.

By using strong words—"emotionally and mentally traumatizing"—and by describing herself as someone who doesn't cry easily and yet who cried for the rest of the weekend, Melanie emphasizes how difficult RC's have been for her. Importantly, she presents the difficulty as both emotional and cognitive.

Melanie struggles to articulate what is so difficult. "I think," "I guess," and "I don't know" indicate that she is still not sure, but she speculates nonetheless. Again, she focuses on the other's pain: "Seeing and hearing the hurt come out of these individual people." But here she adds the effect on her of witnessing that pain—the realization that *she* may be implicated in other's suffering. Notice that Melanie shifts verb forms—from "because of what I had done" to "I could have done something" to "I caused a lot of hurt." The first and third phrases indicate that she feels she *has* done something that specifically harmed a person of color; the second phrase indicates that she thinks she hasn't but can imagine that she *might* have. In either case, she places herself in the position of white people in general who *do* cause harm even if unintentionally.

Throughout this entire account, Melanie does not attempt to distance herself from the three white students who were in the fishbowl. Rather, her response to hearing the students of color's stories suggests that she identifies with those white students. She could have been one of them. Her story is not about trying to defend herself from students of color's charge that white students' actions sometimes exhibit racism. Her story is about hearing that others are hurt by racism and about her realization that as a white person she may have unknowingly engaged in racist actions that caused others pain.

Melanie does not pick up on my statement, "it changes your sense of who you are," but that statement captures one plausible interpretation of her self-construction. To hear, to acknowledge, to accept nondefensively that you have caused or could have caused another pain *is* painful. Even if you *intended* no harm, looking at that harm squarely means acknowledging that you are a person who is capable of hurting others. Melanie seems to say: "As a white person who has not been conscious of my white privilege and how racism operates in everyday interactions, I probably have harmed people of color. This means I have not always been the good moral person I think of myself as being. Now I know that good intentions are not enough. In a situation where people of color get hurt because of the actions of white people like me, I need to change." Melanie's account highlights the pain wrapped up in this new sense of self. This realization—about self and other —is "emotionally and mentally traumatizing." It is "life-changing." Melanie continues:

*Melanie:* Both times I went [to RC]
It just makes me really want to then challenge the things that get said in the classroom
Or just from my friends or whatever
Because I know that a lot of the things get said in the classroom
Outside of the classroom
And whether students of color are present or not
So I think I've sort of taken that as a personal challenge to continually be combating those issues that come up
So from that conference on I then joined White Students Resisting Racism.

Here Melanie introduces what she has done to change her actions as a result of her experiences at RC. After her first RC, she joined WSRR, and since then she has made an effort to challenge racist statements she hears in various contexts on campus.

At this point in her narrative Melanie recounts two stories about friends of color who told her about racist encounters with white students. The first is about a Caribbean woman, Shana, whom she befriended during a study abroad trip.

*Melanie:* A lot of our conversations were about really ignorant statements being said by a lot of the white students on this trip
The first couple of times that we had these conversations I was like
"Wow I'm really sorry
I don't know what to do here"
You know because this was the first time this was happening to me
Where a student of color was sharing their experience
And here I'm like having to *do* something I felt
And she's like
"You know what?
I just want you to sit there and just listen"
And so it was really good to have her tell me that
Because I wouldn't have known otherwise what I was supposed to be doing with that

But I think
Yeah I think she really gave me that experience of
"Ok sometimes students of color just want a listening ear with their white friends"
So I think I developed a really close trust with her in that I didn't—
I wasn't invalidating her experience
I was taking it in and being like
"Oh my god that's *ridiculous*."

As Melanie describes how her friendship with Shana developed, she emphasizes her uncertainty about how to respond to Shana's stories about other white students' racist comments. Melanie presents herself as wanting to take action, and she presents Shana as teaching her that she just wants Melanie to listen. This, then, could be interpreted as a story about a student of color taking the role of educator. What is the difference between Shana's apparent willingness to educate Melanie and CU students of color's resistance to taking that role on campus (see Rachelle's story in chapter 4)? The difference may have to do with context. Shana teaches Melanie what she needs in the context of their friendship. By contrast, CU students of color embrace the role of educator when they offer educational events through their student organizations; the white students they resist are those who fail to attend those educational events but still ask to be educated about race.

In her account, Melanie expresses gratefulness for Shana's willingness to educate her. Melanie learns that "just listening" can be a powerful way to support another person, a form of support that produces trust. She learns that listening can be a matter of acknowledging the other's perception of reality. Her double negative—"I wasn't invalidating her experience"—implies that she felt Shana was accustomed to having her experiences invalidated.

The second story is about Melanie's friendship with an African student, Ayo.

*Melanie:* We've developed a really really close friendship over these past couple
    years
And he's had some recent incidents come up
Where he feels a lot of people on his floor [in the residence hall] have been pretty
    racist to him
And I think in my work towards being an ally is finding ways to help combat these
    situations
And not only being a listening ear for him
So like I went out
Did some research
And found a possible route we could take to address this on an institutional level
Like get this to the dean [of students] so he knows about it
But like obviously you know—
Ultimately it comes down to Ayo's decision

You know whether or not he wants to do it
But I would really like to do it [laugh]
But obviously his decision
I'll do whatever he wants because it's directly affecting him
But I think my role is at least to find outlets
That we can directly act upon these different ways that friends of color have experienced racism.

In this story, Melanie embraces the identity of a white person who is "work[ing] toward being an ally" to peers of color. Her use of the term *work* reflects her involvement with the interconnected group on campus that advocates for social justice. In addition, her statement that she is working *toward* being an ally—rather than claiming that she *is* an ally—reflects a subtle linguistic distinction within social justice discourse as it gets expressed at CU. Those on the privileged side of a social difference—in this case, white people—can aim toward action that supports those on the nonprivileged side of that difference. But it is those on the nonprivileged side who *define* what constitutes supportive action for them. This distinction explains why Melanie emphasizes that it is Ayo's decision—not hers—about what action they take. Although she states, with a laugh, that *she* would like to take his complaint to the dean, she prioritizes what Ayo wants. In a passage not cited here, she acknowledges that she can understand why he might not want to do that: "It's just such an emotional drag to have to go through all that crap." By "crap" she means the official process of filing a complaint and talking to people who may or may not see his point of view.

In another passage not cited here, Melanie told me that the first thing she did after Ayo told her about his experiences in the residence hall was to discuss the problem with White Students Resisting Racism. It was in that group that she learned that there *is* a formal grievance process on campus through which such incidents can be addressed. As we shall see in chapter 8, WSRR is a major source of support for white students who are trying to figure out what it means to work toward being allies to students of color.

In this story, Melanie brings her experience of hearing the voice of the other into her account of how she is developing *her* voice. She has moved from being speechless with emotion at RC, to learning to listen to a friend of color's stories about racist experiences, to seeking support from WSRR, to being ready to act—to speak—in support of a friend's grievance about racism. Like Kia's and Rachelle's narratives about developing their voices, Melanie's narrative about developing her voice is about learning to speak out about social justice issues that concern her. Melanie's desire to take Ayo's complaint to the dean is about wanting to take action in a way that could affect the institution's response to racist incidents in the residence halls.

Toward the end of the interview, I brought Melanie back to the issue of sexuality, asking whether she has gone through any other transitions in that aspect of her life. She said that she is now out on campus as a lesbian and that she is "really close to some gay and lesbian students." But she also expressed disappointment in some GLBT students' failure to think critically about race and sexuality.

*Melanie:* You would think that in coming to terms with an oppression that you have
That you then take that and say
"Oh maybe I'm not the only one oppressed"
Or "maybe there are other forms of oppression that I'm not aware of"
And want to support these other groups of people who aren't as privileged as you are
You know or like just become aware of other things that are going on
But I'm finding that like
*Errrrrrrrr* [emphatic expression of frustration]
In the GLBT community there are some of the most racist—
God there's even people that even have gender and even sexuality issues
I'm like
"How are you able to function as a human and not be aware of these other things?"
Like [there's] still stereotyping going on within the lesbian community
*Susan:* Stereotypes about what?
*Melanie:* Stereotypes about gay men
Like they'll see what you would think of as a stereotypically gay man
And they would say like
"Oh my god he's so *gay*"
And I'm like "*what?*"
*Aaahhhhhh* that just bothers me *so much*
And some of my really close gay and lesbian friends still make really racist comments
And so my biggest challenge has been—
Right now to work with some of my really close friends who are white and address those issues.

Melanie presents herself as more knowledgeable than her gay and lesbian friends about social justice issues, including intersections among them. She is impatient and frustrated with GLBT friends who express racism and lesbian friends who reinforce stereotypes about gay men. She presents herself as not understanding how people who experience one form of oppression in our society could fail to translate that experience into empathy for people who experience another form of oppression. For Melanie, this inability to connect with another's experience amounts to an inability to "function as a human."

Here again we get a sense of how Melanie integrates the voice of the other

—people of color, gay men—into her narrative about her own voice. She indicates that she uses her voice to resist her close friends' racism and homophobia. She brings the voice of the other into her conversations with friends.

*Susan:* What about the other side or the flip side
In the groups that you're involved with that are dealing with racial issues
Is there homophobia there?
Is homophobia dealt with in those groups?
*Melanie:* I think so yeah
I mean a large part of RC isn't just to address the white students
It's to address different stereotypes that students of color have as well
Because we all grow up in this society having stereotypes about different groups
    of people
It's not just white people
But yeah I think the facilitators do a good job of saying
"For you students of color you need to check your sexuality issues your homo-
    phobia" . . .
And particularly on this campus it's been really cool to have some really strong
    [administrators] who are out GLBT individuals
And see the way that students change their attitudes towards gays and lesbians
    because of [those administrators].

Notice that as Melanie answers my questions, she speaks generally rather than personally. She does not talk about how *she* has encountered homophobic attitudes or participated in conversations about sexual orientation at RC. She does, however, acknowledge that at least some students of color who attend RC need to learn to resist homophobia and stereotypes about GLBT people that they have absorbed from the society at large (or perhaps from their religious communities, as Rachelle described in chapter 4). But unlike her talk about white GLBT friends whose racism frustrates her immensely, Melanie does not express frustration here. Like the members of the GLBT Organization who spoke about the administration's support in response to the antigay incidents in chapter 3, Melanie focuses on the broader context of support for GLBT students on campus. Here she mentions that administrators who are out on campus have influenced some students to rethink their attitudes toward GLBT people. Speaking about a particular administrator of color, Melanie said, "I think a lot of the students of color that come into this campus possibly with homophobia issues, but who work really closely with Mr. Jones, they realize, 'oh!'" Melanie continues:

*Melanie:* I see race as my primary issue that I would like to deal with
Rather than sexuality
But [sexuality] is still very important to me
And I'm still trying to find the ways that race and sex intersect.

How do we understand a personal narrative in which a white woman—who has come out as a lesbian during her college years—constructs race as a more compelling social justice topic than sexuality? At least part of the answer has to do with CU's narrative environment. As we saw in chapter 3, race is the most prominent and contentious diversity category on campus. According to Mr. Robert, race is also the most difficult diversity conversation on campus. According to the students involved in the GLBT Organization—as well as several other groups of students I interviewed—CU's administration has been more proactive in supporting GLBT students than students of color. Although the interconnected group addresses many different topics, race is at the forefront of their activities. At the same time, though, as the GLBT students pointed out, there is no counterpart to RC for sexuality (although sexuality gets some attention at RC). In this narrative environment, it makes sense that some students, like Melanie, would take up race as their primary focus.

And yet CU's narrative environment does not *determine* Melanie's narrative—the details of her biography and her sense of self also come into play. Not every white student who attends RC has as powerful a reaction to hearing students of color's stories. Not every white student who hears those stories cries for the rest of the weekend. Not every white student who attends RC ends up joining WSRR. Not every white lesbian student feels compelled to resist her GLBT friends' racist comments. While Melanie's narrative about integrating the voice of the other into the development of her voice on campus is intelligible within CU's narrative environment, it is not the only possible story.

## Narrative Patterns

Each of the narratives presented in this chapter is infused with the biographical details of the narrator's life. Each student's specific life experiences certainly shape what stands out to them as they recount what they are learning at college. And yet there are also patterns among these narratives. As a whole they display what Mark Freeman calls "relational thinking"—an orientation to the relationship between self and other that "shift[s] the angle of vision and thereby open[s] up new, more fully human ways of figuring human lives."[3]

These narratives suggest that exposure to or contact with people whose social locations and identities differ from one's own is a necessary but *in*sufficient condition for hearing the voice of the other.[4] In parts of their narratives not presented here, Sydney and Hannah describe their high schools as more racially diverse than CU, but both also say that race was not discussed in their high school classes, extracurricular activities, or friendships. Their narratives indicate that they experience CU as giving them more opportunities to think and talk about diversity than their high schools did. Sydney states that she has been exposed to the GLBT community because her sister is a lesbian, but she recounts the Kinsey workshop as more influential in learning what it is like to be "other." Although Madison states that at CU she has been exposed to many more out GLBT students than in her hometown, her narrative is about more than mere exposure to gay peers—it is about going to gay clubs with her gay friends and listening to her gay friend speak at the rally. Steven acknowledges that his ex-girlfriend pointed out his sexism, but he could not hear what she was saying at that point. Ramita has been exposed to class inequalities in her home country all her life, but it took a conversation with another international student for her to realize that she has been indifferent to homeless people there. Melanie describes CU as "much more racially diverse" than her high school, but it wasn't until she attended RC at a friend's urging that she paid attention to the experiences of students of color on campus.

The students' stories about epiphanies transform the cliché about putting yourself in another's shoes into a narrative truth.[5] As she listens to her gay friend at the rally, Madison realizes how awful it would be to have to pretend she is someone she isn't. As she listens to her African American classmate, Hannah realizes that being frightened of him just because he is a black male constitutes racism. During the Kinsey workshop, Sydney gets a taste of what it is like to be the one who is different in a group. As he works on his sexism, Steven imagines that it must be just as difficult and exhausting to be a white person working on racial issues. As she thinks about the class privilege she takes for granted at home, Ramita takes the point of view of homeless people there. As she listens to students of color during the fishbowl exercise at RC, Melanie hears how painful their experiences are.

These narratives suggest that putting oneself in another's shoes requires a concrete experience. These and other CU students (in stories not cited here) talk about how experiential or embodied knowledge of others' perspectives is more powerful than theoretical or intellectual knowledge. The former invites one to hear the other's voice in a way the latter does not. Hannah contrasts an intellectual understanding of white privilege to the impact of her peer's story about white women locking their doors when they see him. Madison recounts the impact of her gay friend's story at the rally. Like Melanie, several white students describe (in narratives not cited here) how students of color's personal stories at RC make racism real to them. Definitions of race and racism that they have learned about in other contexts fail to accomplish that. A general understanding that students of color get treated differently because of their appearance also fails to accomplish that.

Although others' personal stories feature heavily in students' descriptions of concrete experiences, some present other experiences as concrete. Sydney contrasts her inability to understand theoretically what it is like to be the only person like oneself in a group to the impact of that embodied experience at the workshop where she was the only one standing at the heterosexual end of the continuum. And Steven uses his concrete understanding of how exhausting it is for him as a man to work on his sexism to imagine that it is just as difficult for white people to work on their racism.

And yet, what turns a concrete event into an epiphany in which a student hears the voice of the other is not predictable. Another student at the same time and place—at Madison's campus rally, at Sydney's workshop, in Hannah's classroom, in Steven's feminist class, in Ramita's conversation, at Melanie's RC retreat—might not experience those events as they did. Why *this* event becomes an epiphany for *this* student has to do with the intersection of the student's biography, the event itself, and the narrative environment. What these narratives have in common is a construction of *this* concrete event as inviting them to put themselves in another's shoes, as allowing them to hear the other's voice in a way they haven't before.

In one way or another, questions about the self—who am I? who am I becoming? what kind of person do I want to be?—are embedded in each of these narratives. As they listen to the voice of the other, these students experience the other as speaking to *them*. Further, they understand that the other is speaking to them as a person with certain social identities—as a heterosexual, as a white woman, as an upper-middle-class person, as a man of color. These narratives are about learning to see oneself in terms of those social identities. As she works at becoming a person who cares about others' rights and experiences of discrimination, Madison learns to see herself as having heterosexual privilege. As she listens to her African American classmate's story, Hannah sees herself through his eyes as a white woman who locks her car door when he passes by. She wants to resist that nonconscious racism in herself. Steven learns to see himself as having male privilege, and he works at being a man of color who resists rather than perpetuates sexism. Ramita learns to recognize how her class privilege operates at home. She wants to be a social justice advocate not only at CU but also at home. Melanie sees herself as a white woman who has probably caused peers of color pain even though she hasn't meant to. Melanie brings the voice of the other to bear on how she develops her own voice on campus.

Finally these narratives reflect various layers of social contexts in which CU students are living and learning, social contexts that foster conditions in which listening to the voice of the other *may* happen, and at least sometimes *does* happen.[6] One layer consists of specific, concrete social contexts. Hannah and Steven speak about certain courses and classrooms in which listening to the voice of the other takes place. Sydney's narrative features the Kinsey workshop and Madison's features a campus rally. Melanie highlights the power of RC. Like Ramita, whose account features a conversation with another international student, these and other CU students speak about relationships with significant others—friends, peers, mentors on campus—as influencing them to listen to the voice of the other.

At the same time, these narratives reference broader contextual layers. Although it is clearest in Madison's narrative (and Mason's in chapter 1), these narratives reflect the preferred story that educators expect to hear from traditional-age students who attend liberal arts colleges: a story about opening their minds to new ideas and their eyes to a broader world. In addition, these students tell a story that makes sense *on this particular campus*—a story about learning to listen to the voice of the other, the voice of those whose lives, identities, and social locations differ from one's own. Indeed, these narratives provide further evidence that "diversity is out there on the table" at CU. Specifically, these narratives reflect social justice discourse as it gets expressed at CU. That discourse includes an emphasis on dialogue. Learning to listen is as important to dialogue as learning to speak.

# PART THREE

# Students' Protest and Response

# 6    *Creating a Voice of Protest*

Now I return to the Activists' story, part of which I told in the introduction. The Activists were an ad hoc group of about forty-five students of color and a few white students who came together to protest what they perceived as the university's failure to live up to its diversity commitments, especially concerning race.

The Activists formed in the context of specific events. Two Asian American students had attempted to complain to Professor Thomas about what they saw as his unsatisfactory treatment of race in one of his courses. According to the students, he refused to meet with them. According to Professor Thomas, their request to meet was not guided by an interest in respectful conversation. The students spoke with administrators, who attempted to mediate the situation, but the students were not satisfied. In the midst of these administrative mediations, the students expressed their complaints in a letter in the student newspaper. Professor Thomas wrote a rebuttal, defending both the content of his course and his pedagogy.[1] Both statements were controversial, and the controversy continued in the opinion section of the newspaper. Some people defended the students and some the professor. Although the conflict between the students and the professor—and how administrators handled it—is important in itself, my focus is on CU *students'* narrative reality. Here that means I focus on what happened next—the formation of the Activists.

For many students of color, the publication of Professor Thomas's rebuttal was the last straw. Its content upset them, but equally if not more upsetting was that the newspaper editors allowed Professor Thomas three times as many words as their editorial policy permitted, while they had required the two students to adhere to the policy's word limit. Students of color interpreted this differential treatment by the newspaper as shaped by race and status, as privileging a white professor's voice over theirs. Thus students of color began to view the situation with Professor Thomas as merely one instance of a broader set of problems on campus that they had been dealing with for a long time.

This shift to a broader, long-term perspective is seen in Kia's response when I asked her and May—the two students I interviewed as members of the Southeast Asian Association (SAA)—what has been important to them this year:

*Susan:* This year has been a really active year in terms of diversity issues on campus
Maybe you all could tell me what *you* think the big issues have been for *you* all
What's been a big deal this year for you guys?
*Kia:* I feel like there's been a lot going on the last four years that I've been here
And it's really just culminated this year . . .
I remember looking through some of my papers
Because we're told to keep everything until we graduate
And there was a flyer in one of my SAA files
And it was about students talking to administrators about cultural diversity
And the racial tension or feelings on campus
And so these agenda items were already brought to the administrators' attention
But they weren't dealt with
And they're pretty much the same issues that we're tackling this year.

Although I asked about *this* year, Kia focuses on the last *four* years and her realization that this year's issues are a repeat of the past. Similarly, during my interview with the Black Collegians, when I asked about the curriculum, and specifically whether there are "courses and departments that are more supportive" in terms of addressing diversity, Tanya said:

*Tanya:* I wouldn't say any department on campus necessarily excels more than another
I would say there's individuals in departments and in classes who do well
And who try to integrate diversity into their curriculum
But generally it's a problem with the educational system as a whole
A lot of the information we are learning does not deal anything with diversity.

Like Kia, Tanya directs attention away from specifics to broader problems, in this case, the curriculum's failure to address diversity adequately. Indeed, several documents confirm these students' perspective that diversity issues have been raised before and not fully addressed. Based on focus group research conducted in the late 1990s, two members of the Faculty Diversity Group wrote a report documenting widespread dissatisfaction on campus with the cultural diversity requirement and classroom climate. In the mid-2000s, a white senior wrote her honors thesis on the history of the cultural diversity requirement, showing that despite periodic attempts to revise it, it has been changed only slightly since it was instituted in the late 1980s. Students can still fulfill the requirement without taking courses dealing with race (or any diversity categories) in the U.S. context. And the year before my study, the white editor of the student newspaper published a front-page article on diversity-related efforts at CU. Among other things, the editor showed that the curriculum, classroom climate, and campus climate have been topics at CU for a long time.

Students of color's shift away from the specific conflict between the two students and the professor to a broader, long-term perspective was pivotal in the formation of the Activists. That group was made up of members of the Southeast Asian Association, the Black Collegians, as well as students in several other student of color organizations.

In this chapter, I present the Activists' voice of protest: their message and the strategies they used to get it across. I show that the Activists' voice of protest was grounded in the strong community of color they had already built across different racial groups of color. And I argue that the Activists' protest was at least partially effective. Accounts by some faculty and administrators show that they were influenced by the Activists to treat racial issues—particularly concerning the classroom and curriculum—with greater urgency than they had in the past.

## A Voice of Protest

The Activists expressed their protest in two major ways: the silent rally and an official document that they sent to CU's administrators.

### The Silent Rally

In the introduction, we heard Kia and May portray the silent rally as a strategy for communicating that students of color haven't been heard in the past at CU, and as a strategy for getting heard *this* time. They also criticized as unjust the stereotype of the inherently angry student of color. At this point —having characterized CU's narrative landscape in part I, and having explored students' personal narratives in part II—I can augment our understanding of the silent rally.

Kia and May's perspective that students of color have been treated unjustly at CU clearly draws on social justice discourse that is familiar in American culture at large. But two aspects of their account indicate that they draw on the particular form of social justice discourse that circulates at CU, particularly within the interconnected group (see chapter 2). First, they focus on the importance of dialogue, on speaking and listening. Their complaint is that their repeated attempts to speak and get heard have failed because others have not listened. Second, by acknowledging that they *are* angry about the state of affairs on campus, they embrace the idea that dialogue about racism can be emotionally volatile. They reject the racist image of the unreasonably angry person of color, but they express confidence that they have good reason to be angry. Kia and May indicate that the problem is not students of color's anger but others' failure to listen to what they are angry about.

In addition, we can now understand the Activists' sense of entitlement to speak out about the racism they experience on campus. That sense of entitlement is facilitated by CU's narrative environment and in particular by the ongoing work of the interconnected group. As we saw in chapters 4 and 5, programs such as the Race Conference encourage students of color to speak in a context that encourages others to listen. In the narrative community fostered by the interconnected group, students of color learn what it means to speak directly about their racial identities and experiences and about race relations on campus. They carry that sense of entitlement to speak and get heard into the broader campus community. They certainly expressed that sense of entitlement in the silent rally.

### The Official Protest Document

A week after the silent rally, the Activists sent a letter signed "the Activists" (without individuals' names) to the administration, faculty, and staff, in which they announced the existence of their group, summarized their protest, and called for a public reply. They also presented the administration with a four-page, single-spaced document outlining their protest. Members of the Activists told me that together they brainstormed ideas for this document and that they wrote it collectively. In presenting it here, I have paraphrased the wording of the document in some places and deleted some details as a means of shortening it.

> Background on how we got to this level of frustration and concern [shortened and paraphrased]
>
> Our frustration has been building for a long time, but at this point we feel bombarded with incidents that make CU's environment as a whole feel unwelcoming and unaffirming. While the administration responds quickly to other incidents concerning intolerance and discrimination (e.g., incidents of homophobia on campus), the administration does not respond quickly to issues and incidents regarding race. When the administration does respond to our concerns, those responses feel like band-aids rather than real solutions.
>
> Concrete issues and concerns [main points only, details for each point excluded]
>
> • Lack of diversity among faculty and staff regarding *domestic* people of color
> • Problematic tone and content of the student newspaper regarding issues and experiences students of color face

• Weakness of and problems with the cultural diversity requirement in the curriculum
• Lack of clarity about the grievance policy and about procedures, resources, and support for dealing with conflicts around diversity that aren't necessarily grievances
• Tokenism/invisibility/misleading/exclusive/over-representation of people of color in the university's promotional materials, website, and photos in administrative offices
• Tone and organization of the student government is not inclusive or welcoming of students of color and their needs, experiences, and programs
• Overall campus climate concerning racial issues (insensitivity in the residence halls; lack of racial education for white students; targeting of advocates who challenge racism, insensitivity, or the status quo)
• Problematic classroom climate for students of color

Recommendations for immediate responses [presented in full]

• Written response to the Activists acknowledging the problems, issues, their experiences and that the climate on campus regarding diversity, and in particular race, is not conducive, ideal, or what we want it to be
• Meetings to be held between the Activists and the administration
• Written communication to the entire campus acknowledging the issues, the climate, the shortcomings, the experiences of many students of color, and plans for addressing these
• Series of public forums/discussions about the issues, inclusion, diverse perspectives and experiences as it relates to student life, students of color, and diversity
• Commitment to develop a plan for diversifying the faculty and staff by forming an ad hoc committee

Recommendations for long-term responses [presented in full]

• Concrete and intentional plan for recruiting, retaining, and supporting faculty and staff diversity, especially for domestic faculty and staff of color
• Better "student-friendly" evaluation process for courses, professors, and the cultural diversity requirement
• Clarify the relationship between the cultural diversity requirement in the curriculum, CU's mission and diversity policy, and undergraduate student life
• Create and implement a diversity campus survey (perhaps using outside facilitators/researchers) to assess the climate and make recommendations regarding diversity
• Training/assistance/professional development for faculty regarding leading, facilitating, encouraging difficult diversity dialogues and discussions. Staff and students may also be able to take advantage of training/professional development opportunities
• Intentional recruitment and student involvement from diverse student groups

in all major evaluative and/or decision-making bodies (e.g., curriculum committee; faculty searches)
• Demystify the ambiguous concept of "the administration" by helping students understand what the protocols are, what the distinctions are between academic and student affairs, and who is responsible, can be of assistance, and held accountable for various parts of the student experience (i.e., who will respond to their needs, questions, etc.)
• Do the same to demystify the concepts of "the faculty" and "academics" so that students have a better understanding of the faculty committee and governance structure.

In this official document, the Activists use a voice that is familiar in any bureaucratic organization. They provide historical background, a list of specific problems that currently need to be addressed, and recommendations for short- and long-term solutions. This voice—or method of communicating—is frequently used by administrators in bureaucratic institutions to formulate strategic plans and the duties of taskforces and committees. The Activists presented to CU administrators a document that they would recognize and understand. In this format, the Activists' voice does not sound angry.

Also familiar is the content of the Activists' document. Students of color on other campuses might draw up similar lists; indeed, these issues are rife in the literature on diversity in higher education.[2] I doubt that the problems the Activists identified surprised CU administrators. In addition, the Activists' recommendations are about activities that are already part of the routine practices and ongoing life of the university: recruiting and supporting faculty, evaluating courses, determining how students should be involved in committee work and in the governance of the university, clarifying grievance processes, and conducting research on campus climate. And they are about the university's official commitments and policies: its mission statement, cultural diversity policy, and the undergraduate curriculum's cultural diversity requirement. Administrators would surely welcome most of the recommendations the Activists outlined and would be delighted to create opportunities for students to be educated about "the administration," "the faculty," and how the university works as an organization.

At the same time, though, embedded in the recommendations is the demand that institutionalized racism be addressed. That demand has radical implications for a predominantly white campus.

### Divergent Strategies for Speaking Out

In both strategies for speaking out—the silent rally and the official document—the Activists use the discourse of social justice to express their frustration with what they perceive as the administration's long-term failure to address racial issues on campus. And yet, the differences between the voice the Activists used in the silent rally and the voice they used in the official document are striking. The creativity of their voice in the silent rally—using silence to communicate that they have spoken many times in the past and not been heard—emphasizes their determination that "this time it will be different." The bureaucratic character of their voice in the official document expresses their understanding that changing the organization requires the use of organizational language.[3]

The audiences also differ. The silent rally got the attention of fellow students, including the student reporters who published an article about it (even though the Activists refused to talk to student reporters at that point; see chapter 7). It also got the attention of the student government representatives who later debated whether the Activists' silent presence at their meeting called for a response (see chapter 3). But the official document got the attention of CU administrators. It made the discourse of social justice bureaucratically palatable.

## A Collective Voice of Protest

The silent rally and the official protest document tell us what the Activists were communicating and how they got their message across to different audiences on campus. But how did these students come together to create this voice of protest in the first place? As stated earlier, the ongoing narrative work of the interconnected group at CU facilitated their sense of entitlement to speak out. In addition, my group interviews with the Black Collegians and the Southeast Asian Association, along with my ethnographic observations, show that the Activists developed their voice of protest on the foundation of a community of color they had already achieved across racial groups of color. Their collective identity as "students of color" made their voice of protest possible.

But further, as the collective nature of their protest becomes clear, so does a more nuanced understanding of the *content* of their protest. We gain a deeper understanding of what they are saying has not been heard. They articulate their needs as students of color, but they also articulate *white* students' need for education about race, and the *university's* need for students of color's contributions to campus life.

### Our Community of Color Is Very Strong

Near the beginning of my group interview with them, six African American women members of the Black Collegians told me about their many activities and events throughout the year. When I asked, "Do you get a good audience, do people come?" they told me that the same people come to their events time after time: "It's rare that you see a whole lot of new faces." At this point, Marshan jumped in:

*Marshan:* CU has a really strong community of color
Our community of color is very strong
But as far as the white community—
The white people on this campus—
They come from very monoracial environments
So this is very cultural
And I think they feel like this is too cultural for them
And they get scared
I mean they honestly are scared
They feel like they're not supposed to be there or they're not invited
*Others:* [Overlapping talk]
*Marshan:* When [an event we put on] is open to the campus
And really it's not just for us
It's to educate.

Although these students had been telling me about the Black Collegian's events, Marshan shifts to speaking about the "community of color" on campus, a much broader group than this particular student organization. As we shall see, this double racial identity—as members of specific racial groups as well as of the broader category "students of color"—characterizes the Black Collegians' and the Southeast Asian Association's talk.[4]

Marshan not only *states* that their community of color is strong, she also points to a specific *effect* of their strong community on campus: white students who grow up in white environments are "scared" in the face of that community and do not feel invited to events sponsored by student of color organizations. Marshan's statements are supported by student journalists' (and others') talk about their discomfort interacting with students of color (see chapter 7).

By pointing out that their educational events are open to all, Marshan implies that the problem lies not in the students of color's actions per se but in the nature of race relations on campus. Marshan is suggesting that—even on this predominantly white campus—the strong community of color affects race relations to an extent that many white students are uncertain about how to interact with students of color. Further, she indicates that this unintentional effect has a specific problematic result—white students do not attend their educational events.

When I asked what makes their community strong, the Black Collegians spoke first about Mr. Robert, the director of Multicultural Affairs, who serves as their mentor and whose office sponsors many programs that bring together students from the various racial groups of color. These include the annual student of color orientation for first-year students, the annual student of color retreat for all students of color, and the annual Race Conference. Then the Black Collegians talked about how relationships have developed across the different racial groups of color.

*Tanya:* Well my freshman year we did have connections [across racial groups of color]

But they were more on an individual level

Like we just had friends as individuals

But we didn't necessarily collaborate and work together

It just happened gradually as [we] realized that our struggles are so parallel and similar

It's like "why are we fighting these separately?"

*Others:* Right [overlap]

*Krystal:* And I started seeing that when I went to the student of color retreat

And I think that that's where I started realizing that the experiences are so similar

Because we talked a lot about stereotypes and so many different issues that all of us have to face

And I think that brought us a lot closer

And that was real deep for me

And I know that I connected with a lot of the other students

And that's how we started building friendships and relationships on this campus.

Tanya and Krystal explain that individual relationships with students of other racial groups of color have deepened into collaborative relationships as the students learned that they face similar problems, such as racial stereotypes.[5] One stereotype that the Black Collegians and the Southeast Asian Association (as well as other students of color) talked about was "the angry student of color." As I showed in the introduction, Kia and May depicted white students as mobilizing the racist image of the inherently and unreasonably angry person of color to dismiss students of color's complaints. And recall from chapter 4 that Rachelle narrated her attempts not to "snap" and therefore not to embody the stereotype of the angry black woman.

In addition, both groups—without my prompting—talked about specific incidents faced by members of other racial groups. The Asian American students described an incident the year before during a student government meeting where two African American women were referred to as "black bitches."[6] And the African American students talked about the two Asian American students' frustrations with Professor Thomas. All of these students constructed a narrative in which students of color have learned to see racial issues faced by other groups of color as akin to their own.[7]

## We Need Others to Respect Our Strong Community of Color

In the excerpt above, Krystal mentions the student of color retreat as a place where cross-racial relationships develop among students of color. As they continued, the Black Collegians explained that they have had to fight with the student government to keep the student of color retreat in their budgets. (Several student of color organizations include the student of color retreat as a line item in their annual budgets.) According to the Black Collegians, the student government budget committee removed this item during the budget negotiation process, but later reinstated it. This fight upset the Black Collegians (and other students of color) because the student of color retreat plays such an important role in their lives at CU.

*Krystal:* [Almost shouting with enthusiasm]
I remember my freshman year
I don't even remember the [???]
*Others:* [Enthusiastic confirmation]
*Rachelle:* Like all your memories of CU start at the student of color retreat
*Others:* [Laughter]
*Dorie:* My freshman year it was just like a big burst of fresh air
Especially seeing all the students of color
You might not see them on campus—
*Others:* Right [laughter]
*Dorie:* We're kind of spread out [on campus]
[But] you get to the student of color retreat
And it's like
*"Oh my god!"*
*Others:* [Laughter]
*Dorie:* And then after the student of color retreat you start to know where people hang out
*Others:* Yup right.

As they describe the student of color retreat these students express immense pleasure. The way they speak—their enthusiastic overlapping—conveys Marshan's earlier statement that their community of color is strong. In this group interview, more than any of the others, the students constantly overlapped and confirmed each others' statements. That's why I sometimes write "these students" rather than referring to individuals' statements. As they narrated various aspects of their campus experiences, the Black Collegians constructed a group identity as a strong community of color.

At the same time, their enthusiastic description of the retreat points to problems they face on campus that make programs designed specifically for them necessary in the first place. In statements not cited here, the Black Collegians described these programs as counteracting their isolation in classes and other campus contexts where they are one of a few students of color. They also said these programs provide relief from the "culture shock" they experience on CU's predominantly white campus if *they* went to high schools or grew up in neighborhoods where *their* racial group was in the majority. Finally, they described these programs as fulfilling *their* need to be educated on racial issues, because they, too—like white students—grew up in racist America.

Speaking in general of the Office of Multicultural Affairs' programs for students of color, Marshan sums up the problem:

*Marshan:* That's what the white people on this campus don't understand
Why those programs [that are specifically for us] are necessary
*Others:* [Overlap, confirmation].

These students claim they have achieved a strong community of color across various racial groups of color, but they have not achieved white people's (students', faculty's, administration's) respect for their need for that strong community. They want white people on campus to understand their need for a strong community of color, not to be uncomfortable with it or intimidated by it. And they want white people to understand that respecting that need includes providing resources for programs designed specifically for students of color.[8]

This need for respect for their strong community of color on a predominantly white campus is not explicitly articulated but is implicit in the Activists' official document of protest. The need for changes in interracial relationships—how white people relate to that strong community of color—is embedded in the demands for changes in policies, curricula, the racial composition of the faculty and administration, and how the student government and student newspaper go about their business.[9]

### White Students Need Education about Race and Racism

As Kia and May told me about the official protest document, they focused on problems that students of color have encountered with the student government and the student newspaper.

*Kia:* And I think [these problems] stem from white students not being educated about the issues
And CU doing a disservice to white students in not challenging them and questioning them
And making sure that when they leave CU they have a good idea of what race and racism [are].

Kia's view that CU offers a flawed education about race and racism differs radically from that of some white students. Some white students view as unfair coercion the idea that one course on race in the United States should be mandated as part of the cultural diversity requirement. (See chapter 7, and recall Kane's description in chapter 2 of diversity education on campus as "crap.") But Kia formulates white students—not just students of color—as having educational needs when it comes to racial issues on campus. She adds to CU's social justice discourse the idea that those who are racially *advantaged* would benefit from an education in race and racism because that would help them understand the social worlds they study, work, and live in.[10]

On a more subtle level, Kia expresses a certain confidence here. She is confident about an idea that runs counter to common sense thinking—being educated about race and racism helps white students not just students of color. She is confident that solutions to racial problems serve a common good. Kia continues:

*Kia:* And you know when students of color or people of color in general are angry
*Why* are they angry?
*Susan:* So if white students normally react to anger like
"What's your problem?
I didn't do anything"
To be able to think about or to ask
"There must be a reason why they're angry
Maybe I should listen"?

Like the Black Collegians, Kia uses the collective term "students of color." Here she gives a specific example of what the education of white students about race and racism should include: an understanding of the anger of people of color. In other words, she calls for an education in which white students would learn to listen to a specific aspect of the voice of specific others: the anger of people of color. This excerpt shows that I attempt to articulate the shift that white students need to make—a shift from defensiveness to listening—but, as we see below, my attempt does not capture fully what Kia is trying to tell me, and so she explains further:

*Kia:* Right right there was a lot of that you know
But I think a lot of the frustration also comes from white students who ask that
    question
And students of color answering it
And then they go on
But then a new white student asking the same question
So you know the cycle continues
And I think that's why the theme was that these issues have been here for so many
    years
And it hasn't been dealt with on a systematic or institutional level.

Kia captures a persistent complaint of CU students of color: they are constantly asked to educate their white peers on issues of race. Recall that in chapter 4 Rachelle described the Race Conference as a productive site for cross-racial dialogue, but she also complained that it benefits white students more than students of color because students of color are often called on tell their painful stories for the sake of their white peers' education. I heard this complaint in other interviews and it appears in the Activists' official document under "problematic classroom climate for students of color."

This problem as well as the one Marshan articulated earlier—that white students rarely attend their educational events—create intense frustration for students of color. They *do* provide educational events—educational activities are mandated by the student government bylaws for advocacy organizations—but few white students (or faculty) show up. At the same time, students of color are confronted in other contexts, such as in classrooms, with the demand to educate white students. At that point, students of color experience white students' interest in education as disingenuous.

Thus Kia argues that the racial education of white students is the *institution's* responsibility. While the Activists' official document of protest also points to the institution's responsibility for white students' racial education (in the critique of the cultural diversity requirement), here Kia points to something that is only implicit in the official document: the *relational* consequences of the institution's failure to take up that responsibility. Interracial relations among students—in the classroom, in student government meetings, in exchanges in the student newspaper—are fraught with misunderstandings that result from white students' ignorance about race and racism. Kia suggests that relations between students of color and their white peers would shift if students of color did not bear the burden of white students' education. She seems to say (I'm speculating here) that if the institution took responsibility for educating white students about race and racism, white students would understand why students of color sometimes get angry.[11] They wouldn't be so surprised by or defensive about or intimidated by students of color's words and actions. White students would also be more likely to show up at students of color's educational events.

Kia's focus on the institution's responsibility for white students' racial education echoes a theme in the literature on diversity issues in higher education. Antonio and Muñiz write, "Research on intergroup relations . . . consistently places *institutions* at the center of race relations phenomena, implicating administrators as orchestrators of campus climate through policies affecting intergroup cooperation, racial attitudes, diversity in the curriculum and cocurriculum, and opportunities for formal and informal interracial interaction" [emphasis added].[12]

## CU Needs Our Work and Contributions

As I listened to the Black Collegians and the Southeast Asian Association, I heard them express a third need that was also fundamentally about relationships and that was not articulated in the official document of protest:

the *university's* need for the contribution students of color make through their many activities. In the following, the Black Collegians speak very directly about CU's reliance on their work.

*Krystal:* If we didn't put on a Black History Month celebration *there wouldn't be one!*

*Others:* Right!

*Krystal:* So they fail to realize that it's not just this group of students who are doing this for themselves

We're doing this for this campus because *without us what would you have*?

*Rachelle:* I mean how would that make CU look if there was no recognition of Black History Month?

*Others:* [Overlap, confirmation, laughter]

*Rachelle:* It *astounds* me

And that's the word

*Others:* [Laughter]

*Rachelle:* How often we have to *fight* for the things that we do

And what they don't realize is that if we went on strike for a year . . .

That would mess with money

That would mess with alumni participation

It would mess with so many different things

That they don't even know is incorporated with our participation on this campus . . .

*Others:* [Confirmation throughout this speech]

*Rachelle:* And not just our organization

I'm talking about all of the student of color and advocacy orgs on this campus—

And even with the recruitment [of new students of color]

*Others: Right!* [overlap]

*Marshan:* A lot of people come here because of us

And they fail to realize that.

These students argue that their contributions to campus life are not recognized as such. Rather than having their work acknowledged as an important gift to the campus, they have to fight for resources in order to put on their events. (Rachelle may be referring to battles with the student government over funding.) When Rachelle asks rhetorically, "How would . . . CU look if there was no recognition of Black History Month?" she suggests that the Black Collegians' events allow the university to claim that it supports diversity initiatives. She suggests that their events bolster the university's institutional narrative about its commitment to diversity.

Are these students' claims plausible? Would alumni of color withhold financial support from CU if students of color were to go "on strike" for a year? Would recruitment of students of color flounder? I cannot answer these questions definitively, but I do know that the university depends on students of color to help with recruitment. And the Black Collegians do have strong relations with at least some alumni, as evidenced by the recent celebration of the thirty-fifth anniversary of the founding of their organization. That weekend-long celebration drew many Black Collegian alumni to campus, some of whom spoke about their CU experiences as part of a panel discussion.

In any case, by listing negative consequences for CU if they were to withdraw their labor, these students express confidence that their activities make important contributions to campus life.[13] Their confidence echoes Kia's confidence that an education about race and racism would benefit not just students of color but white students as well. The Activists' official document does not articulate CU's need for the activities of students of color, yet this is another relational need implicit in their protest. CU *needs* their work to be what it claims to be—an institution committed to diversity—and students of color *need* respect for that contribution.

### CU Is Like Two Worlds

At one point in their group narrative, the Black Collegians portrayed succinctly their perspective on the nature of interracial relationships on campus:

*Rachelle:* CU is like really two worlds
*Others:* Yeah! It really is! Right! [laughter].

The metaphor of CU as two worlds captures both the sustenance students of color receive from their strong community of color and the disconnection they feel between themselves and white people on campus. The Activists' official protest document does not explicitly articulate two worlds on campus, but that view of interracial relations underlies the document.[14]

I attended the Office of Multicultural Affairs' annual awards ceremony, an event that embodied the idea of CU as two worlds. About 250 people attended the ceremony, two-thirds of whom were people of color. Administrators, staff, a few faculty, and some parents were present. Of the students of color, the most prominent groups were Asian Americans and African Americans. Sixty-three seniors were recognized as soon-to-be-graduates—students of color, international students, and a few white students who had been involved in OMA's activities. Here is an excerpt from my field notes about the event.

> After dinner the evening consisted of a long series of awards in categories such as academic, service, leadership, and multicultural ally, as well as faculty and staff awards. There was also a special award given by the OMA director and one named for Ms. Ida Brown, the much-loved and much-respected former OMA director who is now elderly but who managed to be present this evening.

The students were incredibly enthusiastic throughout the ceremony. The names of the award winners were not in the program, and so they were a surprise. Each award-giver talked about the winner at length before announcing the name, and so everyone was trying to figure out who had won. The descriptions of each award recipient were very individual and personal. There was nothing generic or bureaucratic about this award process. When the winner's name was finally announced, the crowd burst into applause, of course, but further, every winner received a standing ovation. I saw Marshan walk into the room just as a description of her was being read. When her name was announced, she was so surprised and overcome with joy. It was fun to watch her.

Mr. Robert, the current OMA director, was wearing a light blue traditional African garment. He was in charge of this whole event, but he wasn't always in the forefront. He led with a confident and generous spirit. Many different people gave out the awards, including students, staff, and a few faculty.

In the middle of the awards ceremony, Diana, an African American student, suddenly interrupted the program to give an award to Mr. Robert. This came as a surprise to him as well as to most people in the audience. Diana read out loud a letter she had written to him, and as she did so, one by one, thirty or so students came up and gave him a personal letter each had written. He was visibly very moved; he stood quietly with his head bowed and humbly allowed the students to honor him. I have never seen such a warm and moving recognition of a mentor by students. It was creative, spirited, well-planned, and well-executed.

The OMA awards ceremony celebrates the students' strong community of color and their contributions to campus life. It also helps to reproduce that community. In addition, the way the students successfully and collectively orchestrated a stunning tribute to Mr. Robert embodies their active role in creating that community of color.

The sense in which this community constitutes a world distinct from white students' world is captured in an observation Professor Moore shared with me a few days later. Professor Moore, who is white, attended the OMA awards ceremony as well as CU's honors day event. She told me that few students of color were present at the honors day event and that very few received awards. She said it was as if the OMA awards ceremony was for students of color and the honors day event was for white students.

In sum, the voice of protest with which the Activists "spoke" during the silent rally and in their official protest document is grounded in their strong community of color. Although the term "people of color" is sometimes critiqued as erasing racial, ethnic, and cultural differences, in CU's narrative environment, "student of color" facilitates students' understanding of their common experiences on CU's predominantly white campus. The group interviews discussed above as well as Kia's and Rachelle's interviews discussed in chapter 4 suggest that CU students of color do not always arrive on campus using this term to identify themselves. Rather they *learn* to use it within CU's narrative environment. OMA's programming encourages a common identity as students of color and many students embrace it.

When CU students call themselves "students of color" they claim a pan-racial identity whereby race is meaningful as a category beyond one's particular racial group. In CU's narrative terrain, this panracial identity—this community of color—made it possible for a multiracial group of students to come together to voice a collective protest. In fact, the group of five students the Activists sent to represent them in meetings with CU administrators was multiracial: one Latino, two African American women, and two Asian American women.

But further, excerpts from the group interviews and from my observations at the OMA awards ceremony invite us to see that the students' construction of their strong community of color also shapes the *content* of their voice. We hear them articulating a set of interrelated needs concerning interracial relationships on campus. They need white students' respect for—not discomfort with or fear of—their strong community of color. White students need to be educated about race and racism for their own good. And the university needs their contributions to campus life in order to fulfill its commitment to diversity. These needs are embedded implicitly in the changes in policies, practices, and curricula that the Activists' official document calls for.

Finally, the students' collective identity as a strong community of color shapes *how* they voice their protest: they express confidence that the racial education of white students is for white students not for themselves, and that white students' racial education is the institution's responsibility, not theirs. They express confidence that their educational programs and events make important contributions to the campus at large and should be recognized as such. Most generally, their strong community of color grounds their confidence that what they have to say is important. It grounds their sense of entitlement to speak out and get heard.

## An Effective Voice of Protest

In what sense was the Activists' collective voice of protest effective? The Activists *did* get heard—at least in some ways and in some quarters. Here I address faculty and administrators' accounts, which show that the Activists influenced them to treat racial issues with greater urgency. Chapters 7 and 8 address how different groups of white students responded to the Activists' words and actions.

In their official document, one of the Activists' recommendations for immediate responses was "written communication to the entire campus acknowledging the issues . . . and plans for addressing these." Within two weeks, the president of CU sent a letter to all arts and science faculty, staff, and students about "concerns raised in recent weeks . . . regarding the university's overall commitment to diversity." The Activists were disappointed by the vagueness of this letter, and yet the president did respond publicly. Another of their recommendations for immediate responses was "meetings to be held between the Activists and the administration." Before the end of the semester, two such meetings were held (more about them shortly). One of the upshots of those meetings was the idea of the Activists meeting with the editorial staff of the student newspaper. That meeting also took place before the end of the semester (more about this meeting in chapter 7).

As the Activists point out in their document, meetings and written statements sometimes amount to lip service. In what follows here, though, I focus on faculty and administrators' accounts that address either direct or indirect ramifications of the Activists' protest.

### The Cultural Diversity Forum

About a week after the silent rally (but before the Activists sent their official protest document to the administration), the faculty curriculum committee hosted an open forum for faculty, staff, and students on the cultural diversity requirement in the curriculum. Although this forum was organized before the silent rally took place, faculty and administrators told me that the silent rally lent it a sense of urgency and probably boosted attendance. A faculty member who gave me a copy of extensive notes she took at the forum said that about one hundred people attended, an unusual number for a college meeting. As the forum's organizers, the curriculum committee sat at the front of the room. An administrator gave a history of the cultural diversity requirement and then the floor was opened to attendees in an open-mike format. The meeting lasted more than two hours, and forty-eight different people spoke, more than a third of them students, including several members of the Activists.

Although the cultural diversity forum was not a direct result of the Activists' actions, it could be seen as an instance of one of the recommendations for immediate responses in their official protest document: "public forums/ discussions about the issues." Indeed, the faculty member's notes show that several problems the Activists outlined in their official document were also raised at the forum, most notably that classroom climate is often difficult for students of color; that many faculty do not know how to lead discussions about race; and that students can fulfill the cultural diversity requirement by taking courses on European history, cultures, and languages, thus never taking any course that specifically addresses race (or ethnicity, gender, sexual orientation, age, or ability) in the United States.[15] When one of the Activists asked during the forum, "What are university officials going to do about all of this?" there was a huge round of applause.

Faculty and administrators generally viewed Dr. Miller, a white member of CU's central administration, as the person who was most responsible for responding to the Activists and for doing something about the concerns they raised. In the following excerpt from his interview with me, Dr. Miller is speaking about the cultural diversity forum.

*Dr. Miller:* I'm glad the students [the Activists] raised the issue
[He means problems with the cultural diversity requirement]
I think the forum that was held on cultural diversity
I think that was a major event in our diversity life . . .
It was useful for students because . . . they saw that the process itself is important
And just because ten students complain about a requirement
You don't turn it over and change it
The faculty has thought very carefully about what it does
On the other hand I think it was good for the faculty to be challenged by the students
And I thought it was delightful that suddenly the students were interested directly in the curriculum
*Susan:* Their own education
*Dr. Miller:* Their own education
I thought that was monumental
I wish I had the whole thing on film.

Dr. Miller presents the forum as a significant event in CU's "diversity life," as an event that influenced both students and faculty in positive ways. At the very least, by mentioning the Activists in the first line above, he intimates that their actions pushed the issue of cultural diversity in the curriculum into the limelight. Nonetheless, the Activists would take issue with two statements here. First, they were a group of fifty students, not ten. (Their decision not to include their names in their initial correspondence with the administration may have contributed to this misperception.) Second, and more seriously, the Activists would be offended by the statement that they were "suddenly" interested in the curriculum. The Activists' argued that students had been pointing out problems with the curriculum and classroom climate for years, but had been ignored. Dr. Miller continues:

*Dr. Miller:* And as a result we've got another committee in the college working now—
We have a retreat every year for the college faculty
And the next retreat will be devoted entirely to issues of teaching including diversity.

Dr. Miller indicates that the focus of the upcoming faculty retreat on teaching is a direct result of questions raised in the cultural diversity forum, a result that bears the Activists' imprint. He continues:

*Dr. Miller:* Because a lot of what has come out—
And some of the things that really kind of surprise me
Were what happens in classes where all of the intentions are good
But nobody understands how many feet they are stepping on when certain things
    are said
The classic example was
"What do your people think of this?"
As a question coming from a white professor to an Asian American student or an
    African American student
With no consciousness of how complicated how complex how inappropriate that
    is . . .
So we're going to have an opportunity now to revisit this.

By stating that he was surprised by what he heard at the forum, Dr. Miller indicates that the forum *educated him* about how classroom climate can be especially problematic for students of color when faculty do not know how to conduct discussions about race. "What do your people think about this?" treats students of color as spokepersons for their entire race, a common complaint by students of color.[16] It may also be an example of white professors relying on students of color to educate their white peers. In any case, Dr. Miller suggests that he learned something new from the forum. He has heard the voice of the other—students of color—and he indicates that he will lead the faculty in addressing the problem.

A week after the cultural diversity forum (at which point Dr. Miller would have received the Activists' official protest document), he sent a full-page memo to all faculty about what faculty need to do next—in particular, focus on the question of classroom environment:

> How best might we shape and monitor our own classroom preparation to make sure we are doing everything possible to provide both an intellectually challenging yet positive, non-threatening and safe learning environment for both teacher and student alike: an environment in which all are willing and able to take the risks necessary to learn? How well are we doing in this matter and how do we know?

Although Dr. Miller mentions students in this letter and "their increasingly diverse backgrounds, traditions and orientations," he does not specifically mention race or students of color. Nonetheless, the Activists' voice of protest reverberates in his statements. He shows that he has been convinced that the faculty needs education about classroom dynamics.[17]

All of the faculty, staff, and administrators I interviewed were well aware of the Activists' actions on campus as well as related events, such as the cultural diversity forum. During my individual interview with Professor Wilson, a white faculty member in the social sciences, he commented on the forum.

*Prof Wilson:* I think that's a good example of what we do right

I think for a small number of students that was extraordinarily important

Faculty that feel particularly strong about that requirement of the college curriculum felt like

"Maybe these students have a point

Maybe the way that it got raised [the two students of color publicizing their complaint about Professor Thomas in the student newspaper]

Was you know slightly too personal or not professional

But now that the conversation is happening

What do we need to talk about?"

Have a forum

Talk about cultural diversity as a bigger thing

Not as a specific thing about one class

And what's the requirement supposed to do?

Then there'll be training that comes out of that for faculty

"If you're going to teach a course that offers this college curriculum designation

Here are the expectations."

In describing the cultural diversity forum as "a good example of what we do right," Professor Wilson uses the collective "we," by which he seems to mean the campus community or at least the faculty at large. At the same time, by talking about faculty who "feel particularly strong" about the cultural diversity requirement, he indicates that he is not among them. Indeed, he told me he is a mentor for *conservative* students on campus. He quotes faculty who feel the Asian American students' letter in the newspaper was "unprofessional," by which he may mean that they did not follow appropriate procedures for addressing a complaint about a professor. (Recall that the Activists' official document included a demand that such procedures be made clear to students.)

Nonetheless, even as Professor Wilson distances himself from these concerns, he presents himself as knowledgeable about them, and he suggests that the students' action opened up an important conversation: the CU community has taken the students' action and turned it into a productive dialogue about cultural diversity. In addition, his shift from the specific incident to a broader perspective is reminiscent of the Activists' shift from the problem with Professor Thomas to the bigger picture of race on campus. Thus even in the account of this faculty member who does not know the Activists personally and who is not directly involved with diversity initiatives, we hear reverberations of the Activists' voice of protest.

When I interviewed Professor Hall, a white faculty member in the sciences, I asked whether the recent discussions on campus about cultural diversity affect her and her science colleagues:

*Prof Hall:* Yes it affects us because there's a great interest on the part of the administration that the sciences offer cultural diversity courses

But cultural diversity as part of the sciences—
Those are really sociology issues
"Why aren't there more students of color majoring in the sciences?"
That's not a science question
That's a metascience question
When a sociologist or an anthropologist studies a culture they're doing their sociol-
  ogy their anthropology
When we're asking cultural questions we're not doing mathematics
We're not doing physics or chemistry
We can ask what mathematic systems were used in primitive cultures
But then we're looking at the *history* of mathematics as opposed to mathematics
And so there's been a lot of discussion on Wednesday afternoons—
The math department hosts a tea
And so faculty from other departments come by
Mostly from the sciences
And so last Wednesday we had a long discussion
On exactly where does cultural diversity fit into the sciences
And how do we bring it in?

Like Professor Wilson, Professor Hall does not know the Activists personally and she is not involved in any diversity initiatives. Here she focuses
on ramifications within the science and math departments of Dr. Miller's insistence that dialogue about cultural diversity include those faculty members
as well as those in the social sciences and humanities. Professor Hall distinguishes between scientific and cultural questions and thus resists the administrative push to have all departments consider how their curricula might
contribute to the cultural diversity requirement. And yet it is noteworthy that
conversations are even taking place within the math and science departments
about cultural diversity. This may be a ripple effect of the Activists' actions
on campus. At the very least it speaks to CU's narrative environment in
which "diversity is on the table."

The following exchange took place during my interview with four members (three white women; one Latino) of the Faculty Diversity Group (FDG),
which has been meeting monthly for many years to discuss diversity in higher
education. Unlike Professors Wilson and Hall, these faculty members know
many of the Activists. They told me that the twenty or so members of the
FDG disagreed about the Asian American students' publication of their complaint against Professor Thomas. Some felt it was a reasonable action to take;
others felt it was inappropriate because the students stepped outside of normal bureaucratic procedures. Nonetheless, the FDG as a whole applauded
the Activists' push for changes on campus. As Professor Young begins, she
is talking about attitudes among faculty in general:

*Prof Young:* And there's been a real mixed sense of like
"Go students!" versus

"Oh my gosh where did they get this?"
*Others:* [Agreement]
*Prof Young:* And I think it's pretty easy to see where they get it.
Like you [Professor Turner] said
It's out on the table
This is an environment that is going to push these harder issues
*Prof Kelly:* Yeah
*Prof Young:* And I think that's where we're getting Dr. Miller taking a kind of step
   that he hasn't taken before.

Professor Young points to the narrative environment on campus—one in which "diversity is out on the table"—as shaping the Activists' ideas and actions. Further, she suggests that the interplay between CU's narrative environment and the Activists' actions has influenced Dr. Miller to push the faculty to consider classroom climate in a way he hasn't before. More than other faculty I spoke with, Professor Young and her FDG colleagues saw the Activists as having had direct effects on Dr. Miller and the faculty generally.

*Prof Young:* So I see us as getting ready to move
But it's a difficult move to this next level of commitment
Where all faculty are really going to have substantial time spent on developing
   skills in this area in terms of classroom climate
We still have I'd say a fair amount of resistance from certain groups of faculty that
   [say]
"This infringes on my academic freedom"
*Prof Garcia:* Right
*Prof Young:* "Who are you to tell me that I don't know how to teach?"
And they feel improperly upbraided by the administration on these issues
So I think we're at a point where we're struggling to move to that next level
*Prof Turner:* I think you're right
And I think one of the issues in the move to the next level
Is trying to figure out what it's going to look like
I don't think we know what it's going to look like
And that's part of the fear whenever you're at that critical juncture . . .
We can't go backwards and what is the forward going to look like?
And I think probably every faculty member would say they are concerned about
   academic freedom
So what is academic freedom going to look like within this context?

These faculty members present this as a crucial moment on campus. Like Professor Wilson's use of "we," Professor Young uses "us" to refer to the faculty as a whole. While Professor Young speaks about faculty who are resistant to the administration's new push to develop skills needed to lead productive classroom discussions about diversity, Professor Turner raises an issue that all faculty are concerned with in one way or another: academic freedom.

But rather than posing the problem as one of opposition—academic freedom versus learning about classroom climate—she poses it in a way that encompasses both concerns: what is academic freedom going to look like in a narrative environment that treats classroom climate as important?

At one point, Professor Turner specifically emphasized that the Activists have played a central role in the new conversations taking place on campus:

*Prof Turner:* I think it's the forum and continued pressure from the Activists—
The work of the Activists I think has been—
I think if it had stopped with the forum nothing—
It would not have happened
I think the continued pressure of the Activists has been crucial.

By "continued pressure" Professor Turner means the Activists' presentation of their official protest document to the administration as well as their meetings with the administration.

### The Meetings between the Activists and the Administrators

Five representatives of the Activists and five members of the central administration met twice before the end of the semester during which the protest took place. (Later, I was told they also met during the break between semesters.) In the following, Mr. Davis, a senior administrator who attended these meetings, describes the first one.

*Susan:* Have those [meetings with the Activists] been productive?
*Mr. Davis:* I think they've been very productive
I think [the first meeting] humanized who the Activists were in the eyes of Dr. Miller
I think, again, it was a lot of listening
And as a result learning from students around these same things [classroom climate]
So to hear the experiences of students confirmed to him that there was work to do with the faculty
And that that was his job.

Like the professors above, Mr. Davis presents Dr. Miller as the key figure in what will happen next on campus in response to the matters the Activists raised. In addition, he presents the Activists as having shaped Dr. Miller's understanding of the importance of classroom climate. According to this account, Dr. Miller listened to the Activists in ways he hadn't listened to students of color before. In other words, this is a story about Dr. Miller hearing the voice of the other. Mr. Davis continues:

*Mr. Davis:* The second time we met was really focused
A lot of the focus was on student government—
The Activists' distrust and dislike of student government and of the newspaper
And those are really tough things
Because at CU those two entities are pretty independent
They do have advisers but it's minimal advising
And I think the question's kind of on the table—
Should that change?
Should the administration come in and say
"We need to find a way to have more—
I don't know—
Have direct engagement with the advising"?
Should it be much clearer?
Or much more?
And I don't mean anybody thinks they ought to control it or tell them
"You can't write this or you can't write this"
But I think [the student newspaper and student government] have run their own
    show for so long
That sometimes they make mistakes about perceptions
And there's a lot of feelings that probably could have been avoided
If somebody could have read the paper and said
"I'm not sure this is a good thing to write here"
But that's not been the culture of that newspaper.

Mr. Davis describes the second meeting between the administrators and the Activists as focusing on other specific complaints in the official document: the insensitivity of the student government and the student newspaper to racial issues. He indicates that this conversation with the Activists has influenced him (and his administrative colleagues) to reconsider the laissez-faire policy CU has had concerning advising these student organizations. By referring to the "culture" of the student newspaper, he indicates that change will not come easy. Like Professor Turner, who asked what academic freedom will look like in a narrative environment where classroom climate is taken seriously, Mr. Davis asks what stronger advising of the newspaper and the student government will look like in a narrative environment where race is taken seriously. This gets to the problem of white students' need for racial education and the university's responsibility for providing it. In addition, Mr. Davis is talking about the role of dialogue between advisers and students, and about the quality of relationships between students of color on the one hand and students who publish the newspaper and lead student government on the other hand.

Finally, here is Dr. Miller's story about a particular interaction during one of the meetings with the Activists:

*Dr. Miller:* We were talking about some of the current issues and challenges and
   problems
And [one of the Activists] said
"We know that the reason we have these issues is because of our success
If nobody was trying to do anything about diversity
If nobody was interested
We wouldn't be having these discussions
We wouldn't be saying
'Yeah but this isn't working yet'"
And it helped actually
It helped me to be reminded of that
Although good grief I'm old enough to be that student's grandfather
It was a nice reminder from somebody who was herself at the time
Rather frustrated by some things
And yet she was able to see that.

This story captures a theme that was expressed in several of the excerpts
above: the Activists have given Dr. Miller an education about race on campus. By remarking that he is old enough to be the student's grandfather, Dr.
Miller indicates that he normally thinks of himself as helping students along
in *their* education. But in this case, he suggests, the student's comments expressed wisdom that helped *him*. Even though the student was frustrated (by
the conversation during the meeting? by events in general?), she formulated
the current state of affairs for him: the conversations between the administrators and the Activists about current challenges on campus reflect "our success." My guess is that "our success" means the interconnected group's
success in supporting students of color so that they feel entitled to speak and
be heard. In any case, by repeating this student's words—and especially by
using direct speech to do so—Dr. Miller communicates that he has heard
her voice, that he has learned something from her framing of the current
state of affairs. She has taught him both how far CU has come and how far
CU has yet to go in terms of addressing racial issues on campus.

   In sum, these professors' and administrators' accounts suggest that the Activists' collective voice of protest was effective in a number of ways. Dr.
Miller learned from listening to the Activists—both at the cultural diversity
forum and in the meetings with the Activists—how important classroom climate is, among other things. Being educated in this way spurred him to take
responsibility for leading the faculty in *their* education about classroom climate. The FDG, for whom diversity topics are central to their professional
lives, constructed the Activists' voice of protest as pushing forward a new
agenda that addresses the relationship between cultural diversity, classroom
climate, and academic freedom. Even faculty such as Professors Wilson and
Hall, for whom diversity is not central to their professional lives, express ripple effects and reverberations of the Activists' protest.

## The Activists' Protest and CU's Narrative Landscape

The Activists themselves orchestrated their protest. Together they brainstormed how to bring long-neglected racial issues to the campus's attention. No one told them what to do. *They* came up with the idea of the silent rally, and *they* wrote the official document. Mr. Robert told me that some people on campus held him and other members of the interconnected group responsible for the Activists' actions. This accusation upset him because it was untrue. The students acted on their own.

The Activists alone were responsible for their actions, but their protest did not come out of nowhere. A focus on the reflexive interplay between the Activists' protest and CU's narrative landscape offers a particular lens on what happened at CU that semester. As Professor Young said, "It's pretty easy to see where students get it. . . . [Diversity] is out on the table [at CU]. This is an environment that is going to push these issues harder." The interconnected group that advocates for social justice on campus has created a narrative niche in which students have learned to question taken-for-granted cultural assumptions, especially cultural assumptions (like color blindness) embedded in the discourse of abstract inclusion. Students have also learned to question taken-for-granted institutionalized practices. The Activists questioned a student newspaper editorial decision that the student journalists viewed as giving Professor Thomas a chance to defend himself in public (see chapter 7). The Activists viewed that editorial decision as privileging a white professor's voice by giving him three times as many words as were given to the students of color complaining about him. They questioned a cultural diversity policy that the university touts as central to its educational mission and yet allows students to fulfill that requirement by taking courses in European history, languages, and cultures. They questioned the administration's greater responsiveness to issues of sexual orientation than to issues of race. They questioned a host of other taken-for-granted practices that come to light as problematic through a social justice lens. Among other things, that lens turns attention to the ways that race shapes social identities, locations, interaction, and institutions.

In addition, the Activists have learned to understand *themselves* as entitled to speak and get heard, an idea that is only radical because, historically, universities have not treated students of color as entitled in that way.

It would be a mistake, though, to see the Activists' protest as *determined* by CU's narrative environment or by the interconnected group's distinct narrative community. In any particular context and at any particular moment, human interaction and narrative realities are much more complex than that. They are malleable and unpredictable. If any part of this situation had unfolded differently, the entire story might have been different. If, for example, the newspaper editors had required Professor Thomas to adhere to the word limit, students of color might not have experienced his rebuttal as the last straw and the Activists might not have formed in the particular way it did—or at all.

In their protest, the Activists communicated their discontent with the university's failure to address racial issues. Even though their protest was not determined by the narrative environment, the character of the narrative environment made it possible for others to hear their protest in particular ways. An environment in which "diversity is out on the table" and in which the interconnected group keeps social justice discourse on the table made the Activists' protest intelligible to many on campus. Equally important, the Activists' protest disrupted the narrative environment in ways that had consequences for others on campus. At least some faculty and administrators began to listen and speak in ways they hadn't before. And as we shall see in chapters 7 and 8, the Activists' protest had consequences for various groups of white students who interpreted it in different ways. Thus CU's narrative environment not only shapes what it is possible to say or to hear—it is also an ongoing accomplishment that is constantly reconfigured as people on campus address the issues that concern them.

# 7 Walking on Eggshells (And Other Responses)

White students' accounts about the Activists' protest ranged from dismissive to hostile to engaged. In this chapter I explore an example of each, drawing from three group interviews with CU students. The first group —students who live together in a residence hall—included some who were only vaguely aware of the Activists' actions and who dismissed the protest as something they didn't need to attend to. The second group—members of a student organization called the Conservative Students—was quite knowledgeable about the Activists' actions but expressed hostility toward them. The third group—student journalists—recounted their direct engagement with the Activists (who had critiqued the newspaper's treatment of race) and expressed ambivalence about what the Activists were telling them. They felt they had to walk on eggshells. The Activists' voice of protest held meanings and consequences for each of these groups of white students—though in very different ways.

## Dismissal

Alan, a white student who is a resident adviser in one of the residence halls, pulled together a group of students on his floor to meet with me in the lounge at the end of the hall. All except Alan were first-year students. Five were white and one was an international student of color. As usual, I opened the interview with a general question: "What kinds of issues have come up for you guys in the residence hall this year?" They offered a list: trash in the hallways, drinking-related problems (such as vomit not cleaned up), students' disrespect for others' property, and resident advisers' inconsistency in enforcing the rules.

When I asked what diversity issues have been most prominent on campus this year, they talked about the antigay incidents and the administration's public condemnation of the perpetrators' actions. This was the only group of students I talked with (out of twelve groups) that viewed these incidents as more prominent than racial issues on campus (see chapter 3). As the discussion about the antigay incidents drew to a close, Raul, the international student, said:

*Raul:* There was the protest right?
About the diversity or something—
*Alan:* The Activists, their protest?
*Raul:* I don't know
They were all in black you know
I don't remember exactly
But you know what I'm talking about?
*Others:* No.

Raul, who had been on campus less than a semester at this point, brings up the silent rally without knowing specifically what it was. He struggles to describe it, but apart from Alan, the others in the group do not know what he is talking about. After this exchange, Alan, who knew several of the Activists, launched into an explanation of the silent rally. When he mentioned the two Asian American students' criticism of Professor Thomas's course, some of the students remembered hearing about that controversy. But at best their knowledge about the entire situation was vague. I prompted Raul for more:

*Susan:* And you had mentioned a protest?
*Raul:* Yeah cause one day I saw people wearing black clothes outside [the main administrative building]
*Susan:* That was the silent rally?
*Alan:* Yes
*Susan:* And did the rest of you hear about that?
*Ashley:* I saw the silent protest
But I had no idea what it was about
I walked through it on the way to class
*Susan:* And what did you think?
*Ashley:* I wonder what they're protesting
*All:* [Loud laughter].

Like the exchange above, this one shows that Raul observed the silent rally and that Alan knows about it. Ashley, by contrast, describes herself as mildly curious about but ultimately indifferent to the protest—it was an event she happened to encounter on her way to class. She implies that the protest wasn't an unusual sight on campus *and* that it wasn't something she needed to know about. Although Raul and Alan position themselves differently in relation to the silent rally than Ashley does, the group's loud collective laughter at the end of this exchange captures and supports the tenor of Ashley's account: on the one hand, "Some people do a lot of protesting on campus"; on the other hand, "I don't have to care about this because it doesn't affect me."

This stance is reminiscent of but not quite the same as Kane's in chapter 2. Kane complained that CU's constant stream of diversity-related events and programs produces an environment oversaturated with "diversity," and he indicated that many students are annoyed by others' imposition of their diversity agendas. Ashley, by contrast, is not perturbed. For her (and some others on Alan's hall), the Activists' silent rally registered *as* "protest," but not as a voice she needed to listen to. She recognizes the silent rally as a typical event in a narrative environment where "diversity is out there on the table," and where "somebody is always protesting something." At the same time, she dismisses the possibility that the Activists' protest is speaking to *her.*

## Hostility

Compared to Ashley and her hall mates, the four white students I interviewed as members of the Conservative Students were more knowledgeable about and more exercised by the Activists' protest. In chapter 2 we heard the Conservative Students construct diversity discourse on campus as a matter of political difference—conservative versus liberal. And we heard their view that conservative students are the ones who are most silenced on campus, particularly in the classroom. They drew on discursive resources provided by the national conservative movement in higher education, especially David Horowitz's ideas, to critique CU's social justice discourse. At the same time, they appropriated local social justice terms—such as "advocacy group"—to make their argument intelligible in CU's narrative environment.

### *Black Students Feel Comfortable Voicing Their Opinion*

About halfway through my interview with the Conservative Students, I turned the discussion specifically to diversity at CU.

*Susan:* I'd like to hear you guys talk about your perspectives on diversity issues here . . .
*Jeremy:* I think that in some people's minds it's making a very big step
And I think for some people it really is
For the black students on campus

They really feel comfortable in saying what they want to say
And making a voice
Making an opinion
I think for a lot of students it probably is making a move
They are making headway
But the perspective that I have is that it reaches a point where it's not what I'm
   here for.

I ask for *their* perspectives, but Jeremy begins by focusing on *others'* perspectives before turning to his own. This movement in Jeremy's talk reflects a pattern in the Conservative Students' accounts about diversity on campus.

Jeremy begins by constructing the viewpoint of black students whom he sees as comfortable speaking on campus. He seems to use "it"—"it's making a very big step," "it probably is making a move," "it's not what I'm here for"—to reference the general focus on diversity in CU's narrative environment. Or he may be referencing social justice discourse specifically. In any case, he implies that because "diversity is out there on the table" at CU, some groups of students—such as black students—are comfortable expressing themselves on campus. When he states, "they are making headway," he implies that black students' comfort in speaking out is a step forward compared to the relative quietness of black students on other campuses (or perhaps of other students of color at CU).

One interpretation of Jeremy's account is that he is attempting to take the point of view of the other, a narrative move that I argued in chapter 5 characterizes at least some CU students' narratives of self-development. At best, though, Jeremy's account misrepresents black students' point of view. Jeremy seems to interpret the Black Collegians' (and perhaps the Activists') confidence in their entitlement to speak and get heard as their feeling "comfortable saying what they have to say." But the Black Collegians (and the Activists) would point out that Jeremy's interpretation does not acknowledge the urgency with which they speak. They would also point out that he does not seem to know that *not* being heard time and again constitutes an important part of their protest. As we saw in chapter 6, the Black Collegians (and the Activists) present themselves as having a strong community of color but as *not* heard on the campus at large.

Jeremy's presentation (and misrepresentation) of the Black Collegian's perspective suggests that he is "setting up the talk" so that what he seems to be doing "is giving a fair account of the other party's position, as a *concession* to them," before moving on to make his own point.[1] As we shall see, Jeremy's last statement, "but it's not what I'm here for," foreshadows the Conservative Students' complaint that social justice discourse infiltrates the narrative landscape at CU to the detriment of white students.

### Black Students Want to Force Us
### to Learn about Racism

Later I asked:

*Susan:* Which diversity issues have produced the most contention this year on campus?
*Evan:* The black student issue by far
*Susan:* Which one was that?
*Evan:* Was it about two months ago now?
There was a—
Is it an overall culture class or something like that?
*Olivia:* They wanted CU to change their cultural diversity requirement
And right now you can kind of get away from it by taking these world classes
And you don't have to take any African American history and racism and that kind of thing
And they think that CU students should be able to—
*Jeremy:* Not *able* to *forced* to—
*Olivia:* *Forced* to [take such a course].

In the previous exchange, when Jeremy speaks about "black students," it *appears* that he means African American students only (although it is possible that he is speaking about the Activists). In this exchange, however, when Evan mentions "the black student issue," it is clear that he *is* talking about the Activists' protest. Nonetheless, the exchange shows that *I* do not know which issue he is talking about, as evidenced by my question—"which [issue] was that?" I am thrown off by his description of the Activists' protest as "the black student issue" because I know that the Activists are a multiracial group. It only becomes clear to me that he is talking about the Activists when he and Olivia describe the Activists' complaint that students can fulfill the cultural diversity requirement without taking any courses on "African American history and racism and that kind of thing."

Thus this exchange shows that Evan treats black students and the Activists as one and the same. He persists in this conflation as he goes on to describe (in talk not included here) the two students' criticism of Professor Thomas. Those two students are Asian American, but Evan calls them "black." Furthermore, the Activists are a multiracial group, but he portrays the silent rally as "a protest by the thirty-five to forty-five black students that we have on campus."

I dwell on this conflation of black students and the Activists because Evan was not the only CU student who made this mistake. Rachelle told me that before the silent rally she anticipated that some people on campus would see the silent rally as the Black Collegian's action rather the action of a multiracial group of students. She was right. In a letter to the student newspaper, a student government representative chided his peers who walked out of the student government meeting when the Activists left to hold the silent rally. He called the silent rally "the Black Collegian's demonstration."

How should we interpret this conflation? One possibility is that Evan and other students simply do not know that the Activists are a multiracial group. While that could be true for Evan, it cannot be true for the student government representative who was present at the student government meeting that the Activists attended and then left. He must have *seen* that the group was multiracial.

Another interpretation is that in American culture African Americans are more susceptible to the "controlling image" of being inherently and unreasonably angry than Asian Americans, and so Evan and the student government representative perceive the Activists through the filter of that image.[2] When I asked Mr. Robert, OMA's director, about this conflation, his comments expanded on this interpretation: "I think that in this country, when white people fear something that has to do with people of color, they immediately attach blackness to it. That's the only way I can explain that. 'Black is what I fear. So what I am experiencing that is making me uncomfortable therefore becomes black.' It's sort of the demonization of black people and black bodies and black ideas that gets extended to others. . . . Black people are demonized and that gets extended to others who make us uncomfortable."[3]

Back to the excerpt above: Evan is in the ballpark when he describes the Activists' protest as including a critique of the cultural diversity requirement, but Olivia's take is more accurate: a student can fulfill that requirement without taking even one course dealing with U.S. racial history and racism. Jeremy interrupts Olivia to emphasize that the Activists want all students to be *"forced"* to take such a course.

College students at any institution must fulfill a range of requirements in order to earn their degrees. By using the word *forced,* Jeremy and Olivia present the idea of a required course on race and racism in the U.S. as unreasonable, as unlike other requirements they have to fulfill. Like David Horowitz, these students focus on the curriculum as the site of conservative students' oppression. Their account also reveals the image of "two worlds" that we encountered in chapter 6. Drawing on social justice discourse, the Activists interpret revisions that would strengthen CU's cultural diversity requirement (for example, requiring one course on U.S. race relations) as a racial education that would benefit white students, as a racial education that white students *need* in order to live and work in a multiracial world. Drawing on political difference discourse, the Conservative Students interpret such a requirement as unfair constraint, as liberals oppressing conservatives like themselves. They view such a requirement as having no benefits for them, but as a social justice agenda that liberals want to impose on them.

### Black Students Get More than Their Share
### of the Student Government Budget

At another point in our discussion, I asked the Conservative Students whether they feel there are "any diversity-related programs that are useful or successful" on campus.

*Dan:* One of the successful things on campus is the Southeast Asian Association
The Black Collegians is hugely popular
The GLBT group is actually very popular even with a lot of straight students
They put on a lot of all campus events that are in my understanding pretty popular.

Like Jeremy in the first excerpt above, Dan does not begin with *his* perspective. Rather he begins with these three student organizations' popularity with students *in general*. By presenting a general perspective, he implies that he is giving a neutral report about campus life. By contrast, of course, students of color view attendance at their all-campus events as disappointing.

As he continues, Dan shifts to what is clearly his perspective:

*Dan:* And having sat on the [student government] committee that decides budgets
  for these groups
I can tell you that they get a *monstrous* amount of money
On the one hand they're upset
They're fuming mad because they are represented only by—
What is it—
By [x] % minorities on this campus?
*Olivia:* Yeah
*Dan:* It is a pretty white campus
We know that
So on the one hand they're fuming mad because there's not enough of them here
*Jeremy:* [chuckle]
*Dan:* On the other hand the Black Collegians *alone* gets more *money* than *twenty*
  organizations *combined*.

When Dan acknowledges that "it is a pretty white campus," he seems to concede that students of color have reason to be angry about that. But he expresses outrage about the disproportionate share of the student government budget that goes to advocacy groups, particularly to student of color organizations, and very specifically to the Black Collegians.

To emphasize the unfairness of the situation and the seriousness of his claim, Dan exaggerates and uses what Charles Antaki calls "extreme description."[4] The other Conservative Students and I know that the Black Collegians' budget is not more than that of twenty other organizations combined. I don't know, however, whether the Black Collegians' budget that year was larger than that of other student organizations.[5] But more important to my analysis than "the facts" is the striking contrast between Dan's complaint that the Black Collegians (and other advocacy groups) get more than their share of the budget and the Activists' complaint that all of the student of color organizations (and other advocacy groups) have to fight for their budgets. In the section on the student government in their official protest document, the Activists wrote: "Receiving adequate funding is always a challenge as students of color and other diversity organizations routinely have a difficult time winning support for their bills, resolutions and funding requests."

At the very least, the contrast between the Activists' and Dan's perspectives is evidence of tension between students of color and some members of the student government, a tension that gets played out in student government deliberations as well as in the accounts students offered to me. As we saw in chapter 3, quantitative and qualitative content analyses of the student government minutes show that race is the most prominent and contentious diversity category in that context.

On one hand, then, Dan expresses outrage about what he sees as a violation of the principle of fairness—shouldn't every student organization get a fair (equal) share of the funds? On the other hand, the Black Collegians (in chapter 6) express outrage about the lack of respect for the needs of their strong community of color. They present the budget battle as one in which the student of color retreat (a line item in every student of color organization budget) is in jeopardy. From their point of view, the student of color retreat is not optional and it is not a recreational activity; rather, it is fundamental to their well-being on campus as students of color. Their account raises the question of whether a numerically equal share of the budget is "fair." Do all student organizations have the same needs? Do they all use their budgets in the same way?

Again, in this clash of perspectives, we get a strong sense of "two worlds." We also hear conflict between the discourse of abstract inclusion (everyone deserves an equal share) and the discourse of social justice (justice requires attention to differing needs). It is noteworthy that while the Conservative Students develop a discourse of political difference in much of their account, Dan uses the discourse of abstract inclusion to express his views here.

### White Students Pay for Black Students' Programming

As Dan continues directly from the above, he is talking about the Black Collegians:

*Dan:* Now granted they are successful in the events they do
They are celebrating their thirty-fifth anniversary year

They're doing a lot for this campus
Well not necessarily for this campus
They do a lot *on* this campus *for their group* [words spoken distinctly for emphasis]
*Evan:* Yeah it's kind of weird how like the—
*The smallest* minority group on campus
Gets one of *the largest budgets*
Out of *our student fees* [words spoken slowly and distinctly for emphasis]
*Dan:* It's aston—
*Olivia:* [loud] That are paid mostly by white students!
*Dan:* [loud] It's it's *astonishing*!

Here again, Dan begins by presenting his sense of the general perspective on campus—that the Black Collegians are successful. As evidence of that general perspective he points to the Black Collegians' recent celebration of their thirty-fifth anniversary. (In chapter 6, the Black Collegians also mentioned that anniversary event as evidence of their clout on campus.) But as soon as Dan acknowledges the Black Collegians' contribution to campus life, he corrects himself and renders *his* perspective: the Black Collegians' programming serves not the campus at large, but themselves. Evan chimes in to point out once again the contradiction between their small numbers and their disproportionate share of the student government budget.

Olivia's interruption, her incredulous statement—"[Fees] that are paid mostly by white students!"—and Dan's affirmation of her statement need careful attention because they capture the racial logic embedded in this exchange. That logic goes like this: All students pay fees that support student groups. The Black Collegians get more than their share of those fees. Most of the students paying fees are white students. Thus white students are paying for the Black Collegians' programming. That programming is basically self-serving. So, white students are paying the Black Collegians to take care of themselves. Olivia's and Dan's tone of voice communicates their feeling that this state of affairs is outrageous.

This racial logic resonates with a cultural discourse that is deeply embedded in American society: white people belong in the center because that's the way it's always been and they deserve to be there. Some racial theorists would call this a thinly veiled version of white supremacy.[6] In any case, this discourse makes it possible for Dan, one of the students in charge of the student government budget, to view himself as wanting to "give" students of color their "fair share" of the budget that belongs, for the most part, to white students in general. With that "fair share," he implies, students of color can do what they want—their own self-serving programming. This discourse treats white people as beneficent and thus as justly indignant when people of color fail to be grateful for what they've been "given" or when people of color demand more than their "fair share." People of color are portrayed as freeloaders, as usurping resources that belong to white people and as failing to be grateful and deferent when white people share "their" resources with black people.[7]

### They Don't Know How Damn Lucky They Have It Here

This racial logic gets further expression in Dan's statements below, which he offered toward the end of my two-hour interview with the Conservative Students:

*Dan:* What causes the most contention [on campus]
There's nothing even close
It is race
And until I'm willing to accept the fact that I have everything handed to me
[That] my life is going to be full of six figure salaries and boats and yachts
Because I am a white male
*Evan:* Conservative [softly]
*Dan:* Then I need to feel guilty
Then I need to bend over backwards to make life easier for a lot of people
When in *fact* all I'm here to do is the same thing that everybody else is doing
Go to class
Do an internship
Do homework
Get a degree and get a job
And I think that's *that's* really what gets lost in all the ranting we do in our diversity policy
Every week there's another workshop
There's another rally
There's another cause of the week
And *all we are is students*
*Evan:* Yeah
*Dan:* Whether I'm white
Whether I'm adopted by a Korean family . . .
Whatever it is
That really gets lost in the fray . . .
The other schools around here don't have [names of majors]
They don't have [names of departments][sneering tone]
They don't have [names of courses]
And I think a lot of these groups need to take stock of what we *do* have
And what a *lot* of other schools don't [have]
Cause they don't know how *damn* lucky they have it here.

Throughout this speech the hostility in Dan's voice escalates. By the time he mentions specific majors, departments, and courses, he is sneering. The intensity of his emotion—and of all four Conservative Students' emotions in other parts of their account—communicates that something important is at stake.

The Conservative Students were the only group I spoke with at CU who expressed this level of hostility toward the advocacy groups on campus, toward the Activists' protest, and more generally, toward social justice discourse. Other students, like Kane in chapter 2, were annoyed by what they experienced as the narrative environment's oversaturation with diversity discourse, but that annoyance did not reach the level of the Conservative Students' antagonism. These students' emotional intensity built during the two hours I spent with them and culminated in Dan's statements above. What is this hostility communicating?

After pointing to race as the most contentious diversity topic on campus, Dan critiques social justice discourse which he interprets as requiring him to feel guilty about his privileged status as a white man. (Evan slips in that being conservative is also relevant.) Dan expresses his frustration through exaggeration and sarcasm (for example, "my life is going to be full of six figure salaries and yachts because I am a white male"). In his view, social justice discourse turns race relations upside down. Within that discourse, he argues, he becomes a guilty, spoiled white man who must bend over backwards to support *other* students who, it turns out, are actually the ones who are spoiled. This echoes the Conservative Students' construction (in chapter 2) of conservative students as the ones who *really* are disadvantaged on campus (as opposed to students in the advocacy groups).

As he counters social justice discourse, Dan proposes the discourse of abstract inclusion: we are all students and we all want the same thing: internships, degrees, and jobs. At the same time, he draws on discourse that presents the goal of higher education as preparing students for good jobs, as opposed to opening their minds, as liberal arts discourse presumes. And yet what comes next indicates that something else is operating in this account.

Dan compares CU to "other schools around here," which he claims don't have diversity-related courses, majors, and departments. Throughout their talk with me, Dan and the other Conservative Students used a nearby university as their major reference point. They told me that that university has a much more conservative culture than CU. A CU administrator who used to work at that university also told me that its culture is much more conservative. The Conservative Students also said that they have forged ties there and frequently go there for conservative events and to hear conservative speakers (such as Ann Coulter whom Olivia mentioned in chapter 2). Even though Dan doesn't explicitly evoke the discourse of political difference here, he evokes it implicitly through his critique of the (liberal) curriculum at CU and his comparison of CU to other universities. Recall that David Horowitz's major focus is the curriculum.

Dan goes on to argue that "a lot of these groups"—by which he means the advocacy groups at CU—"don't know how *damn* lucky they have it here." He seems to mean that the advocacy groups at CU have much more support from various university structures (certain offices and programs; the curriculum) than their counterparts on nearby campuses. So what, he asks implicitly, are the advocacy groups complaining about?

As I thought about how to interpret Dan's hostility, I considered that it might be related to the prominence of race in contrast to the obscurity of class in CU's narrative environment, and especially to the relative lack of attention to the disadvantages working-class students experience on campus. When he speaks sarcastically about six-figure salaries and yachts that will be thrown his way because of his race and gender, Dan's talk is clearly class-inflected. But he is not a working-class student. Evan and Jeremy grew up in working-class families, but Dan's and Olivia's class backgrounds are middle class to upper-middle class (see appendix C). In terms of class, Evan and Jeremy have more in common with the Black Collegians and the Southeast Asian American students I interviewed than with Dan and Olivia. Although class may shape in some way what is going on here, I don't think it produced the Conservative Students' hostility.

Furthermore, as discussed in chapter 2, the Conservative Students have successfully pursued professional connections off-campus: some have traveled to Washington, D.C., to attend the Conservative Political Action Conference with funding from CU's student government, and as a group they accepted an invitation to meet David Horowitz at the state capital. When I interviewed Evan individually, he told me about an impressive political internship he had landed in Washington, D.C. And Jeremy told me about his successful bid to secure funds from CU's student government for a recording studio on campus and his plans to start his own recording company using the new studio's equipment. (I did not interview Olivia and Dan individually.) Thus it would be inaccurate to view these students as lacking opportunities to pursue their professional goals, which is what Dan (and Evan and Jeremy) specifically say they want to focus on while they are at college.

A more plausible interpretation of Dan's and the Conservative Students' hostility has to do with the cultural discourse of white centrality that is embedded in their talk. The Conservative Students' hostility to the Activists' protest, to the advocacy groups on campus, and more generally to social justice discourse, is grounded in their sense that their taken-for-granted position as privileged white students is being undermined in CU's narrative environment. The Conservative Students' assumption that white people are the norm or center around which other racial groups revolve on campus is challenged by CU's diversity policy, diversity workshops, by at least some parts of the curriculum, and by protests like the Activists'. In other words, the Conservative Students' strong emotions—their outrage and frustration with race relations on campus, and their hostility to the Activists—become intelligible within cultural discourse that takes white centrality for granted.

The Conservative Students' hostility to the Activists and the advocacy groups generally is far from unique. It echoes one response in the broader culture to arguments for social change and social justice in many institutional contexts. At the same time, though, these students' hostility is shaped in part by CU's narrative environment. At the more conservative university nearby, conservative students are probably not provoked to express such hostility toward students of color on campus.

## Walking on Eggshells

Unlike the two groups discussed so far, student journalists engaged in direct conversation with the Activists about their protest. The idea for this conversation came out of the second meeting between the Activists and the administration. Before I explore the journalists' account of that conversation, I offer some background about the student newspaper's relation to diversity at CU during the year the protest took place.[8]

### The Student Newspaper and Diversity

*The Race Column.* From their point of view, the newspaper staff was already taking major strides in taking race seriously. The paper's white faculty adviser, Professor Collins, was a member of CU's NCORE group that year. That group consisted of sixteen CU faculty, students, and staff who had attended NCORE in May and who were charged with finding ways to educate the campus about racial issues during the next academic year. The NCORE group proposed to the newspaper editors that a regular column on race be published in the paper, to be written by members of the NCORE group. The editors accepted that proposal. This was an unprecedented step in the history of the newspaper: no other group on campus had ever been given a regular column. Mr. Robert, OMA's director, pointed to that column as evidence that "there is less resistance [now] to talking about [diversity] issues" on campus. He told me that the articles in the Race Column would not have been published in the student newspaper a few years earlier. And he described the current editor-in-chief, as "very good, very supportive. . . . he believes that having diversity integrated into the newspaper is the right way to go."

*The first diversity workshop.* The student newspaper staff had also been engaged—at their own initiative—in diversity workshops, which were facilitated by Professor Garcia, the coordinator of the Faculty Diversity Group. When I interviewed Professor Collins, he told me that the first workshop included "some breakthrough kind of stuff that really opened my eyes to some things that were going on with the newspaper." I prompted him for details.

*Prof Collins:* I can tell you one specific thing because it was so important to me [A student journalist] had made the comment

"I don't know what people are complaining about
Because it's not like we have a sign on the door saying 'whites only' or 'middle
    class only'
Anybody can come in here"
And we were knocking ourselves out
Putting signs all over campus
Having recruitment meetings
Buying pizza
Putting emails out saying
"Come join the newspaper staff"
"We need writers"
"We need you"
And Jessie [one of the journalists] who hadn't said very much the whole time
Just in kind of a quiet voice said
"I had a really hard time coming to the newspaper"—
She's a white woman—
"I had a really tough time"
And everybody sort of got quiet
And she said
"You guys are sitting there
And you're all there in a circle
And you're laughing
And you're talking this newspaper language
And you obviously all know each other really well . . .
But I was determined I was going to be part of this paper
So I didn't let that bother me
But it was really really hard to break into that circle
And I didn't feel welcome at all"
She actually said
"I'm ok now
But imagine if it was a student of color
Or somebody who didn't feel like there was anybody in the room there who they
    could identify with
[Imagine] how much harder it would be for them"
And everybody [the rest of the newspaper staff at the diversity workshop] was just
    like—
Silent.

By stating that Jessie's story "was so important to me," Professor Collins
makes her story part of his own. He presents her story as one in which she
resists the other journalists' defensiveness about their attempts to recruit students to work on the paper. The point of her story—as Professor Collins
tells it—is that the newspaper staff is a close-knit group that is difficult to
break into. (CU is certainly not alone in having a predominantly white student newspaper staff.[9]) Jessie puts herself in the shoes of students of color,

and she speculates that they would feel even more like outsiders than she did if they were attempting to join the newspaper staff. Like the students' narratives in chapter 5, Jessie's story is about learning to listen to the other's voice.

As he retells Jessie's story, Professor Collins uses direct speech for her words and he includes the audience's response: he notes that the other students became quiet as she began to speak and were silent at the end of her story. By using these linguistic devices, Professor Collins highlights the impact of Jessie's story on others, including himself, during the diversity workshop.

As he continued his account, Professor Collins noted that he is always trying to recruit new students because the newspaper staff constantly turns over as students graduate or leave for study abroad. He said he had been aware of the situation Jessie described—of potential recruits hovering around the door of the hot, crowded newspaper office. Then he explained why Jessie's story was important to him:

*Prof Collins:* I'm always trying to get them [potential recruits] to come into the room . . .
But I guess [hearing Jessie's story] was the first time I connected the dots
And saw that as a diversity issue
And that sounds dumb that I didn't get that before
But I didn't
That is a very very salient diversity issue right there
It doesn't matter how much recruiting material we put out in the campus
If people don't feel like they can really be welcome
Why should they take a risk to join this sort of elite group?
*Susan:* So did that event [Jessie's story] kind of turn things around for the whole group?
*Prof Collins:* I think that was kind of an epiphany
And I think that at that point the workshop started seeming less like a class
And started being more about what we can do to change the paper.

Professor Collins presents Jessie's story as an epiphany for him and the student journalists. His view of a commonplace event—trying to get potential recruits to enter the room where the newspaper staff works together—was transformed. Through Jessie's story, that event became a diversity-related event for him for the first time. Embedded in this transformation is a shift from the discourse of abstract inclusion (everyone is welcome) to the discourse of social justice (students of color may need more encouragement than white students to feel welcome in an overwhelmingly white group). Professor Collins's metastatement—"and that sounds dumb that I didn't get that before"—points to the disjunction between those discourses.

*The silent rally.* Shortly after the first diversity workshop, Professor Collins and the editor-in-chief attended a journalism conference to present a paper on their diversity initiatives—their work with the NCORE group on the Race Column and their self-initiated diversity workshops. While they were gone, Professor Thomas's rebuttal to the two students' criticism came out in the newspaper, and in Professor Collins's words, "all hell broke loose." Ironically, as Professor Collins and the editor-in-chief were presenting their ideas to other student journalists about how college newspapers can address diversity on campus, the Activists were charging CU's student newspaper with insensitivity to students of color's perspectives. While the journalists viewed themselves as taking race seriously, the Activists did not.

At the silent rally, which took place ten days after Professor Thomas's rebuttal was published, the Activists refused to talk to student journalists who were attempting to cover the event. The Activists later explained to the journalists that because the newspaper was part of the problem they couldn't trust them to cover their event fairly and accurately. Of course, the whole point of the silent rally was to draw attention to the history of their voices not being heard by the newspaper, the student government, the administration, the faculty, and on campus more generally.

*The second diversity workshop.* By happenstance, the newspaper's second diversity workshop—another three-hour session—took place *after* the silent rally. Professor Collins told me that Professor Garcia, the workshop facilitator, let the journalists vent without judging them. They felt they had been trying hard to attend to racial issues and that the Activists' criticisms were unfair. After letting them vent, Professor Garcia encouraged the students to take the point of view of the other, to try to understand how the Activists could experience the newspaper as insensitive to their perspectives. As Professor Collins described what happened at this diversity workshop, he began with the journalists' perspective:

*Prof Collins:* "They're not assuming that we're acting in good faith"
"They're not assuming we're good people"
"They're just looking at what they see in the paper"
"They're not giving us the benefit of the doubt"
But why should they give us the benefit of the doubt?
They've been burned enough
Why should they assume that we all know what's good and fair?
How we're not racist and all that?
They see a juxtaposition of two articles [Prof Thomas's rebuttal and Carrie Jones's charge that Rachelle's MLK speech constituted reverse racism (see chapter 4)]
Which seem to be without any balance to them
I could argue from a journalist's position
"Oh well balance isn't about what appears on one page of the paper on one day
It's what happens over a length of time"
I could talk about the differences between what's on the opinion page
And what's on the news page

And how we're not saying we endorse anything
I could talk about that
But the fact is people don't necessarily think in that way when they're looking at
    something
They see something that is hurtful to them
And we gave them plenty of reason to think that there's at least a possibility that
    this was sort of like in your face
There were quite a few students who moved quite a ways [during this workshop]
And I did too.

Professor Collins presents three different voices here. First, the journalists' voice. They feel the Activists are misjudging them and are not giving them "the benefit of the doubt." In American culture, the latter is often treated as a ground rule for productive discussion. To fail to give an interlocutor the benefit of the doubt is to derail the possibility of dialogue, of listening across divergent perspectives. Professor Collins uses direct speech for this voice, highlighting its poignancy for him—these are students he works with on a daily basis and whose intentions he knows are good.[10]

Second, he presents the Activists' voice as reasonably challenging the journalists' desire to be given the benefit of the doubt. Given the history of race relations on campus, and particularly with the student newspaper, the Activists have good reason to doubt that the journalists understand their point of view.

Third, Professor Collins presents the voice of professional journalism. The concept of balance, the difference between news and opinion, and the principle of editorial neutrality with respect to the opinion page guide newspaper work. And nonjournalists don't necessarily understand that.

In this account, Professor Collins juxtaposes these three voices, giving each its due. And yet he ends up emphasizing the movement within the second diversity workshop toward an understanding of the Activists' voice. He suggests that both he and the student journalists began to see how students of color could be angry when they saw Professor Thomas's and Carrie Jones's statements on the opinion page and no representation of their point of view.

### Our Meeting with the Activists Was Productive . . .
### But We Got Blasted

As usual, I began my group interview with the journalists—six white students—by asking, "What have been the major issues for you guys this year?" Nick said they have been "confronting diversity issues on campus," and within moments they were talking about the controversy over the length of Professor Thomas's rebuttal and about their attempts to report on the silent rally even though the Activists refused to speak to them. Before long, Nick launched into a description of the meeting the journalists had with the Activists. That meeting took place several weeks after the silent rally, and it was facilitated by Mr. Davis, a senior administrator; Mr. Robert, OMA's director; and Professor Smith, a member of the Faculty Diversity Group who is trained in conflict resolution. As we shall see, the journalists were both influenced by the Activists' voice and felt ambivalent about it.

*Nick:* We met with some of the Activists
And we just sort of sat down and had this big off-the-record meeting
And that's where a lot of this came from
Where they started telling us why they weren't cooperating
And how we got things wrong.

Nick's description of this as a "big off-the-record meeting" underscores the journalists' understanding that they were there to learn about the Activists' complaints about them rather than to gather information for an article. While the Activists had refused to talk to the journalists during and after the silent rally, the Activists explicitly told the journalists their grievances during *this* meeting. Nick states, undefensively, that the Activists told them that they did not cooperate with the journalists during and after the silent rally because of their long-term frustration with the newspaper's treatment of race.

What were the Activists' complaints about the student newspaper?[11] The Activists pointed out that the names of students of color are sometimes left off photos or are incorrect. They stated that the editors' decisions about which articles and opinion pieces to print often resulted in a newspaper that did not affirm and support students of color and their experiences. They raised questions about accountability and responsibility. To whom are student journalists accountable? What is the role of the faculty adviser to the newspaper?[12] What are the ethical standards for and responsibilities of the newspaper? And, of course, they were angry about the editorial decision to allow Professor Thomas three times as many words as the newspaper's policy permits. They argued that this decision privileged his voice over that of the two Asian American students who had criticized Professor Thomas.

Fundamental to these complaints is the question of the role of a student newspaper on a college campus. Although the Activists and the student journalists enter this conversation from different social locations and with different perspectives about the newspaper, both groups understand that the topic is ethics and responsibility in college journalism—in relation to race relations on a predominantly white campus.

The journalists continue directly from Nick's statements above; they are still talking about their meeting with the Activists.

*Grace:* A really really really big meeting
It was like two hours
*Others:* Yeah
*Grace:* Quite productive

*Jessie:* I guess when we went into it
I don't know if any of us really knew what to expect
I was afraid that we were going to get *blasted*
But it ended up being actually I thought a pretty good conversation
*Grace:* We did get blasted a little
*Nick [or Phil]:* We did get blasted
*Jessie:* Yeah but I don't know if it was necessarily undeservedly [laugh]
Cause there's just a lot of things we don't know
And now we do know more than we did before that
And I thought it was good.

This exchange captures the journalists' ambivalence, which was a theme throughout their interview with me. On the one hand, Jessie (the student whose story Professor Collins incorporated into his account) describes the dialogue they had with the Activists as productive in the sense that they learned a lot, including learning about their own ignorance. On the other hand, Grace and Nick (or Phil) feel they got "blasted," a word that captures the intensity of the Activists' anger, at least as the journalists experienced it. Although Jessie suggests they may have deserved that anger, the others seem more hesitant about that. Again, the underlying issue is the newspaper's role on campus: to what extent are the journalists responsible for understanding and presenting in the paper the experiences and perspectives of various communities on campus?

### The Activists Want Us to Build Relationships with Them

At this point, the journalists discussed how they've struggled to cover diversity-related issues in the paper without really knowing much about diversity. This led to a description of the diversity workshops that Professor Collins told me about. Eventually they returned to their meeting with the Activists.

*Phil:* They wanted us to build relationships
So that maybe starting to cover an event—
Covering more events is good—
But if the reporter can say
"Hey my name is John Doe
I work for the student newspaper
I'd like to talk to you about your event"
Even if that story doesn't run for some odd reason
You've still made that connection that said
"I'm here
I'm at your event
I care."

Phil describes one of the concrete changes the Activists asked the student newspaper staff to make—to build relationships. In so doing, Phil articulates the Activists' point of view and shows that he has heard their voice. What he has heard fits well with the Activists' request (as articulated in chapter 6) for shifts in interracial relationships between themselves and their white peers.

More evidence that the journalists were influenced by their conversation with the Activists lies in the difference between two editorials they published during these events. After the publication of Professor Thomas's rebuttal but before the silent rally, they wrote an editorial in which they explained why they had decided to publish the professor's letter even though they were violating their own policy about length. They stated that the two students' criticism created an unusual situation because of the students' accusation that the professor was refusing to meet with them to discuss his course. They also explained that they had already worked with the professor on the length of his letter—the published version was less than half of what he had first submitted to them—and further cuts would have distorted his argument. Finally, they explained the principle of free speech and pointed out that the opinion section of the newspaper is a public forum open to all views, some of which some readers may find inflammatory.

In the second editorial, which was published *after* the meeting between the journalists and the Activists, the editors made a dramatic shift. This time they began by reflecting on the underlying issues in this case. What is the difference, they asked, between criticism and personal attack? Was the students' criticism of the professor a personal attack? Was the professor's criticism of the students a personal attack? They acknowledged the wide range of perspectives on these questions among various groups on campus and they stated that the answers are far from clear cut. They pointed out that *they* had been criticized by those who felt they shouldn't have published one or the other or either letter. At the same time, they took responsibility for their editorial decisions. Most notably, they apologized for their decision to give the professor three times as many words as their policy permitted, while they had held to the word limit the two students who had criticized him.

In addition, in this second editorial, the journalists acknowledged that their reaction to the criticism they received in this case was to retreat defensively into the newspaper office and to whine that no one understands how hard their job is. Realizing that such defensiveness is unproductive and leads to missed opportunities for conversation, they announced that they would create a new, clearer editorial policy about the opinion section of the paper. They printed a draft of the new policy and invited all members of the campus community to an open forum to discuss it. The proposed policy included the creation of a five-person board that would review all opinion pieces concerning length, content, and risk of libel, and would ensure that editorial policies are upheld.

The shift from the first to the second editorial—from defending to apologizing for the violation of their policy—was a public demonstration that the journalists had heard the Activists' voice. Their actions—the second editorial as well as the work on the policy—provide evidence that the Activists' voice of protest was effective: the journalists heard them. The conversation between the journalists and the Activists (facilitated by two administrators and a professional mediator) may have produced conditions that made it possible for the journalists to hear the Activists' voice. Mr. Davis, one of the administrators present at this meeting, told me, "That was one of the best learning situations. . . . The [journalists] began to understand how others felt about the newspaper."[13]

The movement between the first and second editorials also includes a shift in the journalists' articulation of the role of the newspaper on campus. In the first, they relied on the right to free speech to defend their decision. In the second, the editors addressed the complexities of free speech and of decisions they make every week as they publish the paper. Implicit in their more nuanced reflections is a sense that as journalists they have responsibilities to all campus constituencies.

### What Are We Supposed to Do Now?

About halfway through my conversation with the journalists, I asked, "Are there any parts of this that you're *not* comfortable with or that you think aren't right, or are you pretty much all on board with this?" By "this" I meant the dialogues they had been talking about—the diversity workshops, the meeting with the Activists—and the subsequent shifts in their thinking about their responsibilities as journalists. After Grace acknowledged the changes that the newspaper needs to make (such as making the newspaper office a more welcoming environment for newcomers and building relationships with a broader range of groups on campus) she raised a new question:

*Grace:* Has anyone heard anything recently from the Activists?
More stuff they've done since the protest?
Cause I feel a little bit alienated
Almost because they got really angry
Did a lot of protest
And called us on some stuff
And now they've kind of disappeared
And so we're left doing as much as we can
Or as much as we do I guess you could say
And I don't feel like there's any more feedback
And I don't think one time is enough one protest is enough
To tell us exactly what we should all be doing
When we don't really know
*Phil:* And a silent one at that.

Grace implies that the Activists have left the journalists in the lurch. She suggests that the idea Phil expressed earlier—the Activists want us to build relationships with them—is not specific enough for the journalists to figure out what to do next. Phil's comment at the end here supports Grace's complaint. Although Grace and Phil, like the other journalists, understand that the Activists did not talk to the journalists at the silent rally as a way of protesting the newspaper's treatment of race, something about the Activists' actions rankles. Grace's and Phil's words—"I feel . . . alienated," "they've disappeared," "a silent one"—point to their feeling of disconnection from the Activists. This problem, they imply, is not their fault alone.

One interpretation of Grace's account is that it is a request to continue to be educated by the Activists. As we have seen, students of color depict as problematic white students' requests to be educated about race. Students of color *do* embrace the role of educator when they put on educational events, but few white students attend those events, and so white students' requests to be educated often come off as disingenuous. But another interpretation of Grace's complaint is that she literally lacks information about what the Activists have done since the silent protest. In their four-page official protest document, the Activists had asked the administration to communicate with the entire campus. As mentioned in chapter 6, CU's president did so, but his letter was so vague that even if the student journalists had read it, they would have no idea that the Activists had been meeting with the administration and that together they were planning to work on specific issues.

Interestingly, the Activists also expressed frustration about this lack of communication. In her individual interview with me, Marshan said:

*Marshan:* It's frustrating because we feel like we need to make statements to the campus
But we don't want to stop our progress with [the administration]
We don't know if they would be ok with that
And that's what we really did want to happen [open dialogue with the administration] . . .
We've been asking the administration to make public that we're doing something about stuff
And they haven't done that
And we've been asking them to do that for a really long time.

Now that they are meeting with the administration, Marshan suggests, the Activists' hands are tied. She may be acknowledging one of the costs of "going through proper channels," of trying to make change by following the rules within a bureaucratic organization. The Activists want the campus at large to be informed about how the administration is taking up their demands, and they expect the administration itself to do that informing. Failing that, Marshan indicates that the Activists themselves want to "make statements to the campus." But doing so might jeopardize their collaboration with the administrators.

This is a significant dilemma, one that has consequences for the relationship between the Activists and the journalists. If the journalists actually knew specifically what the administration and the Activists were planning, the journalists might have had a stronger sense of what they should do next in relation to the issues the Activists raised. At the same time, if the journalists had already built relationships with the Activists, they could simply have asked their peers what was going on. In any case, the journalists' lack of information and the Activists' inability to provide them with information exacerbate tension in the narrative environment. This is a situation where stronger leadership from CU's administration—providing clearer information—would help students navigate their precarious cross-racial relationships. In addition, those who mediated the meeting between the journalists and Activists could improve the situation by following up with both groups and perhaps facilitating another meeting between them.

As the journalists continued talking about the issues Grace raised, they addressed the question of who is responsible for doing what in this situation. Then Nick summed up the issue of responsibility.

*Nick:* Yeah, I'm in both boats actually if I can be that [laughter]
Because on the one side you think like
"What the hell?
They yell at us
And then they go away
And so what are we supposed to do about it?"
You know it's like your dad getting angry with you
And you're like "why?"
And he walks away
*Others:* [Loud laughter]
But on the other side you're absolutely right
I mean I think this is our responsibility
And I think some of this is our initiative to take
*Others:* [Confirm with "hm hmm" throughout Nick's speech].

Nick expresses the ambivalence that runs through this group's dialogue about the problem they now face—not knowing what to do next. By using the analogy of a father yelling at his kid, Nick places the students of color in a position of authority and the journalists in the position of children. This analogy implies that the one in authority has the greater responsibility, at the very least to explain, to guide, to help the children understand their responsibility. At the same time, though, Nick embraces the idea that the journalists *do* have the responsibility to initiate action. Nick expresses the ambivalence as a split between the journalists' emotions—confused and frustrated by the Activists' anger—and the knowledge that they have a responsibility in this situation.

As their conversation continues, these students first follow up on the idea of *their* responsibility. They brainstorm about specific actions they can take: Nick suggests that he and the other journalists who are graduating can personally contact the graduating seniors among the student of color leaders. They decide that they should make an effort to show up at student of color organizational events. They reject the possibility of having another open forum because that method of soliciting feedback about the newspaper hasn't worked in the past. (For example, when they held the open forum on the new editorial policy for the opinion section of the paper, few people showed up.)

These ideas are examples of ways to build relationships with students of color on campus. Even though the journalists don't know what the Activists and the administration are up to now, this brainstorming shows that the journalists have been influenced by the Activists to consider how they can listen more fully to students of color and thus improve race relations on campus.

### We're Trying. . . . Can't You Give Us the Benefit of the Doubt?

Toward the end of the conversation, Grace followed up on the other side of the group's ambivalence.

*Grace:* This is me sticking my neck out again . . .
This is my main thing
I talk about this a lot.

Grace uses these metastatements—talk about her talk—to preface her account. Her metastatements indicate that she feels she is entering controversial territory and that she feels strongly about what she is about to say.

*Grace:* The biggest frustration like inside myself that I feel right now is that
I feel *so* on board
*So* motivated
*So* focused
*So* part of the group that's trying to help with the GLBT students
But I completely shrink away—
And I can't help it—
But I feel that way with students of color
Because I feel that they're so angry that they don't talk to me
I've had people just look away if they recognize that I'm with the student newspaper
*Phil:* Yeah.

Grace focuses on her *emotions*, her frustration, discomfort, and confusion about the Activists' anger. She contrasts the connection she feels with GLBT students to the disconnection she feels with students of color. The difference, she explains, lies in the students of color's anger. Although she implies that their anger is directed against her as a journalist, rather than against her personally, she indicates that their anger affects her personally. It makes her "shrink away." Apparently Phil has felt the same thing.

*Grace:* And like just the way that I feel
I completely feel like they don't want me to help
They don't want to talk to me about it
Maybe they do in theory
But like I feel completely uncomfortable talking with them
Cause like they're
I mean like
I can understand the anger
Sort of
I mean as much as a white person can
I guess
Maybe I can't
But I understand why they're angry
At least I try to
But just for me personally
I find it really hard to jump on the bandwagon to try to help and do what I can
Cause I don't feel like I'm comfortable among the ranks
The GLBT students I feel like I can
And I do what I can
And I go to the rallies and things
But I would feel uncomfortable I think going to a rally [of students of color]
Because I think people would pretty much be like
"*Eeeeww* newspaper people" [imitating a tone of disgust].

In this account Grace stumbles and hesitates and qualifies her statements in ways that are uncharacteristic of her talk in general. As such, this is an instance of "disrupted talk."[14] The disrupted character of her speech may indicate that she is listening to herself speak, listening to how what she's saying might sound to others and how others might respond.[15] She communicates that she is "sticking her neck out" here, that she is saying something risky.

What risk is she taking? Grace is trying to acknowledge the validity of the students of color's anger, yet she knows that she may not really understand their anger because of her social location as a white student. But when she contrasts the comfort she feels in providing support for and reporting on GLBT events to the discomfort she feels with students of color, she implies that at least part of the problem lies in the student of color's anger. That is where the risk lies: Grace is implicitly criticizing students of color for the way they express their anger, and that critique could be heard in CU's narrative environment as insensitive, ignorant, and racist.

Nick continues her train of thought:

*Nick:* Well I think the thing you mentioned that I've found too
There's that sense with GLBT and with the Students for Disability Rights
Cause I covered some of that stuff last year
There's that sense that you can walk in there
And say something stupid
And make a mistake
But still be ok
They'll be like
"Oh it's ok
No that isn't right but here's why
It's understandable"
And kind of educate you
But you make a mistake with students of color
A lot of times and it's like well—
*Phil:* "You're racist"
*Nick:* "You're not being my friend
And I guess we won't talk anymore."

Nick supports Grace's idea that reporting on issues important to GLBT students and students with disabilities is much more comfortable than reporting on student of color issues. He suggests that it's possible to make a mistake with these groups and get corrected without incurring their wrath. With students of color, though, a mistake has dire consequences—the charge of racism, personal rejection, and silent treatment. By acknowledging that he does make mistakes, Nick presents himself as willing to be corrected, to hear the point of view of the other. What disturbs Nick, Grace, and Phil is anger that they feel they don't deserve, that doesn't give them the benefit of the doubt, and that seems to deny them the chance to continue a conversation.

It is noteworthy that this is the only instance in the journalists' talk (that I have presented) that includes the use of reported speech for students of color's perspectives. Nick uses reported speech to contrast what the members of the GLBT Organization and Students for Disability Rights have said when he has made a mistake and what students of color have said in that circumstance. As Richard Buttny points out, reported speech is sometimes used to accentuate a negative portrayal of "the racial other."[16] In this case, reported speech bolsters Nick's (and Phil's) implicit claim that no white person would want to be talked to in the ways that they claim students of color have talked to them.

Interestingly, these students had recently published an editorial that raised

questions about why race is a more difficult topic at CU than sexual orientation. They asked why straight people easily come to the defense of the
GLBT community on campus and why only a few white people support
protests by students of color. They asked why homophobia receives more
attention than racism. This editorial expresses public support for students
of color on campus. It also points to the need for greater understanding of
why that support is not often forthcoming at CU. Remember that during the
same months when racial issues were coming to a head at CU, the campus
experienced several antigay incidents. As discussed in chapter 3, almost all
of the students I spoke with, including the GLBT students, agreed that the administration responded more quickly and directly to these incidents than to
those involving racial issues. Read in light of their conversation with me, the
questions the journalists ask in this editorial can be heard as questions they
are asking of themselves. What they don't say in the editorial, though, is that
they experience the anger of students of color itself as an impediment to dialogue.

Nick continues from the above:

*Nick:* Just to clarify
Just afraid of an overgeneralization
This isn't everyone
*Grace:* Right
*Nick:* I think
At least my experience
It's been
It's a lot of these people
The students of color that are leading these things
That are you know leading the Activists
Leading the protest
They're the ones that I've felt have sort of littered this campus with eggshells
*Grace:* Yeah it's definitely not everyone.

With Grace's support, Nick makes a distinction among students of color
—it's the *leaders* who are causing problems on campus. As Margaret
Wetherell points out, this distinction can be a discrediting narrative move.
Nick implies that most students of color are like the journalists, doing their
best to deal productively and reasonably with diversity issues. The distinction
places the leaders outside the mainstream at CU and thus as "hearably illegitimate." Illegitimacy can be further established by constructing "a sense of
suddenness, an 'out of the blue'-ness, a sense of coming from nowhere." This
sense was explicit in Nick's earlier account of how being criticized by students of color was like being yelled at by one's father and not understanding why. It is also present here in that the leaders' anger is portrayed as
"uncaused." Wetherell argues that in this type of account, "The other social

groups involved and the history of conflict disappear, while the actions of those one disagrees with become meaningless, frenzied, and inexplicable."[17]

Furthermore, Nick's metaphor—it's the leaders who have "littered this campus with eggshells" imputes interactional power to those leaders. He suggests that the leaders of the Activists express their anger in ways that leave well-intentioned but unknowledgeable white students with no options but to tiptoe around their anger. The leaders have littered the narrative environment with their anger.

The journalists' accounts and their editorials show that they have heard the Activists' voice in some ways, they have taken public action in support of students of color, and they take their responsibilities as journalists seriously. At the same time, they construct the Activists' anger as confusing, frustrating, painful—and even illegitimate. They are at a loss about what to do about that anger.[18]

## Dismissal, Hostility, Eggshells . . . and CU's Narrative Landscape

The Activists' voice of protest holds different meanings and has different consequences for each of the groups whose accounts I have explored in this chapter. Several of the first-year students on Alan's hall dismiss the Activists' silent rally as just another protest, a familiar event, but one that doesn't speak to their lives. The Conservative Students express hostility toward the Activists (and more generally, the advocacy groups), whose protests they experience as unwarranted and as undermining their sense of what race relations should look like on campus. The journalists struggle to understand their responsibility toward the Activists and they express confusion and ambivalence about the Activists' anger.

These widely varying responses show that CU's narrative environment does not *determine* students' accounts and understandings of diversity-related issues or events on campus. Of course, some narrative environments— such as courtrooms and psychiatric wards—*do* exert significant control over people's stories about their selves, lives, and realities.[19] But, by and large, universities constitute more diffuse narrative environments where a range of discursive resources and narrative possibilities coexist (and often conflict), and where a wide range of ideas gets expressed. The latter is certainly the case at CU.

At the same time, all three responses to the Activists' voice reflect the particular character of CU's narrative environment. All three orient to the "big story" about diversity at CU—that "diversity is out there on the table." The first-year students' dismissal implicitly acknowledges that diversity is frequently topicalized and that rallies are common occurrences at CU. The Conservative Students' hostility reflects the conspicuousness of social justice discourse at CU. On another campus, an equally conservative group of students may not be confronted so directly with this discourse, and thus their accounts of events on campus may not express such intense antagonism about race relations. The journalists' ambivalence points to a narrative landscape in which speaking and listening across differences is valued in some quarters but is not frequently modeled on the campus at large. On another campus, where diversity is *not* out there on the table and where the student newspaper is not a target of protest by students of color, student journalists probably don't walk on eggshells like the CU journalists do.

To say that these responses are shaped but not determined by CU's narrative environment is to say two things at once. First, each of these responses *makes sense* within CU's narrative landscape. They show the influence of—an orientation to—the "big story" about diversity at CU. Second, these responses show the narrative work each group engages in as they construct accounts about what's going on at CU. In other words, these students do not passively reproduce ideas that are presented to them. Their accounts show how they *work* to make sense of what's going on at CU and of their relation to those events.

These responses to the Activists' voice of protest also show that CU's narrative environment, although particular, is not an isolated enclave, free from the influence of broader narrative environments. In order to understand the Conservative Students' hostility, we need to understand not only the Activists' voice and CU's narrative environment but also the national conservative movement in higher education. The Conservative Students' antagonism is fueled by that movement—and specifically by David Horowitz's critique of the "liberal curriculum." The intensity of the CU Conservative Students' hostility is intelligible in relation to the clash between Horowitz's ideas and social justice discourse at CU.[20]

Similarly, in order to understand the journalists' ambivalence, we need to understand not only the Activists' voice and CU's narrative environment but also discursive resources in the field of journalism. The commonsense view within American culture is that journalists are objective reporters, news articles are neutral presentations of events, and opinion pages represent the principle of free speech. Within the field of journalism, these truisms are complicated by questions of ethics, the nuances of free speech, and the idea of a newspaper's responsibility to the community it serves. However, the relationship of these complexities to diversity topics on college campuses is less frequently addressed in the profession of journalism. The CU journalists' ambivalence about the Activists' anger makes sense given their profession's lack of guidance about how to address diversity. These students are just beginning to have contact with those involved in the interconnected group at CU who could provide them with resources for thinking more concertedly about diversity. The two diversity workshops provided a beginning—and the meeting with the Activists furthered their education—but it is fair to say that they don't have the resources they need for dealing with the most diffi-cult, highly emotional conversations about race and journalism.

Finally, each of these three responses consists of accounts constructed at a specific point in time. During their college careers, the first-year students on Alan's hall may develop new accounts that sound more like those of the Con-servative Students or like those of the journalists (or like those of the white allies in chapter 8). They may also develop accounts that differ completely from any I heard during my research. Similarly, as a result of new events, new encounters, new relationships, or new conversations, the Conservative Stu-dents and the journalists may also alter their narratives over time.

# 8    *Doing the Work of Allies*

Five years before my study, the white students who attended the National Conference on Race and Ethnicity (NCORE) as part of CU's NCORE group returned to campus with a desire to cultivate a deeper understanding of white privilege. They created an informal group called White Students Resisting Racism (WSRR). WSRR's founders published a letter in the student newspaper inviting other white students to join them in learning about race at personal, organizational, and societal levels. Since the founding of WSRR, a group of eight to ten students have met regularly to study race and racism, reflect on their racial identities, and consider how to support their peers of color on campus.

During my study I met five members of WSRR: Melanie, Sarah, Mark, Connie, and Kate. Kate was a new member; the others had been active in the group for several years. Sarah and Connie had been members of NCORE groups, and Connie had written some of the Race Columns in the student newspaper. Melanie, Sarah, Mark, and Connie had attended CU's local Race Conference several times during their college careers and the latter three had served as group facilitators there. These four students were also involved in many other organizations associated with the interconnected group at CU: for example, a campus peace organization, the Feminist Majority Leadership Alliance, Men Against Sexism, Community Commitment, and Habitat for Humanity. Sarah and Mark occasionally wrote letters to the student newspaper about various issues of social justice. Sarah, Mark, and Melanie were on the student government committee charged with supporting advocacy groups, a committee where the question of how the student government treats race was frequently aired. WSRR also had informal connections with antiracism groups in the city, such as the local chapter of The People's Institute, the National Fellowship of Reconciliation, and Jewish Community Action.

Thus, even before the events that led to the formation of the Activists, these white students were already highly engaged with racial issues. They had already established trusting relationships with peers of color, relationships that were missing between the journalists and students of color. Unlike the white students whose accounts we heard in chapter 7, members of WSRR understood the grievances of their peers of color. Their listening provided the foundation for their supportive work as allies.

In this chapter I begin with WSRR's response to students of color's request for their support during the tumultuous events preceding the silent rally. Then, taking a broader view, I show how these white students make cognitive and emotional shifts as they talk about race, which allow them to hear the voices of their peers of color and thus to do the work of allies.

## Providing Support and Taking Action

As students of color debated what to do in response to the publication of Professor Thomas's rebuttal, they reached out to members of WSRR. During her individual interview with me, Connie described the situation.

*Connie:* Well what happened is like—
What Joe [a student of color] had wanted to do was have us [WSRR] write a letter
   to the student newspaper
Kind of reframing the issue . . .
He wanted it to come from us rather than him
And we didn't actually do that
Because we decided we wanted to wait and have some time to talk about it.

Connie presents Joe as wanting the white students to take supportive public action *as* white students. Embedded in such a request is the assumption that white students who speak out about racism will not be seen as self-serving and thus will boost the credibility of the students of color's claim that they are not being heard.[1] Connie's description of this interaction implies that the relationship between Joe and the white students was already one of trust. As Connie continued this account, she described the meeting that may have been the birth of the Activists.

*Connie:* We met with them
It was like maybe four or five of us from WSRR
Met with Joe and other students of color who were concerned about [Prof
   Thomas's rebuttal] and the cultural diversity requirement
And these are the same students who are involved in all of the antiracist things
So we already know them
So they asked us to meet with them to talk about it

And so it was late one night . . .
And we just talked
It was mostly just getting some of the emotions out there
And just being there to listen
And just kind of talking about how frustrating it was.

Connie recounts the white students' role during this meeting as one of listening, making space for their peers' emotions, and sharing their frustrations. Not long after this meeting, the white students decided that the best way to support their peers of color would be to create a zine about institutional racism on campus. During my group interview with WSRR (which included Sarah, Melanie, Mark, and Kate, but not Connie), Sarah explained:

*Sarah:* A lot of white students that we talk to didn't get it
They didn't know what was going on
And they might have had Professor Thomas [for a class]
And felt that he was a good professor
And that he was being attacked
And so we thought that people don't get that the cultural diversity requirement is not working
So let's put something out that's about that.

Sarah indicates that in creating the zine WSRR took on the role of educating other white students. Echoing Kia's and Tanya's comments in chapter 6, she suggests that WSRR wanted to move attention away from Professor Thomas as an individual to the broader issues. Here she specifically mentions the curriculum.

Interestingly, WSRR present themselves as not only in the position of educating white students but also of explaining to white professors what was going on.

*Mark:* Professors were feeling on edge and I guess some even felt threatened
Because the Activists sent out a letter [to all faculty, staff, and students in the college]
And everybody wanted to know who that was
And they didn't know how many students were involved
And so there was like . . .
There was just kind of a general—
*Melanie:* Uneasiness
*Mark:* Yeah uneasiness
Kind of like panic [on professors' part]
Like "how do we respond?"
*Melanie:* Talking to a couple of professors before the cultural diversity forum
I know that they were really worried that students were going to single them out individually and attack

Which didn't happen at all
And that was a strategy from the beginning
That we were going to keep this at an institutional level and not a personal level
   discussion
And I think some professors were really happy about that
*Sarah:* Yeah because even the ones that were really supportive and excited about
   the Activists
They would ask us questions like
"How many students are in the Activists?"
"What are you guys doing?" [imitating an anxious tone of voice]
Like they were asking all the white students to tell them about the Activists.

According to this account, the Activists' initial refusal to identify themselves as individuals made many white professors uneasy, even panicky. Although the Activists were not anonymous at the silent rally, they did not sign their names to the letter they sent to administrators, faculty, and staff after the silent rally. At that point, it may have been difficult for others on campus to make a connection between the silent rally and the letter. Of course, there was already controversy on campus concerning the two Asian American students' criticism of Professor Thomas and his rebuttal. Mark, Melanie, and Sarah describe this tense narrative environment as making professors worry about being singled out. Again, like Kia and Tanya, Melanie reiterates that the Activists were more interested in addressing the issues at an institutional than a personal level.

Sarah points out that even professors who were sympathetic to the Activists were asking *white* students (she probably means members of WSRR) what was going on. She implies that white professors were more comfortable talking to white students than students of color about this race-related conflict. At the very least, this observation indicates WSRR's sense of the importance of white people in antiracism work.

The zine, which WSRR distributed widely on campus before the cultural diversity forum (which Dr. Miller discussed in chapter 6) was a twelve-page pamphlet focused primarily on flaws in the cultural diversity requirement. In the zine WSRR used the metaphor of "naming the elephant" in two ways. First, they reprinted the ancient poem, "Elephant in the Dark," which is about a group of individuals, each of whom describes an elephant incorrectly because they cannot see it and each one touches only part of it (trunk or tusk or ear). They used that poem to encourage participation at the upcoming cultural diversity forum, organized by the curriculum committee, at which, presumably, the many perspectives offered by different community members would help to illuminate "the elephant."

Second, they named "the elephant in the room," what everyone knows but is afraid to talk about: racism and its effects it "on who we are and what we do." They defined the concept of institutional racism as a system of structures, policies and practices that advantage white people and disadvantage people of color. And they identified institutional racism as the source of problematic structures, policies, and practices at CU. They addressed interracial dynamics in classrooms where there are few students of color and the host of problems that arise from the low representation of people of color among CU faculty and administrators. They devoted much attention to the cultural diversity requirement, in particular the fact that students can graduate from CU without taking a class on race or ethnicity in the United States. They grounded their critique of the cultural diversity requirement in the college and university mission statements. They wrote:

> We need to design a plan to make sure that students learn about race because the development of racial awareness and understanding is an important part of becoming a world citizen.

They critiqued CU's flawed process for addressing complaints about professors and courses by using the language of liberal arts and critical thinking:

> Students have a right to question the information being given us, especially when it concerns topics that the institution presents as central to its core values [education about diversity and social justice]. *But CU has no formal written grievance policy.* It is important that students have this information [about how to file a grievance] and its unavailability is negligent at best. Faculty and staff need to be responsive to student concerns. It is, after all, our education. [emphasis in original]

They took the student newspaper to task for printing Professor Thomas's long rebuttal while limiting the students' criticism to the official word limit, presenting this, too, as an instance of institutional racism.

> By making *selective* exceptions [to the policy limiting letter length], the newspaper is vulnerable to accusations of bias, even in so-called unusual circumstances. . . . The student newspaper passively accepted the professor's claim that this conflict is rooted in personal attacks rather than institutionalized racism. [emphasis in original]

Finally, they described the history of WSRR, their goals and activities, and they invited others to join them in their antiracism work.

In terms of format, the WSRR's zine differed dramatically from the Activists' official document. The zine was a pop culture artifact that included drawings, a poem, and an argument aimed at persuading readers that institutional racism was the source of conflict on campus. The WSRR sought a broad audience for the zine. They distributed it widely across campus, dropping off copies in administrators' offices, in the student cafeteria, in the lobby outside the auditorium where the cultural diversity forum took place, and in other high traffic areas. By contrast, the bureaucratic form of the Activists' official document—a list of problems and demands for action—suited the limited audience the Activists targeted after the cultural diversity forum: administrators.

Despite differences in format and audience, the complaints outlined in WSRR's zine and the Activists' official document are essentially the same. This similarity of content reflects the collaboration between the students of color and WSRR, as well as their joint involvement in the narrative community of the interconnected group on campus.

Like their peers of color, WSRR argued that current racial problems on campus are not new. During the group interview, Mark and Sarah talked about CU students' efforts three years earlier to direct administrators' attention to racial problems, efforts that included a sit-in, a formal list of demands, and a public forum to address the issues. Then they explained how the protest was different this time.

*Mark:* But I think the difference between that and what's happening now is that the Activists was initiated by students of color
There were students of color that were part of the sit-in [three years ago]
But it was a lot of white students too
And a lot of first-year students as well
*Sarah:* Yeah
*Mark:* It's interesting going through this
And being a part of the Activists
Because these sort of things they go in circles
And they pop themselves back up
And it seems to be the same issues
*Sarah:* But the administration is responding a lot differently now
Because I think they are realizing how urgent it is
And I really think it's the leadership of students of color that's making them realize that
And just the amount of people that were at that protest [silent rally]
And the people they've been meeting with [meetings between the Activists and the administrators]
They're the *best* students on campus [she names several of them]
They're just like—
You can't argue with them because they're just so smart! [laugh]

According to Mark and Sarah, this time is different because students of color rather than white students are leading, because the leaders are juniors and seniors rather than first-year students, and because the leaders are so persuasive with their arguments. In any case, Sarah suggests that this time students of color have successfully communicated to administrators the urgency of the problems: the administration is listening in a way they haven't in the past. In other words, according to this account, students of color have reshaped the narrative environment in ways that have jolted others into listening.

## Doing the Work of Allies

Students of color were also successful at enlisting WSRR's help. Because these white students were already practiced in listening to their peers of color, they were able to act quickly to create and publicize the zine—an instance of antiracism work on the part of allies. But what does it mean to say that these white students knew how to listen to their peers of color? What does that listening entail? These students' accounts and narratives show that they make a series of conceptual and emotional shifts that allow them to hear their peers' voices and thus do the work of allies.

### We Do What We're Asked to Do

Shortly after the excerpt above, I asked Sarah, Melanie, and Mark about their role as members of the Activists. In the book's introduction I presented this excerpt in a shortened form; here I include more detail in order to interpret more fully what they are communicating. Bold text indicates what I excluded from the earlier version of the transcript.

*Susan:* **And so there's been kind of a shift in those three years**
**The leadership had been white students and now a shift to students of color being leaders**
**And the white students in the Activists are—**
**How would you describe that role?**
*Sarah:* Uh we do what—
*Sarah and Melanie:* [Laugh]
*Melanie:* **What we're asked basically**
*Sarah:* **[Overlapping with Melanie]** What we're asked to do [laughing voice]
**I mean** it's a very quiet role
*Melanie:* Yeah
*Susan:* **And how does that feel?**
*Melanie:* Yeah I think
**I don't know** for me personally **like**
**It was [pause]**
It was really interesting to go to the first couple of meetings [of the Activists]
**And [pause]**
**Sort of** have a *background* role
Because **[pause]**

In all the organizations I'm in . . .
I have a pretty vocal role
But then to be a part of *this*
And **sort of** [pause]
**Be you know kind of in the back** *back*ground—
**I don't know if that's the right word—**
**But** have a more silent role
It's *unusual* for me anyways
So **it was—**
It's been interesting to be part of this group
**And experience that**
**I don't know**
**It's been interesting.**

When I presented parts of this account in the introduction, I focused on Melanie's and Sarah's comments about how unusual it is for them to be in the background because they are leaders in their other campus activities. By including more of the transcript here we can interpret their account more fully. First, this version shows that as Sarah and Melanie begin to answer my question, they talk at the same time, use the same words, and laugh together. This suggests that they are articulating a shared experience. Second, their overlapping statement "we do what we're asked to do" is perplexing. Do they mean this literally? At the very least, it suggests that they experience themselves as followers rather than leaders in this context, and thus it highlights the quietness, silence, and sense of being in the background that the first version of the transcript included. Third, this transcript includes Melanie's pauses, stumbles, repetitions, qualifications, and her metastatement after using the word *background* for the second time—"I don't know if that is the right word." These linguistic practices communicate that she is struggling to find the words to describe this new, unfamiliar relationship with peers of color.

Listening to this fuller transcript in light of my analyses of CU's narrative landscape in part I and of students' narratives and accounts in parts II and III also sheds further understanding on what these white students are communicating.

The theme of voice and specifically the transformation in their voice runs throughout this account. Sarah uses the words "*quiet* role." Melanie describes it as a "*silent* role" which she contrasts to her typical "*vocal* role." This emphasis on voice, of course, is embedded in social justice discourse as it gets expressed at CU. But the transformation moves in the opposite direction from what we usually think of as the development of voice regarding social justice topics. Kia's narrative highlighted her transition from being silent to having a quiet but confident public voice of authority. By contrast, these white students are learning to be quiet and to stop leading. To be quiet, stop leading, move to the background, and do what others ask one to do is to engage in new, unfamiliar relationships. By talking about their voices *in relation to students of color's voices,* they indicate that in order for someone to step forward to speak, someone has to step back to listen. I suggest that Melanie finds these ideas hard to articulate and perplexing because they are not often expressed in American culture. Stepping forward to speak out can be a culturally laudable action, but stepping back to listen doesn't have the same cultural cachet. Who wants to be the one who steps back to listen? Frances Kendall speaks to this unfamiliarity when she offers this guideline for white people during difficult interracial conversations: "Don't just do something, stand there. . . . The point is just to stand and wait and think."[2]

Sarah and Melanie continue from the above:

*Sarah:* At times it's been really exciting
Especially the first couple meetings
It was just like *exhilarating*
*Melanie:* Yeah
*Sarah:* Because it was like
*Melanie:* [Overlap unclear]
*Sarah:* "This is the way it's *supposed* to happen!"
*Melanie:* Yeah
*Sarah:* "This is the role I'm *supposed* to be playing
And I'm not supposed to be out there"
**Whereas at CU a lot of times since it's so small**
**You have to be like doing work**
**But it was just**
**Like it was *so* cool to—**
**Especially because the students of color that are leading it are really amazing**
**And other times it's been kind of uncomfortable**
**because you don't know like**
**like if you have a thought**
**if you should say something**
**or if you have an idea or a question . . .**
**But I think it's been really cool**
We were talking about how it felt like a SNCC meeting the first one we went to
*Sarah and Melanie:* [Laugh].

Sarah's comment that because CU is so small "you have to be doing work" reflects the importance of "the work" to social change on campus, another aspect of CU's social justice discourse. Along with the theme of "voice," their focus on "the work" signals WSRR's participation in the narrative community created by the interconnected group.

When Sarah describes the shift to a quieter role as exhilarating, as reminiscent of interracial cooperation in SNCC (Student Non-Violent Coordinating Committee) during the civil rights movement, she frames that shift as part of something larger than what is going on at CU. She brings historical knowledge about the civil rights movement to bear on what is happening on her campus. Although stepping out of the limelight is an unfamiliar role for these students, Sarah recognizes that it has historical precedents.

Sarah and Melanie don't talk explicitly about listening to their peers of color, but that activity is implicit in their talk. At this point, we can hear how complex that listening is. "We do what we're asked to do" *sounds* like passivity or obedience, but in light of Connie's account above, we know that it is not. Joe asked WSRR to write a letter to the student newspaper, but they decided to create the zine instead. So, "we do what we're asked to do" does not mean "we obey others' commands" but something along these lines: "Students of color asked for our help, we listened, and we responded in the way we thought was best." In the zine, WSRR used a confident, creative, and forceful public voice. In the account above, though, they show their flexibility—their ability to shift from that forceful public voice to a quiet presence during the Activists' meetings.

Finally, Sarah's comments about how the Activists' meetings are sometimes uncomfortable show how difficult it is to listen well. She knows that students of color need and want to lead—are *entitled* to lead—because *their* voices need most to be heard on campus right now. But she wonders: Does moving to the background mean I shouldn't speak at all during the meetings? In other words, what does it mean to listen well in this new relationship? Sarah suggests that the basic principles governing their relationship with students of color are clear—sometimes stepping back to show support and sometimes stepping forward to show support (e.g., publishing the zine). At the same time, Sarah communicates that it is hard to know exactly what to do at any particular moment. And yet, in commenting on that discomfort, Sarah does not complain, ask to be educated by students of color, or seek an easy fix. She simply acknowledges the discomfort of this unfamiliar relationship.

### We Go to Student of Color Events

Later in the group interview, these students talked more generally about what it means for them as white students on a predominantly white campus to support students of color. When I asked about their involvement in student of color organizations, Mark said that he has been a member of the Black Collegians in the past, but not recently. He continues:

*Mark:* What we try to do is go to a lot of student of color events
Because that's a consistent thing that's really frustrating for students of color
Is that they put on all these events
And then people don't show up to them

And on a campus that's predominantly white people
The blame can fall on the white people that don't show up
And I think that's kind of telling about where things are at on campus
So I think that's where we try to get involved.

Mark has heard students of color's persistent complaint that white students do not attend their educational events. He implies that supporting students of color means listening to their frustrations, and specifically, attending their events. Notice that Mark focuses on *what* frustrates students of color, not on the emotion itself. The student journalists, by contrast, vacillated between acknowledging students of color's complaints and focusing on their own feeling of vulnerability in the face of their peers' anger. Of course, unlike WSRR, the journalists have been a recent target of the students of color's anger. But still, Mark positions himself differently in relation to students of color than the journalists do. Mark's focus on *what* frustrates students of color is grounded in his understanding of the nature of race relations on campus. He knows that student of color events on this predominantly white campus are intended to educate white people about race and racism. Low attendance means white people are not taking up that educational opportunity. WSRR's commitment to attending demonstrates that they have listened to students of color's frustration, that they want to be educated about race, and their understanding that by becoming educated they may help transform race relations on campus.

### We Create a Safe Space Where We Can Risk Making Mistakes

Melanie continues directly from Marks's statements above:

*Melanie:* After being a part of this group [WSRR]
I see the importance of having our separate spaces
To talk about issues that we're dealing with
And to be safe in that environment
And I definitely think that conversations do change
And your dialogue changes when you're with students of color in the room
And I think just being able to—
Like especially in this group
Since we are all white students
Being able to say things and make mistakes
And then without hurting someone . . .
So I see the importance of having those separate spaces.

In describing how their all-white group functions as a safe environment in which white students can discuss race and risk making mistakes, Melanie makes two important shifts. First, rather than expecting students of color to educate white students in contexts besides their educational events, Melanie suggests that white students can take responsibility for educating themselves. They can do so by discussing racial issues among themselves (and, as they mentioned at another point, by reading about race and racism). Second, rather than trying to avoid angering students of color, Melanie says all-white group discussions allow white students to make mistakes that might hurt students of color if they were present. This shift from a focus on students of color's *anger* to students of color's *hurt* is grounded in an understanding that what produces the anger in the first place is injury or injustice that consists of various forms of racism. In Melanie's construction, racism is not just inappropriate, it causes harm.[3]

The journalists wanted to be allowed to make mistakes, but they didn't consider having a safe space separate from students of color in which to make those mistakes. They focused on their own intentions—we didn't mean to hurt you—rather than on the hurtful impact of their mistakes. Melanie, by contrast, shifts her attention from intent to impact. This shift resonates with Kendall's advice to white people, "Keep in mind that, even though you have good intentions, it is your behavior and the impact of that behavior that matter."[4]

### We Hear Our Peers' Stories about the Pain Caused by Racism

How do the white students make this shift from attending to intent to attending to impact? How do they learn to hear the injury that underlies anger? In chapter 5, we heard Melanie's account of how the stories students of color tell at the Race Conference (RC) have been crucial to her understanding of how peers have been injured by racism. During their individual interviews with me, Sarah and Connie recounted similar stories. In the following, for example, Connie is talking about the first RC she attended:

*Connie:* I remember hearing—
Really for the first time—
About the history of the Hmong
[Their role in the Vietnam War and their immigration to the United States]
And hearing some of my classmates talk about how—
Or *cry* about how their grandparents have experienced life
And how they feel like they are betraying them in some ways but they can't really
  help it
And that was really powerful
One student that I really remember a lot
Who I really looked up to
She was an African American student and a leader on campus

And she was really strong
And I would never picture her as someone who would cry
But she went up and cried because she was scared of her brother losing his life due
   to police brutality
That was really powerful too.

The powerful stories Connie heard are similar to the stories that Kia talked about the Hmong students telling and that Rachelle talked about the African American students telling at RC (see chapter 4). In their narratives, Kia and Rachelle presented these as stories about race-related pain. Here, Connie (like Melanie in chapter 5) presents herself as *hearing* that race-related pain. She indicates that she didn't expect to hear what she heard: it was her first time hearing about Hmong history and how it affects Hmong families and Hmong college students. By shifting from "talk about" to "*cry* about" she emphasizes the pain embedded in her peers' stories. And it was her first time hearing the strong African American woman cry because of her brother's vulnerability to police brutality. By stating that she didn't expect this woman to cry in public, Connie again emphasizes the pain in her classmate's story.

Like the stories we heard in chapter 5, Connie's narrative is about an epiphanal moment in which she hears the voice of the other in a way she hadn't before. And yet Connie's story (and others like it told by Melanie and Sarah) includes something that is not present in most of the stories we heard in chapter 5. Rather than putting herself in the other's shoes, Connie's account about hearing the other's pain suggests that she understands that she is *not* in the other's shoes. Rather than identifying with the other's pain, Connie's account seems to be about becoming open to or compassionate in the face of the other's pain. Hearing the other's pain in this way seems to be fundamental to the transformation of these white students' racial consciousness.

RC is a site where students of color tell their stories (sometimes for the first time, as in Kia's case) and a site where some white students hear students of color's stories for the first time. But, as Rachelle explained in chapter 4, RC can also be a site where students of color feel the burden of having to educate white students who don't always "get it." During their group interview, as the Black Collegians talked about the difficult but life-changing conversations that happen at RC, they brought up WSRR as an outlet for white students, an outlet that relieves pressure from them as students of color:

*Rachelle:* And they do have a white allies group that they—
*Marshan:* Cause they realized that they have to work on their own issues without
   us teaching them
*Others:* Without us teaching them right right
*Marshan:* Cause that's one of the things that they teach people at RC
That you can't expect—

*Dorie:* And that helped a lot this year
And they helped a lot of the younger white students realize that it's not up to us
And that helped them to realize that they have white privilege
And that they need to understand that before even trying to talk to us about issues
  that we have as students of color
So it's not always us telling them what you're doing wrong
Or what you need to work on.

The Black Collegians' appreciation of WSRR centers on the white students' willingness to work on their own race-related issues, to work at understanding how white privilege operates in their lives, and to resist the temptation to ask students of color to educate them. Notice once again that the term *work* communicates a serious ongoing commitment to social justice. It is noteworthy that as the Black Collegians and the Southeast Asian Association talked with me about their activities and antiracism work, they mentioned WSRR only briefly. By contrast, as WSRR talked with me about their activities and antiracism work, students of color played a major role in their accounts. This contrast references the fundamental shift that the white students make: as they consider recent race-related events on campus, they move to the center of their attention students who exist on the margins of their predominantly white campus.

### We Work with Students of Color on Their Issues

As my group interview with WSRR continued, Sarah and Mark recounted what it is like to join student of color organizations—the awkwardness they felt at first; how that awkwardness dissipated over time; how it is impossible to know if their presence inhibited students of color; and how they suspected that their participation was appreciated. They also talked about how, because of other commitments in recent months, they were no longer active members of any student of color organizations. They did, however, continue to attend student of color organizations' events. Then Mark said:

*Mark:* Going to [student of color organizations'] events is important
But there also has to be some other space
Where [white] students should get involved
Otherwise it's difficult to dialogue
And sort of hear the issues
Unless you have really close relationships with students of color
But then it's only with certain ones.

Mark argues that white students who are committed to antiracism work have to find spaces for interacting with students of color so that they will know what issues are important to their peers. Students of color's educational events do not fit that bill because their aim is often the education of *white* people about race and racism. The aim of those events is not work on issues that students of color prioritize, what students of color need. Mark also suggests that friendships with individual students of color may or may not make it possible for white students to hear fully students of color's concerns. He continues:

*Mark:* If we weren't involved on [a specific committee of the student government]
We never would have got involved in the Activists
And if we hadn't been involved in the Black Collegians [in the past]
We probably wouldn't have known the same people in the same capacity
*Sarah:* Yeah.

Mark speculates: because he, Sarah, Melanie, Connie, and a few other white students had already worked with students of color in a variety of contexts, students of color trusted them enough to ask them to join the Activists. Further, he suggests (in a statement not included here) that the classroom is not a space where interaction is conducive to developing trusting interracial relationships. More implicit in Mark's talk is a shift from inviting students of color to one's own events to joining students of color on *their* turf. This is a shift that the student journalists were just beginning to understand. The journalists knew that the open forum they held on their new policy about the opinion section of the paper failed because students of color did not attend. Their brainstorming about how to reach out to students of color included attending students of color's educational events, but did not go so far as to join committees or organizations led by students of color. Mark continues:

*Mark:* Cause it shows a different level of commitment
It's a situation where you do have to be tested
And you do have to see how are you going to react.

Mark argues that joining students of color on their turf so that one can hear the issues their peers prioritize shows a deeper commitment than simply attending students of color's educational events. Further, he claims that in joining students of color on their turf, white students have to be willing to be tested by students of color. This talk embodies another shift: instead of expecting students of color's gratitude for one's willingness to do antiracism work, white students should expect to be tested.

### We Allow Ourselves to Be Tested

During my individual interview with Mark, he talked about his relationship with John, a South Asian American student and member of the Activists:

*Mark:* He's very uncomfortable relating to white students
And he's very blatant about it
And a lot of my white friends have actually heard him talk about it
And sometimes they're like
"Oh he's taking it too far"
But he's just at that point where he has to say
"I can't trust white people"
And I think that's part of the continuum of racial identity—
"I'm just through with white people"
And he's pretty much committed his life to working in social justice with—
He always says "brown or black people—
That's where I'm going do my work with"
And so those have always been interesting conversations
Because he feels comfortable talking to me about it
And me being a white man obviously
And I don't take that sort of thing personally.

Mark presents John's blatant talk about not trusting white people as offensive to some white people, and he presents his own strategy for hearing that talk. First, he understands it as part of John's racial identity development, an idea Mark learned at RC (as he mentions below). John may be expressing the "resistance stage" of identity development during which a person of color "experiences anger, pain, hurt, and rage" and during which "the effects of racism may appear to be all consuming."[5] Second, Mark resists hearing John's talk as personal, as about Mark himself. But not taking it personally is different from not taking it seriously. He is not dismissing John's talk but working to understand it. Mark seems to be saying: "When John talks about not trusting white people, he's talking about his experience of race relations, about what's important to him right now in his racial identity development, and about his desire to work on social justice with brown and black people after graduation." Mark stakes out a position where he can hear John's words as a commitment to a certain way of living right now. Mark is neither offended by John's statements nor does he dismiss them. As such, Mark exemplifies a shift from defensiveness to hearing the voice of the other.

*Susan:* Why does he feel comfortable with you?
*Mark:* I don't know
He always says
"You're the only white man on campus that I trust anymore"
And I guess it's because I can listen
And I guess he knows how I stand on various issues
And he knows that I'm outspoken
Like if need be when there's racist things printed in the student newspaper.

Mark responds to my question in the terms it implies: how are you different from other white men such that John feels comfortable with you? His response describes what an ally does: listens and takes a supportive stand when the need arises. He continues:

*Mark:* Because I'm sure a lot of those conversations that he has
If he's attempted with other white friends of his
They've probably been really reactionary
Maybe
I'm just guessing
But in terms of like
Well if he would say to his white friends
"I just can't stand going to those parties"
Maybe they'd say something like
"That's reverse racism."

Mark indicates several times—"maybe"; "I'm just guessing"; "maybe"—that he is speaking hypothetically when he imagines conversations between Mark and other white peers. And yet the hypothetical conversations are plausible. The charge of "reverse racism" is prevalent in American culture—white people frequently make this accusation when people of color (or policies) resist the status quo. "Reverse racism" usually evokes the discourse of color blindness and more broadly, abstract inclusion.[6] In this case, Mark describes a hypothetical situation where white peers accuse John of "reverse racism" in response to his resistance to attending parties where white students predominate. Mark's point is implicit: accusing John of reverse racism probably misses what John is communicating.

*Mark:* But I guess I can understand John
Because we talk a lot at RC about different models of racial identity development
I think that's just part of the process
And maybe that's how he will feel all of his life
But I don't think so really
Because I think of him being able to have that relationship with me
I guess that's one white person that he trusts or whatever
And when he says that I know that he really doesn't mean that in terms of
"I can't trust *any* white people"
Cause I *know* there's some [white] professors that he trusts.

Mark returns to the idea of racial identity development, which he has learned about at RC, as an explanation of John's feelings about interracial interactions right now. Although Mark doesn't spell out this idea, he makes clear that it includes the possibility that one's racial identity and how it shapes one's sense of self and one's actions may change over time. Mark speculates that John may feel differently about white people at another point in his life. And he uses John's friendship with him—as well as John's trust in a few white CU professors—as evidence that John does have good relationships with at least some white people.

Note that my original question—why does John feel comfortable with you?—invited Mark to talk about how he differs from other white people. But Mark resists presenting himself as "a special white person." As he reflects on his relationship with John, Mark maintains his focus on John and resists making himself central.

*Mark:* But that's just the way he has to frame it right now
We talk a lot in our white student's group about sort of tests
Like that we have to expect to be tested by people of color
And I think that's part of it
Kind of like saying
"Are you okay with this?
Are you okay with me voicing my frustrations with other white people?
And are you going to respond to that by listening?
Or are you going to respond to that by attacking me about how prejudiced I am?"
So maybe that's why he feels comfortable.

Mark interprets John's statement that he doesn't trust white people as a way of framing his current frustration with race relations. He also interprets it as a test of their friendship. Mark presents John as needing white friends who will listen nondefensively to his frustration with most white people, rather than to critique that frustration as prejudice. By using the metaphor of being tested, Mark implies that is difficult to make the shift from being defensive to listening. At the same time, he implies that the reward of doing the difficult work of listening is an interracial friendship that includes open talk about emotions and race. Equally important, Mark constructs the white student group as a source of support in facing the tests and doing the difficult work of listening.

### We Keep Each Other in Check

A recurrent topic in WSRR's conversation with me was the group's goals—what the goals have been, how they have shifted over time, and what they should be. For example, Sarah spoke about her impatience a few years earlier when older students were first organizing WSRR.

*Sarah:* We [younger students] were kind of at that stage where we really wanted to
*do* things
And we didn't really know yet that it was important for us to keep learning

And get a really good foundation
And also to have constant conversations with other white people.

Sarah describes the desire she had to "*do* things"—to make change happen *now*—as the misguided impulse of a white person with a newly raised racial consciousness. The older students who organized WSRR insisted instead that the group focus on learning about race and that they resist the impulse to "go around on campus being 'the good white students' that know everything about race and racism." Although the group started their self-education with readings, they also began to talk about racial issues they were encountering in their everyday lives. They started to include this kind of discussion after attending a meeting of an antiracism group off campus where they observed others engaging in this form of self-education. Continuing from the excerpt above, Sarah describes how this kind of discussion has evolved over time:

*Sarah:* I think doing the work has expanded to—
Since our group has changed to something where we talk about what we're encountering personally—
It's expanded to
"You're responsible for saying things
Now that we've discussed how you're going to confront the situation
You're responsible for confronting it next time"
So this group helped me to confront racism in my workplace
And I probably never would have done it without being able to talk about it [with WSRR]
But it's like after we talked about it I couldn't *not* do it
That would be totally *embarrassing* [laugh]
So it's been that way where we keep each other in check in some ways
Just because we have expectations
And we help each other.

When she says, "doing the work," Sarah places WSRR's discussions squarely within the narrative community of the interconnected group. She describes WSRR both as a source of support for figuring out what to do when white members encounter racism in their everyday lives and as a source of expectation that they take action once they have received that support. In the previous excerpt, she constructed a white person with a newly raised racial consciousness as tempted to act before knowing what she is doing. Here she constructs a white person who is racially conscious as tempted *not* to act even if she knows what to do. Thus she presents the support of the group as essential in a racially conscious white student's shift from consciousness to action. Through supportive discussion, the group holds members accountable for their actions.

When I interviewed Sarah individually, she told me the story she refers to above, a story about a blatantly racist incident at the restaurant where she works.

*Sarah:* The manager of the restaurant who's a person of color* was like
"So it's Christmas and there's lots of purse snatchings during Christmas
And I don't want to be stereotypical
But it's always black men"
And I was like
*"Oh my god!"*
And so of course I was like
"Umm isn't that kind of racial profiling that we should like—"
Because she was saying
"Watch out for black men"
And she's like
"Oh well you know I'm not prejudiced at all [sing-song voice]
I'm just saying by my past experiences—"
And all the other people in the meeting
Who are all white
Are nodding like
"Yeah sad but true" you know
And so I went home
And I'm like *what do I do?*
And so I talked to the white students [in WSRR] about it
And we talked all night about this
And figured out that I was going to write a letter to the owners of the restaurant
And they helped me figure out what to say and everything
And I wrote this letter.

In telling this story, Sarah constructs a mundane employee meeting as a dramatic moment in which her racial consciousness is called into play. She presents herself as the only employee who speaks up at the meeting, the only one who names the manager's statement as racial profiling. She describes the other employees as colluding with the manager's racist statement, as if they, too, know for a fact that black men are more likely than other people to snatch purses. She focuses not on how she is "the good white person" but on the intensity of her realization that she must take action without knowing exactly what to do. She presents her attempt to resist during the employee meeting as failing and so she turns to WSRR for help. When she states, "we talked all night," Sarah points to the group's collective commitment to helping her respond by writing a letter to the owner.

*I assume the manager is not African American because Sarah says further on that no African Americans work at the restaurant.

*Sarah:* And the owner called me a couple weeks later
And was like "so where do we begin with institutional racism?"
I was like
"*What?*"
He's like—
He had been working on racism stuff at his church
And so he understood where I was coming from
Because what I was concerned about is—
Is this a policy that they like tell [employees to do racial profiling]?
And after that of course I was noticing there aren't very many African American
    customers
There's *no* African Americans working here
Like "what's going on?"
And he asked me what I thought they could do to educate the employees better and
    all this stuff
And he was really responsive.

This story is about Sarah finding a kindred spirit where she wasn't expecting one. She emphasizes her surprise and pleasure that the restaurant
owner wanted to do something to educate employees about institutionalized
racism.

Notice that Sarah implies that in her letter, she asked about the restaurant's *policy*—which managers would presumably have to follow. This is a
strategy of approaching those who hold power in an organization and holding them accountable to their stated commitments. WSRR used a similar
strategy in their zine when they held the college accountable to its mission to
help students become world citizens. And the Activists used the same strategy when they targeted CU's administration and held them accountable to
the university's mission statement and their responsibility for students' education.

Sarah concludes her story:

*Sarah:* [This] gave me confidence in WSRR's process
Because I knew how much harder it would be to just go home
And write my own letter and send it
And be like "well guess I'll get fired now" [imitating dejected voice]
But being able to actually say in the letter
"I'm part of this student group that talks about these issues and we also do ac-
    tivism"
Hint hint like "we'll write letters if you"—
So that was really powerful
I think it also showed me that I can't ignore those issues
And that if I don't [ignore them] something might come out of it.

Sarah describes WSRR as not only helping her brainstorm action she could take but also as a source of further support if her initial action failed. Unlike a lone letter writer, Sarah could hint in her letter that, if need be, WSRR would start a letter writing campaign against the restaurant. Sarah's letter is an example of what Chesler et al. call a "pressure strategy" in that it includes the threat of further action if needed. Interestingly, the restaurant owner responded by talking about the "persuasive strategy" of educating employees about race and racism.[7] When Sarah states, "It also showed me that I can't ignore those issues," she may be referring to what she said earlier, that the group holds members accountable for doing something once they have raised issues. She also presents this instance of successful resistance as giving her hope that when she acts kindred spirits will sometimes be found. Overall, Sarah's story about resisting racism in her workplace exemplifies a shift from isolated individual action to action supported by the group.

## WSRR's Shifts and CU's Narrative Landscape

As they talk about WSRR and their relationships with students of color, these white students make both cognitive and emotional shifts.[8] The shifts are cognitive in the sense that the students resist conventional, institutionalized understandings of race relations. Conventional understandings take white privilege, white centrality, and white dominance for granted. These white students' narratives undermine that privilege, centrality, and dominance by keeping the voices of students of color at the center of their attention. They hear their peers' persistent complaint that white students do not go to their events and so lack the education about race and racism those events are designed to offer. They hear their peers' insistence that outside of those educational events they are not responsible for white students' education about race and racism. They educate themselves by reading about and discussing race and racism in WSRR. Rather than expecting students of color to join white students' groups, these white students make an effort to join students of color on their turf so they can learn about the issues their peers care about. When their peers of color ask them to speak publicly about racial issues, the white students find a way to do so. Equally important, when it is time for students of color to lead and speak, the white students move to the background. These students did not talk explicitly about their white identities, but they positioned themselves as "antiracist allies to people of color."[9]

The shifts are also about attending to their own and others' emotions in ways that undermine white privilege, centrality, and dominance. Again, this is a matter of keeping students of color's voices at the center of their attention. The white students understand that they will make mistakes as they become educated about race, so they create a space of their own where they can make those mistakes without hurting their peers of color. They understand that their peers' anger is grounded not in an abstract notion of racism's inappropriateness but in its harmfulness. They allow themselves to hear, nondefensively, their peers' stories about the pain and harm caused by racism. They understand that racism has painful effects no matter how good someone's intentions may be. Rather than expecting to be given the benefit of the doubt, they work to cultivate students of color's trust. Rather than expecting the other's gratitude for their antiracism work, they expect to be tested. Rather than becoming defensive when students of color test their commitment to antiracism work, they work to understand how their peers' statements make sense under current circumstances. Rather than running away from the discomfort and uncertainty that accompany these ways of interacting with their peers, they acknowledge and live with those feelings.

Because these cognitive and emotional shifts disrupt conventional, institutionalized race relations, they constitute hard work. These white students' narratives demonstrate that their mutual support and accountability make that hard work possible.

These intellectual and emotional shifts also speak to these students' maturity. Indeed, it is easy to think of these students as exceptionally strong individuals just as it is easy to see the leaders among the Activists in that way (as Sarah and others pointed out a number of times). But it would be a mistake to view these white students' (or the Activists') maturity *only* in terms of their individual strengths. An individual-level explanation misses one of the main points of this book. These students' speaking and listening make sense within and contribute to a narrative environment where just this kind of maturity becomes . . . not inevitable, but *possible*.

Like the Activists, the white students in WSRR are active participants in the interconnected group that advocates for social justice on campus. Their talk about "the work" signals their membership in that narrative community. Within that narrative niche these white students have learned to question taken-for-granted cultural assumptions about race and racism. An example is Mark's resistance to the idea that John's talk about white people is reverse racism and his explanation of that talk as reflecting John's racial identity development. These students have also learned to question institutionalized practices that support the status quo. An example is Sarah's resistance to the restaurant manager's warning to watch out for black men snatching purses.

A common denominator among the WSRR students is participation in the Race Conference, the weekend retreat where space is created for students of color to tell their stories and opportunities are given to white students to listen. As mentioned at the beginning of this chapter, Sarah, Mark, Melanie, and Connie have attended RC several times, and three of them have served as group facilitators there. But it is also important to remember that the narrative community created by the interconnected group on campus has ties to narrative communities beyond CU.[10] NCORE is one such narrative community. Each year, CU sends a different group to that conference, and each year the group brings back new ideas for educating the campus about race. Sarah and Connie have been members of NCORE groups. In addition, WSRR has ties to antiracism organizations in the city where CU is located. One of those organizations gave WSRR the idea of helping each other respond to racist incidents they encounter in everyday life.

Of course, these white students are far from passive recipients of the interconnected group's, NCORE's, or any other community's narrative resources. Their accounts about how they listen to their peers of color show their active narrative work as they sort out what is going on and what they need to do. Moreover, their listening and speaking *influence* what goes on within the interconnected group at CU. For example, as these white students facilitate small groups at RC, they model for other white students what it means to listen to peers of color, to examine white privilege, and to risk making mistakes in a safe space (such as RC's white students' caucus).

WSRR also played a role in shaping events during the Activists' protest. They had already gained the trust of students of color on campus, earned through their various activities on campus and their earlier demonstrations that they know how to listen and to speak when necessary (for example, in writing letters to the student newspaper). Because students of color already trusted these white peers, they reached out to WSRR for support after the publication of Professor Thomas's rebuttal. WSRR listened to students of color's frustrations, helped them strategize responses, attended meetings of the Activists where they stepped out of the limelight, and wrote the zine that they distributed widely on campus.

And yet there was nothing inevitable or predetermined about these specific turns of events or about WSRR's actions. Once again, we need to remember that human interactions and narrative realities are complex and constantly shifting. The possibilities for and the consequences of specific instances of listening and speaking cannot be predicted. Small details can alter the course of a larger story.

The WSRR students laughed at themselves as they told me that they forgot to include contact information in their zine, making it difficult for white students interested in joining their group to find them and making it easy for other students to criticize them as unapproachable. In fact, one member of the Conservative Students specifically called WSRR "elitist." He was under the mistaken impression that a white student had to be *invited* to join WSRR. That was just the kind of mistaken impression that the white students in WSRR knew was being reinforced by their omission of contact information in the zine. Sarah said, "One challenge we always have is that people think we're a really exclusive group and we try not to be and then we accidentally forget to put our contact information on [the zine] and it's like *bad*." They also speculated that their omission of contact information may have added to the uneasiness and tension on campus in the wake of the silent rally, the cultural diversity forum, and the letter to everyone in the college that was signed "the Activists" (rather than with a list of individuals' names).

In one sense, anonymous speech may be easy to dismiss because recipients cannot be held accountable for responding to specific others. But it is also possible that in the particular constellation of events at CU that year these instances of anonymous speech elevated the tension on campus in a way that motivated administrators to respond more quickly. Of course, it wasn't long before the Activists identified by name the five individuals to represent them in meetings with the administration. And because "diversity is out there on the table" at CU, an interested white student who exercised some initiative could find WSRR by asking the right people a few questions.

In any case, CU's narrative landscape not only shapes possibilities for speaking and listening, it is also an ongoing accomplishment. It is constantly reshaped as various groups of people engage diversity topics in specific ways, under specific circumstances, on particular occasions.

# Reflections

What can we take from my narrative inquiry into CU students' engagement with diversity? What practical insights does my study offer?

Because structural factors affect narrative realities, my reflections in this final chapter are most relevant for small to midsize, private, predominantly white colleges and universities. For example, institutions with more racially balanced student bodies are likely to have different racial dynamics than those at CU. And larger universities may include multiple communities that are unaware of and unaffected by each others' activities. Nonetheless, I hope that my reflections will interest all students and educators who care about how diversity gets addressed on their campuses, as well as people in other organizational contexts who care about speaking and listening across differences. I also hope my comments will interest researchers in the fields of narrative inquiry, racial discourse, and diversity in higher education.

## The Collaborative Work of the Interconnected Group

Some of the CU administrators I interviewed had worked at other universities where the commitment to diversity went beyond lip service—as it did at CU. They told me that at some institutions, academic programs (such as women's studies or racial and ethnic studies) took the lead in implementing that commitment. At other institutions student affairs programs took the lead. By contrast, at CU, the interconnected group took the lead. The Office of Multicultural Affairs (OMA) was at the forefront, with strong participation from the Office of Student Affairs (OSA), the Faculty Diversity Group (FDG), student advocacy organizations, and individuals involved in other campus programs.

From my point of view, *the most significant aspect of the collaborative work of the interconnected group is that it created a narrative community that integrated academic and extracurricular arenas. Because it was not limited to one or the other, the interconnected group increased opportunities for students to learn to speak and listen across differences—and opportunities to work together to bring about institutional change.*

In *How College Affects Students*, Ernest Pascarella and Patrick Terenzini summarize three decades of research, which demonstrates that student learning and development take place inside the classroom as well as outside the classroom in informal interactions with faculty and staff, in relationships with peers, and in extracurricular activities.[1] The CU students I spoke with reported that they learned about diversity both in and out of the classroom, but that productive conversations were more likely to happen outside the classroom. They pointed to the Race Conference as the site of the most productive and extensive diversity dialogue.

Interestingly, white students at CU were more likely than students of color to describe the classroom as a place where they learned about diversity, as a launching pad for their involvement in diversity activities in other campus arenas, and as a resource for further learning. Students of color were more likely to place extracurricular activities at the center of their learning to speak and listen across differences. Students of color were also more likely than white students to describe the classroom as a problematic narrative environment. For example, Marshan said that because many faculty members did not know how to lead conversations about race, they did not always correct misinformation that students sometimes brought to the discussion. She dealt with this by doing research on her own and coming to class armed with information. This exemplifies learning to speak, and so it is not a completely negative experience, but without support from OMA and her peers in student advocacy organizations, she might not have had the resources and confidence to speak out in the classroom. Furthermore, as we have seen, students of color experienced the classroom as a place where they were expected to educate other students about race, or to represent the experiences of people of color in general.

Given these differing classroom experiences, the interconnected group played a central role in bringing students together for sustained interaction who otherwise might not have had much contact with each other. Students who developed an interest in diversity topics through coursework could be directed by their professors to campus events sponsored by various student organizations and OMA, and they could be introduced by their professors to students involved in other activities of the interconnected group. Likewise, students who began their engagement with diversity issues through student organizations or OMA could be directed by OMA and OSA staff and administrators to professors and courses where they could further their learning on the academic level.

These interconnections created narrative possibilities that might not have existed otherwise. On campuses where such connections are not as strong, student learning about diversity—and student organizing for social change —might take place in the enclaves of student affairs *or* academic programs.

In addition, working relationships within the interconnected group provided models for speaking and listening across differences. Faculty and staff or administrators sometimes cotaught courses. Faculty, staff, administrators, and students coorganized and cofacilitated workshops and conferences. The NCORE group each year was composed of students, faculty, staff, and administrators. Whenever possible, coteachers, cofacilitators, and the NCORE group were interracial, cross-gender teams. This was not easy on a campus where students, faculty, and administrators are predominantly white.

It is noteworthy that much of the research on student learning about diversity in higher education focuses either on curriculum, pedagogy, and classrooms, or on student affairs programming and student organizations.[2] Some researchers do point out the importance of connections across organizational boundaries. Melanie Bush argues that collaboration between student affairs and academic affairs encourages connections between experiential and theoretical learning.[3] Donna Wong suggests that collaborations among students, faculty, staff, and administrators have been pivotal to change at the University of Oregon.[4] And Leonard Valverde argues that the development of networks across units and ranks and among students, faculty, staff, administrators, and trustees can facilitate institutional change.[5]

And yet, as Mark Chesler and his colleagues point out, barriers often exist to connections between student affairs and academic affairs. Viewing their academic role as distinct and superior, faculty do not usually get involved in student affairs activities. For their part, student affairs personnel may be "loath to cooperate fully with potential academic colleagues."[6]

Because student learning takes place both in and out of the classroom, Pascarella and Terenzini argue that universities should work to overcome barriers to collaboration between student and academic affairs. "Learning-centered organizations will find ways to increase opportunities to link the formal and informal worlds of learning and instruction. . . . How creative can colleges and universities be in eliminating the conceptual and organizational separation of student learning into cognitive and affective, academic and nonacademic? Can structures and practices be developed that recognize learning as ongoing, without regard to time and place?"[7]

## The Role of Personal Narratives in Learning to Listen

For CU students, diversity talk took many forms in many venues—discussion and debate during student government meetings, articles and letter exchanges in the student newspaper, conversations during educational events sponsored by student groups, academic discussions in the classroom, e-mails from administrators about campus incidents, keynote speeches by nationally acclaimed scholars, diversity education in the residence halls, and informal interactions in many settings. All forms of communication about diversity contributed to CU students' narrative reality in which diversity was on the table.

But I found that *one type of diversity talk—personal narratives—played a particularly important role in students' learning to listen across differences.* As we saw in chapters 5 and 8, for some students on the privileged side of a diversity category, hearing "the other's" personal story led to understanding the other's life experience for the first time. Examples of personal narratives include the Hmong students' stories at the Race Conference about their families' immigration to the United States after the Vietnam War, and African American students' stories, also at the Race Conference, about family members' vulnerability to police brutality.

The telling of personal stories was neither incidental nor accidental but was part of the interconnected group's educational strategy. Some Race Conference exercises specifically encouraged personal narratives. A monthly event at CU called My Life consisted of panelists of all races and backgrounds recounting how race has shaped their experiences. Authors of the Race Column in the student newspaper sometimes told personal stories as they addressed topics such as immigration and HIV/AIDs. And some professors used exercises in class where students shared stories as a method of enhancing student learning about an academic topic.

Educators on many campuses use personal narratives as a method of encouraging listening across differences. For example, in the preface to *Making a Difference: Students of Color Speak Out,* Julia Lesage states that she (and a colleague and students) at the University of Oregon gathered the narratives of students of color in order to present them to others on campus (students, faculty, staff, and administrators) who needed to hear them. Because these narratives are available in book and video formats, the students of color themselves do not have to tell their stories over and over for others' edification.[8] Similarly, other books include long personal narratives by students of color, and several films document students' personal narratives as well as interracial dialogue among students—all aimed at audiences who need to learn to listen.[9]

Learning to understand difference is often evoked as a value of a liberal arts education. In *Cultivating Humanity,* philosopher Martha Nussbaum argues that "the narrative imagination" is one of the capacities that a liberal arts education in today's world should cultivate. She defines the narrative imagination as "the ability to think what it might be like to be in the shoes of a person different from oneself, to be an intelligent reader of that person's story, and to understand the emotions and wishes and desires that someone so placed might have."[10] Nussbaum's focus is on the curriculum, and she argues that the humanities play a particular role in developing the narrative imagination.

As we have seen, CU students cultivated the narrative imagination—hearing the voice of the other—not only in some humanities and social science classrooms but also during extracurricular events and activities where personal narratives played a central role. And, as they did so, they developed another capacity that Nussbaum names as belonging to a liberal arts education: "The capacity for critical examination of oneself and one's traditions—for living what, following Socrates, we may call 'the examined life.' This means a life that accepts no belief as authoritative simply because it has been handed down by tradition or become familiar through habit."[11]

In chapter 5, I showed that when CU students heard the voice of those whose social identities and locations differed from theirs, they began to imagine *their* actions and beliefs from the other's point of view. As Hannah listened to her African American classmate recount how white women interact with him in public spaces, she realized that she is more afraid of black than white male strangers. As Melanie listened to her peers' stories at the Race Conference, she realized that she may have inadvertently said or done things that hurt people of color. As students saw themselves through others' eyes, they began to question taken-for-granted beliefs, such as racism being a matter of personal prejudice and good intentions being sufficient for moral action.

Nonetheless, Nussbaum's descriptions of these capacities leave out one pivotal point that I heard in some students' accounts about learning to listen. Some students constructed the other's experience as something they could *not* imagine. I suggest that acknowledging the *limits* of one's narrative imagination is an important component of that capacity. This is not an excuse for giving up on trying to put oneself in another's shoes. Rather it is a realization that the other's story is about experiences that differ so greatly from one's own that one can only imagine *working* toward putting oneself in the other shoes. This acknowledgement prevents disingenuous connections across differences. Madison's story is an example. When she heard her gay friend at the GLBT rally say that sometimes in some places he has to pretend he is someone he is not, she realized that she could *not* imagine what that must be like. Knowing the limits of one's imagination can motivate one to seek further education about the other's experience. Developing a narrative imagination and living an examined life are ongoing educational pursuits.

## The Role of Critical Thinking in Learning to Speak

It is not difficult to argue that "learning to listen" exhibits narrative imagination and critical self-examination in Nussbaum's terms. But I found that *"learning to speak" also requires critical thinking about oneself, one's beliefs, and the world one lives in.* It might be tempting to hear Kia's and Rachelle's stories in chapter 4 as *only* about their psychological development: overcoming reticence in Kia's case, and learning anger management in Rachelle's case. When we think of learning to speak in this limited way, it is easy for educators to relegate it to the realm of student affairs, to those who care about students' personal development outside the classroom. But to the extent that learning to speak integrates personal development, critical self-examination, and development of civic engagement skills, it is a capacity that both academic and student affairs educators should care about. This is why the interconnected group's collaboration across the boundaries of academic and student affairs is so important.

Kia's and Rachelle's personal narratives demonstrate critical examination of themselves and their habits of thought as individuals who were raised in particular environments. Kia grew up in a Hmong family and community that treated women as subordinate to men. She attended a predominantly white school where she internalized stereotypes about Hmong people, and later, a multiracial high school where she learned to resist limiting images of Hmong students. Rachelle was brought up in an African American family, neighborhood, and religious community where the very topic of sexual orientation was taboo. She moved thousands of miles from home to attend a predominantly white, upper-middle class high school so she could get tracked into college.

When they arrived at CU, Kia and Rachelle interacted with others in ways that made sense to them at that time. Kia was quiet and uninvolved; Rachelle was quick to anger and lash out. As they narrated transitions they have gone through during college, they constructed their self-development as including critical examination of their upbringings and of how they relate to others. Kia recounted learning to break through traditional silences: to speak about what is unspeakable in the Hmong community (rape); to speak publicly at the Race Conference with other Hmong students about their families' histories; and to speak with moral conviction at the student government meeting as both the chair of the budget committee and as a person of color. Rachelle told about learning that she can be friends with gay people; learning to resist others' requests that she speak for all members of her social groups; and learning that her tendency to lash out precludes rather than fosters conversation.

Thus Kia's and Rachelle's narratives are not only about psychological development. Their narratives are also about becoming more thoughtfully engaged in various contexts and with various groups of people. My point is not that they made the "right" decisions in each of the situations they faced. Rather my point is that their narratives of self-development *embody* critical thinking about themselves and about how to speak and act as members of their communities.

The skills of critical thinking and civic engagement are also displayed in the Activists' speech and actions. As we saw in chapter 6, the Activists' silent rally, official document, and meetings with administrators reflect a sense of entitlement to speak and get heard as members of the campus community. The word *entitlement* is often seen as pejorative, as a matter of taking for granted and even overstepping the bounds of what one deserves. But for students whose voices have historically been marginalized in higher education, learning to speak requires *developing* a sense of entitlement to speak and get heard. The Activists' protest embodied their understanding that they *and* white students deserve an education and learning environments that take race and racism seriously. Learning to speak in this collective way—to protest what they perceive as an institution's failure to live up to its commitments—involves critical thinking about how the institution operates. It also involves learning how to engage effectively the institution's various communities. Again, my point is not that each of the Activists' actions was "right," but that their actions embody critical thinking about how the university needs to address race and about their and others' responsibility for making that happen.

Educators don't usually treat "learning to speak" as a matter of developing critical thinking skills. My guess is that most educators assume that students come to college already embracing their entitlement to speak and get heard. But when educators make that assumption, they have in mind students on the privileged side of various diversity categories. For students on the nonprivileged side of one or another diversity category, learning to speak is an essential aspect of a liberal arts education.

## Emotional Volatility in Diversity Dialogue

Colleges and universities produce materials—brochures and virtual tours—that show what learning looks like. The images are usually of students with faculty in labs and classrooms, in solitary study in the library, in group discussions outside on beautiful days. In these images students are attentive, reflective, and curious. Sometimes students and teachers are smiling or laughing, indicating that learning can be fun. In the last ten years or so these materials have increasingly included images of students studying abroad, expanding their horizons through exposure to other cultures.

But these images don't show that learning to think critically about oneself and one's communities can be emotionally difficult. These images don't include photos of people who are angry, anxious, defensive, frustrated, or confused. Not represented is the idea that some aspects of a liberal arts education might move one to tears or to outrage. Not shown is that examining one's beliefs and traditions could separate one from family and friends, could challenge many ideas one holds dear.

But when diversity is on the table as it is at CU—and when diverse others are right here, rather than far away in other countries—narrative reality is bound to be emotionally volatile, at least sometimes. To the extent that learning to speak and learning to listen across differences involve critical thinking about oneself, others, and the world one lives in, conversations will sometimes be difficult. Pent-up frustration and fear of saying the wrong thing will surface from time to time. Some faculty told me that they tell their students that if they always feel comfortable in the classroom, then something is not right. In chapter 8 we heard Sarah say that she sometimes felt uncomfortable during the Activists' meetings because she didn't know whether or not to speak. Her account indicated that she accepted that discomfort rather than immediately trying to get rid of it. Some faculty at CU and elsewhere use guidelines for class discussion that help both faculty and students when discussions get tense.[12] My favorite is "assume that everyone is doing the best they can," which doesn't mean assuming that what they are saying is "good" or "right."

I am not suggesting that universities should add images of outraged and anxious students to their brochures and virtual tours. Nor that faculty should be trained as therapists. But I am suggesting that *any university that is committed to taking diversity seriously—which includes understanding that learning to speak and learning to listen are capacities that belong to a liberal arts education—needs to recognize, be explicit about, and be prepared to deal with the emotional component of the issues.* Resources need to be devoted to supporting students, staff, faculty, and administrators through the difficult work of taking diversity seriously as an educational endeavor. Resources include budgets, of course, but right now I am thinking of resources that support people interactionally as they deal with the emotional volatility of the issues.

At CU, the Faculty Diversity Group's monthly meetings were a source of support for professors who teach courses that address diversity. Some faculty found that coteaching helped them deal with difficult classroom conversations. For African American women students, the Black Women's Circle, facilitated by an African American woman administrator, functioned as a safe, private place where they could "vent." Other groups of students of color had similar circles. (These groups were different from the student of color advocacy organizations that had a public educational mission.) WSRR served as support for white students who wanted to learn about race and racism in a context that allowed them to speak frankly without hurting their peers of color or expecting their peers to educate them.

Groups such as these are frequently criticized for creating separatism and increasing racial tensions on campus. However, the literature on diversity in higher education suggests that such groups can do just the opposite. In *Can We Talk about Race?* Beverly Daniel Tatum, the president of Spelman College, writes about "The ABC's of Creating a Climate of Engagement." The

ABC's are affirming identity, building community, and cultivating leadership. Tatum states, "As paradoxical as it may seem . . . students who feel that their own needs for affirmation have been met are more willing and able to engage with others across lines of difference."[13] Similarly, in his summary of initiatives that improve universities' diversity environments, Frank Hale Jr. includes "encouraging the social bonding of students from a common culture" and "affirming their right to be drawn to each other and to have some campus space set aside where they can engage in social and educational exchanges."[14] These ideas resonate with what the Black Collegians said in chapter 6: they need respect for their community of color.

CU has another resource that helps students and others navigate the emotional volatility of diversity issues: faculty, staff, and administrators who are trained in conflict resolution. Sometimes they are asked to mediate conversations between various groups in conflict. For example, Professor Smith, a trained mediator and a member of the Faculty Diversity Group, was present during the meeting between the Activists and the journalists that I discussed in chapter 7.

Many universities have an ombudsman or other position devoted to conflict mediation. But Leah Wing and Janet Rifkin point out that mediation practices typically focus on individuals' specific needs and ignore "the fact that society is stratified by *group* membership."[15] Wing and Rifkin developed an alternative mediation program at the University of Massachusetts-Amherst that takes into account people's social locations and social identity development. They offer the example of a team of mediators (one white woman and one African American woman) who helped to resolve, over several sessions, a conflict between an African American woman student and a white woman professor over a grade. The mediators allowed each person to develop her story fully, acknowledged each person's construction of how she was misunderstood, and pointed out how each person's understanding of her racial identity and of racial dynamics in the classroom (where the student was the only person of color) exacerbated their conflict. The professor did not change the grade, but she learned that the student could legitimately interpret her well-intentioned pedagogical strategies as problematic. The student gained satisfaction from the teacher's new understanding. Once each person felt heard, she was able to transform her original story into one that took the other's perspective into account.

At CU skilled mediators provide strong resources for addressing emotional volatility in diversity dialogue. And yet I suspect that *students' needs in this area are easily underestimated.* Anger, frustration, defensiveness, and fear of saying the wrong thing need to be addressed continuously, in both academic and extracurricular arenas. George Yancey's findings are worth repeating here: "Contact that is egalitarian, intimate, voluntary, and cooperative *and is supported by relevant authority figures* is most likely to produce alterations in a person's racial attitudes" [emphasis added].[16] I suggest that it is *educa-*

tors—faculty, administrators, and staff—whose job is to create conditions that encourage speaking and listening across differences, to create conditions that encourage students to understand rather than become overwhelmed by emotional intensity. This, too, is a critical thinking skill.[17]

## The Invisibility of Student Learning

As I listened and observed at CU, I often found myself wishing that some other group on campus could hear what I was hearing. Students who identify with any of the three groups of white students in chapter 7—the students on Alan's hall, the Conservative Students, and the journalists—might learn by listening to Kia's personal narrative about how she was silent and uninvolved when she first came to CU and how over time she developed a quiet voice of authority. They might learn by listening to Rachelle's personal narrative about how she is learning to speak so that others will listen. These white students, as well as some faculty, staff, and administrators might be surprised to learn that the Activists' anger—as expressed in chapters 4 and 6—reflects that they are learning—as all college students need to learn—to think critically about themselves, the university as an institution, and what it means to take their education seriously. The Activists' anger was not unfocused lashing out.

When I attended OMA's awards ceremony, I wished that the same three groups of white students as well as more faculty, staff, and administrators could be there. I wanted more people at CU to hear about students of color's accomplishments and I wanted them to witness the dynamism embodied in the strong community of color on campus. I also wanted them to see that white students, faculty, staff, and administrators are important members of this community.

I wished that CU students, faculty, staff, and administrators could hear the students' stories in chapters 5 and 8 about learning to listen to those whose social identities and locations differ from theirs. I especially wanted students of color to hear these stories because these stories reveal that other students *are* listening in ways that aren't necessarily visible to them. If students of color (and all students on the less privileged side of any diversity category) could hear peers' stories about learning to listen, they would realize that their speaking *does* have an impact on campus. And I wanted students of color to hear the journalists in chapter 7 struggle to understand their responsibilities toward their peers of color. The journalists may be walking on eggshells but they are actively engaging the issues and they care deeply about their journalistic responsibilities to the entire campus community.

I wanted students, faculty, staff, and administrators who have not attended events like the annual Race Conference to know that each year a multiracial group of students on campus is learning the skills of speaking and listening across differences—and that some are learning the skills of leading, facilitating, and mediating dialogue within multiracial student groups.

If people at CU who are trying to bring about institutional change knew how much at least some students (and others) are learning, they might realize how much their work matters. *And knowing that their work matters might help to temper the frustration and discouragement I heard from some among the interconnected group.* Steven, the South Asian American student who turned our interview into a conversation with me, wanted to know what was happening on my campus. When I told him that diversity is not on the table at my university like it is at CU, and that an event like the silent rally either would not happen or would not have much of an impact if it did, he said, "You're putting a smile on my face, but I don't want to get too comfortable with that." He meant that he could see that from my point of view as a researcher the Activists *did* disrupt CU's narrative environment on campus—but he also knew there was more to do.

## The Question of Social Class

The concepts of learning to speak and listen across differences indicate that those who are socially privileged (in whatever way) need to step back from the familiarity of being in the forefront so that others can move forward to speak and get heard. At CU, at the time of my study, it was students of color who were claiming their entitlement to move forward, to speak, to get their agenda on the table. And it was (some) white students who took the unfamiliar step of moving back. By focusing on students' narrative reality in a particular time and place, I ended up highlighting students of color's speaking and white students' listening (and other responses). At other times and in other places, different groups of students might claim entitlement to speak and different groups might learn to listen. Different narrative realities might be created. As I stated in the introduction, I began this study with an interest in how CU students engage diversity, not with the intention of focusing on race per se. I *found* that race was the most prominent and contentious diversity topic on *this* campus at *this* time. At the same time, as the chapters in parts I and II show, talk about other diversity categories also circulated at CU. And sometimes students of color constructed *themselves* as privileged, as needing to listen to the voice of the other. In chapter 5, for example, Steven spoke about learning to recognize his male privilege and Ramita spoke about learning to recognize her class privilege.

Indeed, throughout my study, various people told me that other voices needed to be included more fully in diversity dialogue at CU. The GLBT students felt well supported on campus, but they wished for an event modeled on the Race Conference that would focus on sexuality. The students in the Women's Coalition also felt well supported on campus but wished that an incident of sexual assault the year before had been addressed in terms not only of violence but also of gender. Students for Disability Rights were excited to get their organization up and running but felt frustrated that some buildings on campus remained inaccessible. And the Conservative Students were pleased with professional opportunities that were available to them, but felt they were silenced in the classroom. Faculty, staff, and administrators involved in the interconnected group told me that the next step in their work would be developing new ways to encourage students on the privileged side of diversity categories to participate more fully in diversity dialogue. They specifically mentioned white men and conservative students.

From my perspective as an observer, *the voice of working-class students also needed more attention.*[18] The interconnected group clearly recognized the significance of social class—by including class in the intersections conference and at Race Conferences, by supporting working-class students of various races, ethnicities, genders, and sexual orientations, by getting a speaker for a fall faculty retreat on first-generation college students. In the documents I analyzed—student newspaper, curriculum, student government minutes, events calendar—social class was definitely present as a topic, and much more present than at RU. At the same time, it vied with disability and religion as the least represented diversity categories in CU's documents.

Structural factors make it difficult to bring social class to the forefront in diversity dialogues on campus. Like CU, most universities do not have a student affairs office or even a position devoted specifically to helping students from working-class families learn how to navigate the college environment. Like CU, most universities do not have a student organization chartered by the student government called First Generation College Students or Association for Working-Class Students. There is a financial aid office, of course, and many CU students receive aid and many of them are employed. But working-class students typically get little or no assistance in socialization to the middle- or upper-middle-class milieu of private colleges and universities. The invisibility of social class in this organizational sense shapes its minimal presence in the narrative environment.

Broad cultural discourses also contribute to the difficulty of bringing social class to the forefront in diversity dialogue on campus. As many social scientists have pointed out, social class is at once always present and rarely addressed directly in American society. In the society at large, social class typically marks neighborhoods, schools, occupations, restaurants, stores, and other public spaces. But when politicians and talk show hosts address social class, the deeply taken for granted cultural discourse of individualism usually dominates. According to that discourse, a person who is born into a poor or working-class family can move up the social class ladder through hard work and determination. Failure to do so is the individual's fault.

Because of these structural and cultural factors, when working-class students go to college or university—especially expensive private colleges and universities—social class is not a category with which they are likely to identify themselves publicly. It is not a category around which they are likely to organize. Kia's and Rachelle's narratives offer good examples. Both grew up in working-class families, and their narratives demonstrate that class location shaped their experiences. Kia lacked the cultural capital to figure out how to apply to college. Through A Better Chance, Rachelle attended a white upper-middle-class high school thousands of miles from home to increase her chances of going to college. Yet class disappears as they narrate their college experiences.

In recent years, some colleges and universities have created programs intended to support low-income students who are the first in their families to get a higher education.[19] The need for support is based on their low graduation rates. The Pell Institute reports that only 11 percent of low-income, first-generation students have earned bachelors' degrees after six years, compared to 55 percent of their peers.[20]

An example of a new program is the University of Cincinnati's Gen-1 Theme House, where a small number of first-generation students live together and receive mentoring and advising based on their needs. Rather than stigmatizing them as poor, students reportedly feel that living in the house is "cool."[21] It remains to be seen whether such programs will become institutionalized on U.S. campuses, and if they do, how working-class students will learn to speak about their identities, realities, and communities. And it remains to be seen whether and how working-class students will shape narrative realities on their campuses.

## One Final Thought

As I have said throughout this book, the relationship between narrative practices and narrative environments is reflexive: narrative practices are at once shaped by and shape narrative environments. Narrative reality in any particular time and place is dynamic and constantly re-created. Even so, through the same processes, ways of speaking and listening can become habitual, and conflicts can become entrenched, even institutionalized. In educational institutions committed to the liberal arts, educators need to model the capacities of narrative imagination, critical self-examination, and civic engagement. They need to model speaking and listening across differences. They need to be open to students' narrative practices and their efforts to reshape the narrative environment. Easier said than done, I know.

# Epilogue

Three years after the Activists' protest, I returned to CU for a brief follow-up study. Most of the students I had met in the mid-2000s had graduated, but I showed the Activists' official document to faculty, staff, and administrators who had been on campus three years earlier and asked them whether any of the Activists' demands had been met. Some people were more positive and some more negative in their assessments, but there was general consensus about how the university was moving forward and where it was stalled in its diversity commitments.

One step forward was turnover in the administration. Several senior administrators had retired and been replaced by a white woman, two men of color, and a white man. Faculty, staff, and administrators told me that the new administration was more proactive than the previous one in dealing with diversity. One new administrator was hired specifically to coordinate diversity initiatives on campus. A white male professor who had been at CU for thirty years told me that having even a few people of color in key positions, which CU now had, sent a signal of seriousness about diversity to the rest of the campus.

The faculty had moved forward in some ways but not in others. As Dr. Miller had urged three years earlier, the annual two-day faculty conference was addressing classroom climate and curriculum in more depth than before. And the original Faculty Diversity Group had spawned a spin-off group that was open to staff as well as faculty. A grievance policy (for students with complaints about faculty or others, as well as for all employees with grievances) was now in writing and was more visible to students. The faculty had voted to require that all courses be evaluated by students (tenured professors had previously been exempt from course evaluations). Several new faculty of color had been hired but several had left, indicating that CU had difficulty retaining them. The curriculum diversity requirement had not been revised. CU students could still fulfill that requirement by taking courses in European languages and history. And some people told me that students of color still felt marginalized in the classroom and on campus.

The student newspaper published the Race Column for another year; that ended when those who had initiated the column graduated. Professor Collins, the newspaper's faculty adviser, told me that during a particularly tense race-related incident, the student journalists debated whether to print photos that many on campus felt included racist images. The photos were on the internet and so they were already in the public realm. The question was whether publishing the photos in the student newspaper would inform the campus community about what had happened or would replicate the racism embodied in the images. Professor Collins urged the journalists to consult their peers of color on campus. The journalists did so and followed their peers' advice to print the photos. This shows proactive advising on Professor Collins's part as well as listening on the journalists' part.

The interconnected group continued its collaborative work in many forms, such as the NCORE group, the Race Conference, student advocacy organizations, OMA's and OSA's diversity workshops, interdisciplinary academic programs, the Faculty Diversity Group, and its new spin-off. People in the interconnected group served on the search committees that brought a more proactive administration and more faculty of color to campus.

From my perspective, the main thing that had *not* changed was the general character of CU's narrative environment. Diversity was still out there on the table—contentiously. The discourses of social justice, abstract inclusion, and political difference continued to inform students and others as they engaged in diversity-related debates and dialogue. Race continued to be the most prominent and contentious diversity topic on campus. The student government in particular continued to struggle with racial tension.

I timed my follow-up study so I could observe some events that were part of the university's response to a racial incident that had occurred a few months earlier, an incident that had galvanized the entire campus. A group of white CU students who felt they were engaged in harmless fun had used racial images in a way that some CU students of color and some of their white peers felt was racist.* This is where the student journalists had to decide whether or not to print photos of the images in their article about the situation.

The details of this incident and its implications could be the subject of another book. I will end this book, however, with the university's response to the incident and one particular observation that startled me. What I observed struck me as evidence that—in the midst of all the contentiousness—CU's narrative landscape continued to encourage speaking and listening across differences.

---

*I wish I could be more specific (see appendix A). As anyone who listens to the national news knows, CU is far from alone in continuing to deal with racial incidents.

CU's crisis response group convened immediately after the incident. CU's president held a press conference and promised to treat the situation seriously. An ad hoc committee was formed, including members of the interconnected group. Within two weeks, the committee organized two town hall meetings on campus, one drawing three hundred people, the other, seventy-five. A few days later the Black Collegians sponsored a showing of *Ethnic Notions* (a film about the history of racist images in the United States), and they recruited faculty, students, administrators, and members of the local community to facilitate discussions after the film. The students involved in the incident were disciplined: they were barred from participating in an extracurricular activity for the rest of the semester. And they were required to work with a well-known, well-respected, and well-liked African American mediator in the community who helped them to understand how what they thought was harmless fun could be interpreted as racist and therefore harmful to others, themselves, and the entire campus community.

The ad hoc committee also organized a half-day teach-in, which took place about a month after the incident; four hundred people attended. And they organized a full-day event that took place two months later. The latter included a nationally known keynote speaker, and morning and afternoon workshops on many different diversity topics. Five hundred people attended. The administration did not cancel classes but strongly encouraged faculty to have students attend. Members of the interconnected group did the bulk of organizing and legwork for all of these events, with substantial support from senior administrators. Faculty and administrators told me that the attendance and the conversations that took place during the events marked them as pivotal moments in the life of the university. The energy and resources devoted to transforming the racial incident into multipronged, ongoing occasions for education indicate that the university was moving toward a proactive commitment to diversity.

As I observed the full-day event (and watched a video of the half-day event), I was struck by the prominence of personal narratives in the proceedings. Most striking was that two senior administrators were among those who shared personal narratives to audiences of hundreds of people. I will focus on just one of these. At the beginning of the full-day event, after traditional introductions, Dr. Greg, a new senior administrator who is white, spoke. His job was to set the charge for the day.

At the risk of going autobiographical on you for a moment . . .
I grew up in the Deep South before the end of Jim Crow . . .
Today I keep on my desk a mimeographed sheet of paper—
Two pages actually—
That functions as a reminder for me
[It's] a list of the many people whom I knew
Many of them the fathers of the kids I went to school with

Some of them the fathers of kids I considered my friends
Who were members of or alleged to be members of the KKK
What it has represented for me and still represents
Are the complexities of the issues that we're dealing with today
Of the fact often forgotten that the KKK was—
And I don't mean to make light of it—
An equal opportunity hater
That it directed its hate campaigns of violence against African Americans of course
But against Catholics and Jews as well
So that from the very beginning of my coming to awareness
There was a growing sense, still growing, of what I came to understand eventually
   as otherness
And of the ways in which different people
Sometimes for reasons of race
Sometimes for reasons of ethnicity
Sometimes for reasons of language etcetera
Are put in positions of being other
Of the oppressed
Of the marginalized
In some cases but not always of the hated . . .
I use it as an object to remind me of the struggle that demands of us reflection,
   scrutiny, hard work, collaboration, and dedication.

Dr. Greg begins his speech with a metastatement—"at the risk of going autobiographical on you"—indicating that telling a personal story is not something he usually does in public settings like this. His description of the list of
alleged KKK members as "mimeographed" suggests that the list is decades
old, that it was probably created when he was a child. There are many details missing from this story, such as how he got the list, to whom it was
originally circulated (KKK members and their friends? Those fearful of the
KKK?), and what it meant to his family. Nonetheless, by describing the people on the list as fathers of his childhood classmates and friends, he positions
himself as close to the *perpetrators* of violence. He states that the list reminds
him of how complex the issues are, and particularly of the KKK's equal opportunity hatred, but he does not mention that he is Jewish. He does not
mention that his family could have been among the KKK's targets. Some
people listening to his speech would know that he is Jewish, but some may
not. In either case, in this public setting, he explicitly situates himself as close
to the perpetrators of violence and leaves unstated that he is also close to
their victims.

Dr. Greg's self-positioning evokes a sense of humility and lack of inno-
cence. He presents himself as implicated in social processes that create injustice as well as in social processes that can dismantle injustice. He moves
from his personal statements to a specifically educational stance, which res-

onates with liberal arts discourse. Confronting injustice requires "reflection, scrutiny, hard work, collaboration, and dedication."

When I met with Dr. Greg later, I told him that I had heard his speech at the full-day event. Without prompting from me, he said that it was not typical of him to speak so personally at public events. I commented that CU is the kind of place where people tell stories like that. He said, "Yes it is, and it's important because the issues are not just abstract and theoretical and academic, they are very personal, too."

I already knew from my research at CU three years earlier that personal narratives were central to students' learning to speak and listen across differences. And yet I was startled when I heard Dr. Greg, who was relatively new on campus, using personal narrative in a public setting to address diversity issues, making himself vulnerable in a way he usually didn't and in a way that senior administrators usually don't. I can interpret his speech as shaping narrative reality on that day, as modeling for students in the audience what it means to reflect on and place oneself within diversity dialogue. At the same time, it is equally plausible to interpret his speech as having been shaped by CU's complex narrative reality. A new administrator who is learning how to use personal narrative to speak publicly at CU is one who has been learning by listening to others at CU. Although not a direct effect of the Activists' action, this administrator's speech—his action—may be interpreted as part of their legacy.

# Note to People at CU

I have, of course, changed the name of CU—as well as the names of all of the organizations and individuals I write about. I have also described CU in general—even vague—terms in order to conceal its identity. I have even been imprecise about dates, referring to an academic year "in the mid-2000s" as the time when the Activists' protest took place. These concealments are important, standard, ethical practices in my discipline. Nonetheless, my efforts are not foolproof, and I have no illusions that some industrious sleuth won't be able to uncover CU's identity. Regardless, in my view CU has nothing to hide and actually has much to be proud of.

In several cases I have left out or slightly changed details about people's specific characteristics because including them would have risked revealing them to others *at CU*. There are also several stories I have told in less rather than more detail to protect the identities of those I interviewed. Nonetheless, several people whose accounts I cite in this book will inevitably be recognizable to others at CU because of their positions. I shared with those people the excerpts I used from their interviews as well as what I have written about them. I wanted to make sure that nothing that appeared in this book would make them feel vulnerable if others at CU were to read it. Of those people, one asked me to make a minor change, and I did.

I want to emphasize that this book concentrates on *students'* narrative reality, and so faculty, staff, and administrators' stories are not of foremost importance. They serve as background for my understanding of students' narratives. Like any sociological study, of course, this one ultimately represents *my* understanding of what is significant in the events and accounts discussed here. While my understanding is partial, as any understanding necessarily is, I hope this book offers people at CU helpful ways of thinking about CU's narrative landscape and about how students learn to speak and listen across differences.

Finally, as I state in the preface, I am deeply grateful to everyone at CU who shared their stories and perspectives with me and who made it possible for me to take part in campus activities. This study has been a gift to me.

# Methodological Issues

Here I address methodological issues that I have not discussed in the introduction or elsewhere in the book.

For both the original and follow-up studies, I received approval from my institution's Institutional Review Board, CU's provost, and CU's research administrators. All of the interview material for this study was produced during intensive interviews with me as the researcher and interviewer. I received written informed consent for each interview. I wrote field notes after each interview as well as after each time I observed an event or participated in a program on campus. Individual and group interviews with students lasted between one and two and a half hours. Interviews with faculty, administrators, and staff lasted between thirty minutes and an hour and a half.

Like other narrative researchers, I treat what people told me during interviews as accounts that we "coconstructed," rather than as already formed accounts that the narrator was just waiting to reveal.[1] Coconstruction means that what people told me is shaped in part by my questions and interests, how the narrator chose to take them up at that moment, as well as taken for granted assumptions about what an interview is. In other words, at another time, in a different context, or with a different audience, a narrator might tell a different story. This does not mean that researchers should suspect that narrators are lying. During interviews as well as other interactions, narrators typically hold themselves accountable for the credibility of their stories. Yet we do need to be aware that narrators might include or exclude parts of an experience, or emphasize one experience rather than another, depending on context, audience, and a host of other circumstances such as what is most meaningful or relevant in their lives at that moment.

Keeping this in mind, I noticed that some students offered accounts during a group interview and then talked about the "same" experience somewhat differently during our individual interview. For instance, during my group discussion with the Black Collegians, Rachelle laughed as she told stories about herself as a person who has a real problem with her tendency to speak rashly when she is angry. Her friends laughed boisterously with her, signaling that this is something they knew about her and had talked about before. As she spoke with me individually, however, she didn't laugh about this. Rather, as discussed in chapter 4, she reflected at length about how working on her temperament has improved her ability to speak wisely and effectively about race on campus. Neither her laughter in the group interview nor her seriousness in the individual interview is more "authentic" or "the real story." Rather, the difference shows that Rachelle fashioned her story for different audiences and contexts while maintaining consistency in terms of content.

Misti Sterling transcribed the individual interviews for the study in the mid-2000s. Kathryn MacDonald, another sociology major at my university, transcribed the individual interviews for the follow-up study. I transcribed the group interviews. Once I had full transcripts of all the interviews, I listened to the recordings again and checked the transcripts for accuracy of content and for tone of voice.

Next I imported the interview transcripts into Atlas-ti, a qualitative data analysis software program. After testing an initial set of codes on several interviews, I settled on sixty-eight codes organized around several general themes: self/identity; college transitions/experiences; events/programs/organizations; dialogue/discourse; specific issues; CU's history/structures/policies. I also used Atlas-ti to write extensive memos throughout the transcripts. Then I created a new file within Atlas-ti containing my memos on the students' interviews and another file containing the memos on the faculty, staff, and administrators' interviews. I constructed a new set of codes for these files, focusing on perceptions of CU's strengths and weaknesses in terms of its diversity commitments.

This was my first time using a qualitative analysis software program. In my view, its main value is that it serves as an enormous virtual filing system. As others have pointed out, software programs do not do the analysis for you. Nonetheless, I have returned time and again to my data in Atlas-ti, for example, to quickly find a certain story in an interview; to pull out all of the students' talk about the student government, student newspaper, or silent rally; to pull out all of the students' talk about their voice or the voice of the other; or to pull out all of the memos I wrote about how faculty talked about CU's curriculum. Coding and writing memos on the interviews were extremely time consuming exercises, but well worth the effort. In a project that has taken years to complete, the virtual filing system I created through Atlas-ti served as my memory.

When I got to the point of analyzing specific excerpts from the interviews, I listened again (and again) to the interview tapes. This time, as I explained in the introduction, producing transcripts for close analysis and for presentation in the book was much more than a technical issue.

Here are a few more details about my transcription style. I capitalized the first word of each line simply because it makes the transcripts easier to read. I used punctuation (question marks and exclamation points) only when it helped express tone of voice. Quotation marks show that the speaker is reporting their own or others' direct speech. Ellipses ( . . . ) represent deleted words. Nonlexicals appear in brackets [laugh], as do explanations of deleted material [name of town]. A dash (—) indicates speech broken off or an interruption. Italics show a speaker's emphasis on certain words.

In many cases, I decided that it was not important to include "um's" and repetitive uses of "like," and similar commonplace expressions. When I deleted that material, I did so only because I determined that I did not need it to interpret what and how a speaker was communicating. In some cases, however, I included every sound and word because I deemed them central to a speaker's meanings.

Pseudonyms presented a small dilemma. I heard many students call faculty, staff, and administrators by their first names, but I also heard many students (sometime the same ones) use more formal terms such as "Professor" or "Dr." Of course, how students address faculty and administrators is influenced by context (for example, in or out of the classroom), the individuals' preferences, and the particular relationship between the individuals. For the sake of simplicity, I decided to use last names for faculty, staff, and administrators, and first names for students. I asked everyone to call me by my first name so that's what I used in the transcripts.

Finally, a few words about the Internet, which gave me access to many texts and documents. The downside to this convenient access is that quoting anything that appears online risks revealing CU's identity. So, every time I quoted from a text that is online, I changed the wording slightly so that the quotation could not be easily searched. When I quoted from a text that is not online, I used exact wording.

# APPENDIX C

# Interviewees and Interview Guides

## Group Interviews with Students

Table C.1 lists the twelve CU student organizations with which I conducted group interviews, in the order in which they appear in the book. Table C.1 also lists the names, race, and social class of the students who participated in these interviews. I gathered information about race and class from students' written answers to questions about their backgrounds—they filled out these background surveys at the end of the group interviews. I determined a student's race on the basis of their self-identification and their description of their parents' race. I determined a student's social class on the basis of their parent(s)' or guardian(s)' level of education and occupation. When parents or guardians fit into different class categories, I indicated both, for example, middle class/upper-middle class (mc/umc).

Table C.1 shows that of the forty-eight students I interviewed in the twelve groups, thirty-six are white and twelve are of color. Fifteen are working class; four working/middle class; seventeen middle class; seven middle/upper-middle class; four upper-middle class. (I do not have Sheree's class background.) Thirty-four are women; fourteen men. Not shown in table C.1: four explicitly identify themselves as GLBT, and one has a visible physical disability.

## Individual Interviews with Students

At the end of the group interviews, I asked for volunteers for individual interviews. Table C.2 lists the twenty-five students I interviewed individually, their race, class, and the student organizations they were active in at CU. I use acronyms in table C.2 for organizations that appear in table C.1. The list

**Table C.1.** Group interviews with students

| Student group | Name | Race | Class |
|---|---|---|---|
| Southeast Asian Association (SAA) | Kia | Hmong American | wc |
| | May | Southeast Asian American | wc |
| White Students Resisting Racism (WSRR) | Melanie | White | mc |
| | Mark | White | mc |
| | Sarah | White | umc |
| | Kate | White | mc/umc |
| Students for Firearm Safety & Recreation (SRSR) | Jackson | White | wc |
| | Mason | White | mc |
| | Kane | White | mc |
| Conservative Students (CS) | Olivia | White | mc/umc |
| | Evan | White | wc |
| | Jeremy | White | wc |
| | Dan | White | mc/umc |
| Black Collegians (BC) | Marshan | African American | mc |
| | Rachelle | African American | wc |
| | Tanya | African American | wc |
| | Krystal | African American | wc |
| | Dorie | African American | wc |
| | Sheree | African American | not available |
| Women's Coalition (WC) | Hannah | White | mc/umc |
| | Felicia | White | wc/mc |
| | Camille | White | mc |
| GLBT Student Organization (GLBT Org) | Nathan | White | wc |
| | Rose | White | mc |
| | Sydney | White | mc/umc |
| Students for Disability Rights (SDR) | Madison | White | mc |
| | Lily | White | mc |
| | Charlotte | White | wc/mc |
| | Natalie | White | mc |
| Student Government Representatives | Ramita | South Asian (international) | umc |
| | Julia | White | mc |
| | Asha | South Asian American | mc/umc |
| Student Journalists | Nick | White | mc |
| | Phil | White | wc |
| | Grace | White | wc |
| | Ruby | White | wc |
| | Jessie | White | mc |
| | Ella | White | wc/mc |
| Alan's Floor (Residence Hall) | Alan | White | mc |
| | Raul | Latino (international) | umc |
| | Greg | White | umc |
| | Lewis | White | mc |
| | Ashley | White | wc |
| | Gail | White | wc/mc |
| Chelsea's Floor (Residence Hall) | Lena | White | wc |
| | Nora | South Asian American | mc/umc |
| | Beth | White | mc |
| | Tess | White | mc |

is in alphabetical order by students' names. Two of these students (Connie, Steven) did not participate in group interviews.

Table C.2 shows that of the twenty-five students I interviewed individually, seventeen are white and eight are of color. Six are working class; two working/middle class; ten middle class; four middle/upper-middle class; and three upper-middle class. Sixteen are women; nine men. Not shown in table C.2: four identify as GLBT, and one has a visible physical disability.

## Interviews with Administrators, Staff, and Faculty

I conducted twelve interviews with administrators, staff, and faculty. Two of these were group interviews, so the total number interviewed is sixteen. Table C.3 shows that thirteen are white, three of color; five are women, eleven men. Not shown in table C.3: three are out on campus as gay or lesbian.

## Follow-Up Study

When I returned to CU three years later, I reinterviewed seven people whom I had interviewed for the original study. Their names are starred (*) in table C.3. I also interviewed three recently hired senior administrators (an Asian American man, a Latino, and a white man); a student affairs administrator (an African American woman), and five students (a Hmong American woman, a Southeast Asian American woman, a white woman, and two white men). I gathered documents related to the racial incident described in the epilogue, and I observed and participated in several events on campus that were organized as educational responses to that incident.

## Interview Guides

As the name suggests, my interview questions served as *guides*. The interview excerpts throughout the book show that I asked many questions that are not on the interview guides, questions that prompted for clarification, thoughts, feelings, or for fuller stories about a group's activities, specific events on campus, or about an individual's experiences. Although I, as the researcher, set the overall agenda for the interviews, my aim was to invite the group or the individual to construct accounts as fully as possible.[2] During the group interviews with students, after getting the interview off the ground, I tried to step back and listen to how they conversed about the issues among themselves. This strategy worked quite well, I believe, because each group of students already knew each other well and was accustomed to conversing together during their regular activities. By the time I interviewed students in-

**Table C.2.** Individual student interviews

| Name | Race | Class | Student groups and activities |
| --- | --- | --- | --- |
| Alan | White | mc | NCORE group, WSRR, Community Commitment, GLBT Org, Theatre Student Organization |
| Asha | South Asian American | mc/umc | Student Government, Activists, Asian Student Organization, NCORE group, Student Orientation Team |
| Camille | White | mc | Women's Coalition, Feminist Majority Leadership Alliance, Student Dance Group, Amnesty International |
| Connie | White | wc | WSRR, NCORE group, Activists, Office of Service Learning, Community Commitment |
| Evan | White | wc | Conservative Students |
| Felicia | White | wc/mc | Student Government, Women's Coalition |
| Hannah | White | mc/umc | Feminist Majority Leadership Alliance, Women's Coalition |
| Jeremy | White | wc | Conservative Students, Theatre Student Organization |
| Julia | White | mc | Student Government, CU Student Leaders |
| Kane | White | mc | SFSR, Resident Adviser |
| Kia | Hmong American | wc | SAA, Activists, Student Government, Multicultural Student Group, Committee on Campus Life |
| Madison | White | mc | SDR, Residence Hall Association |
| Mark | White | mc | WSRR, Activists, Students for Peace, Community Commitment, Student Government |
| Marshan | African American | mc | BC, Activists, Multicultural Student Group |
| Mason | White | mc | SFSR, Student Government |
| Melanie | White | mc | WSRR, Activists, Habitat for Humanity, Community Commitment |
| Nathan | White | wc | GLBT Org, Forensic Science Student Organization, Student Government |
| Nora | South Asian American | mc/umc | Asian Student Organization, Student Dance Group, Inter-Greek Council, Habitat for Humanity |
| Rachelle | African American | wc | BC, Activists, Multicultural Student Group |
| Ramita | South Asian (international) | umc | Student Government, SDR, Asian Student Organization |
| Raul | Latino (international) | umc | International Student Organization |
| Rose | White | mc | GLBT Org, Inter-Greek Council, Feminist Majority Leadership Alliance, Women's Coalition |
| Sarah | White | umc | WSRR, Activists, Feminist Majority Leadership Alliance, Students for Peace |
| Steven | South Asian American | wc/mc | Asian Student Organization, Activists, Multicultural Student Organization, Student Government, NCORE group |
| Sydney | White | mc/umc | GLBT Org, Asian Student Organization, Residence Hall Association |

**Table C.3.** Interviews with administrators, staff, and faculty

| Administrators | Position | Race and gender |
|---|---|---|
| Dr. Miller | Senior-level Administrator | White man |
| Mr. Davis* | Senior-level Administrator | White man |
| Mr. Robert* | Director of Multicultural Affairs | African American man |
| Mr. Perez | Student Affairs Administrator | Latino |
| Mr. Jay* (interviewed with Mr. Perez) | Student Affairs Administrator | White man |

| Faculty | Academic area | Race and gender |
|---|---|---|
| Prof Jones* | Humanities | White man |
| Prof Wilson* | Social Sciences | White man |
| Prof Rowe | Humanities | White man |
| Prof Green | Sciences | White man |
| Prof Hall | Sciences | White woman |
| Prof Moore* | Social Sciences | White woman |
| Prof Collins* | Humanities | White man |

| Faculty Diversity Group (group interview) | Academic area | Race and gender |
|---|---|---|
| Prof Garcia | Social Sciences | Latino |
| Prof Young | Humanities | White woman |
| Prof Turner | Social Sciences | White woman |
| Prof Kelly | Humanities | White woman |

*Reinterviewed during follow-up study

dividually, we had already met each other in the context of a group interview, and they had already provided me with written information about their hometowns, high schools, family background, and campus activities, among other things. During the individual interviews, the interview guide again provided a general structure. Yet my aim was to follow their lead and invite them to develop stories as they identified important learning experiences and transitions they have gone through during college.

### Interview Guide for Group Discussions with Student Organizations

1. What are the major issues/activities that your organization has been involved with this year?

2. Does your organization get support for its activities from regional or national-level organizations?

3. How, if at all, is your organization involved in diversity issues? What kinds of diversity issues have you been dealing with this year?

4. What does "diversity" mean at CU?

5. Who are the major players on campus when it comes to diversity? Which students/student groups are involved in these issues? How involved are faculty, staff, administrators?

6. Does productive dialogue about diversity take place on campus? Examples?

7. Which diversity issues have produced the most contention among students this year? How have the conflicts been resolved? Productively? If yes, what worked? If not, what didn't work?

8. Which of CU's diversity-related programs are most interesting/useful/successful? Which are less interesting/useful/successful?

9. How does CU's curriculum address diversity? Which majors/courses do you feel do a good job addressing diversity? Are there any that do not do a good job?

10. What is your perspective on CU's policies related to diversity?

11. Is there anything that you wish were done differently on campus when it comes to diversity?

### Interview Guide for Group Discussions with Students in the Residence Halls

1. What are the big issues (concerns, controversies, etc.) that students in this residence hall are talking about these days?

2. What diversity issues have come up this year for students in this residence hall?

3. [Starting with "What does 'diversity' mean at CU?" the questions are the same as those for group discussions with student organizations.]

### Interview Guide for Individual Students

1. Tell me about your high school years. What were your interests then? Who were your friends? What kind of a student were you? What were your extracurricular activities? Who was most influential in your life at that point?

2. Why did you choose CU? Or, how did you end up at CU?

3. What kinds of transitions did you go through during your first semester and first year at CU?

4. What kinds of transitions have you gone through since your first year here?

5. What have been your most positive learning experiences during your college years?

6. Who has been most influential in your life during your college years?

7. What is your perspective on diversity issues at CU?

8. How did you develop your ideas about diversity? Who or what has been most influential in shaping your ideas about diversity?

9. Can you tell me about a conversation or interaction that was important to you in terms of your understanding of diversity?

10. Do you have friends who are "different" from you in important ways? What do those friendships mean to you? Has that "difference" been a topic in your friendship?

11. In what contexts do you feel you have had the most involvement in— or learned the most about—diversity issues? Classroom? Residence hall? Student organization? CU program or event? Extracurricular activities? Other?

12. [If involved in student organizations] What has your involvement in _____ organization(s) meant to you?

### Interview Guide for Administrators, Staff, and Faculty

1. Your position is _____ here at CU. How long have you been here? In what positions?

2. [For long-term administrators/staff/faculty] Can you take me through changes that [your office/department] has gone through during your time here in terms of diversity issues? For example, policies, programs, priorities, professional development.

3. What do you think CU's strengths are in terms of diversity-related efforts? In what areas do you think CU is achieving its diversity-related goals? If applicable, same question for your office.

4. What does "diversity" mean at CU?

5. In your experience, does productive dialogue about diversity take place on campus? If so, can you give me an example? If not, why do you think it doesn't happen?

6. In recent years, which diversity issues have been most contentious among students? How has conflict been resolved?

7. Can you give me an example of a diversity-related event, policy, or program or aspect of the curriculum that you feel has been particularly successful? What about it works (worked) well?

8. In what areas do you think CU (or your office/department) could do a better job in terms of diversity-related efforts?

9. Can you give me an example of an event, policy, program, or some aspect of the curriculum that you feel has not been particularly successful? What about it doesn't (didn't) work well?

10. Which groups of students do you think are best served by CU's diversity-related efforts?

11. Which groups of students do you think are not well served by CU's diversity-related efforts?

12. Which groups have been the major players on campus in terms of initiating, debating, and resisting diversity-related policies, programs, curriculum, etc.? Students? Alumni? Faculty? Staff? Administrators? Others?

13. What is the level of involvement on the part of the student body as a whole? Are there groups of students who are especially involved? And are there groups who are not engaged at all in diversity-related events, discussions, debates?

14. What is the level of involvement on the part of the faculty as a whole? Are there groups of faculty who are especially involved? Are there groups who are not engaged at all in diversity-related events, discussions, debates, etc.? What about staff? Administrators?

15. From your perspective, what do you think the overall purpose or goal or value of CU's commitment to diversity-related programs/policies/curricula *should* be?

# Detailed Tables and Methods of Content Analysis

Table D.1 is a detailed version of table 3.1 (which appears in chapter 3). Table D.1 shows the three most prominent diversity categories in CU's student newspaper, events calendar, curriculum, and student government minutes. For example, race is the most prominent category in CU's student newspaper: 10.1 percent of all articles published during two years in the mid-2000s included explicit content about race, an average of 2.8 articles per issue of the newspaper. "Articles" includes regular articles, editorials, opinion pieces, and letters.

Table D.2 is a detailed version of table 3.2 (which also appears in chapter 3). Table D.2 shows the three most prominent diversity categories in RU's student newspaper, events calendar, curriculum, and student government minutes. For example, gender is the most prominent category in RU's student newspaper: 5.9 percent of all articles published during two years in the mid-2000s included explicit content about gender, an average of 1.3 articles per issue of the newspaper.

## Methods of Content Analysis

Jessie Finch and Misti Sterling assisted me with the quantitative content analyses of CU and RU's student newspapers, student government minutes, events calendars, curricula, and web sites. We had hard copies of the newspaper and accessed the other texts and documents online. We analyzed every issue of the student newspaper for two academic years in the mid-2000s; every set of monthly minutes for the student government for three years; every monthly calendar for two years; every class in the course schedule for three years; and the web sites during one two-week period. We coded these texts and documents for race/ethnicity, social class, gender, sexual orienta-

**Table D.1.**  Most prominent categories in CU's documents (detailed version of table 3.1)

| | Student newspaper | Events calendar | Curriculum | Student government minutes |
|---|---|---|---|---|
| Most prominent diversity category | Race | Race | Global | Race |
| Percent of all articles, events, or courses that include the most prominent diversity category | 10.1% | 17.9% | 11.3% | |
| Average number of articles per newspaper issue, events per month, or courses per year that include the most prominent diversity category | 2.8 articles/issue | 7.0 events/month | 92 courses/year | 2.04 = average number of times per meeting that race gets raised |
| Second most prominent diversity category | Gender | Global | Gender | General |
| Percent of all articles, events, or courses that include the second most prominent diversity category | 8.1% | 16.2% | 3.7% | |
| Average number of articles per newspaper issue, events per month, or courses per year that include the second most prominent diversity category | 2.3 articles/issue | 6.3 events/month | 30 courses/year | 1.06 = average number of times per meeting that diversity in general gets raised |
| Third most prominent diversity category | Sexual orientation | Religion | General and race (tie) | Global |
| Percent of all articles, events, or courses that include the third most prominent diversity category | 5.6% | 9.7% | 3.4% and 3.4% | |
| Average number of articles per newspaper issue, events per month, or courses per year that include the third most prominent diversity category | 1.5 articles/issue | 3.8 events/month | 28 courses/year (General) 27 courses/year (Race) | 0.96 = average number of times per meeting that global gets raised |

**Table D.2.**  Most prominent categories in RU's documents (detailed version of table 3.2)

| | Student newspaper | Events calendar | Curriculum | Student government minutes |
|---|---|---|---|---|
| Most prominent diversity category | Gender | Global | Global | Race |
| Percent of all articles, events, or courses that include the most prominent diversity category | 5.9% | 12.6% | 5.1% | |
| Average number of articles per newspaper issue, events per month, or courses per year that include the most prominent diversity category | 1.3 articles/issue | 3.6 events/month | 45 courses/year | 0.75 = average number of times per meeting that race gets raised |
| Second most prominent diversity category | Global | Gender | Gender | General and global (tie) |
| Percent of all articles, events, or courses that include the second most prominent diversity category | 3.6% | 8.3% | 2.7% | |
| Average number of articles per newspaper issue, events per month, or courses per year that include the second most prominent diversity category | 0.8 articles/issue | 2.4 events/month | 23 courses/year | 0.44 = average number of times per meeting that gender and global get raised |
| Third most prominent diversity category | Sexual orientation | Race | Race | Class |
| Percent of all articles, events, or courses that include the third most prominent diversity category | 3.5% | 4.5% | 2.1% | |
| Average number of articles per newspaper issue, events per month, or courses per year that include the third most prominent diversity category | 0.8 articles/issue | 1.3 events/month | 19 courses/year | 0.31 = average number of times per meeting that class gets raised |

tion, disability, religion, global/international, and general. We coded for these diversity categories when a newspaper article, a speaker's talk in the student government minutes, an event listed on the calendar, a course title (and/or course description) listed in the schedule of courses, or statements on the web page included "explicit diversity content." Any item could receive more than one code (for example, race and gender). We defined "explicit diversity content" as a focus on any of the following:

- Groups—or individuals that belong to groups—that historically have been underrepresented in the local context or in the broader society, where the idea is that their perspectives need to be heard or their experiences or contributions need to be visible or attended to. These groups include: people of color, working-class or poor people; girls or women; people who are gay, lesbian, bisexual, or transgender; people with disabilities; non-Christians; people from non-Western or non-European countries.
- Organizations specifically for individuals or groups mentioned above, and/or the activities and needs of these organizations, for example, Amnesty International (global); Habitat for Humanity (class); Black Collegians (race).
- The demographic composition of the university's student body, faculty, staff, or administrators by race, gender, class, sexual orientation, ability, religion, or national origin.
- Problems faced by these individuals or groups, including (but not limited to): discrimination, profiling, assault, harassment, hate crimes, accessibility, barriers to religious practice, immigration, lack of or unequal access to resources.
- Racism, classism, sexism, heterosexism, ableism, or religious intolerance.
- Programs, departments, majors, minors, certificates, or curricula related to groups or issues mentioned above, for example, women's studies (gender) or study abroad in non-Western countries (global).
- Policies concerning individuals, groups, issues, or organizations mentioned above.
- Dominant groups (whites, men, middle/upper-class people, heterosexuals, able-bodied people, Christians, Westerners,) if the text is explicitly about their privilege or about their need to attend to the voices of subordinate groups.

The content analyses involved careful decisions about innumerable details. A few examples: whether to count and code ads and photo essays in the students newspapers (ads, no; photo essays, yes, if they were clearly distinct from other articles); what to count as an instance of speech in the student government minutes (a speaker's turn at speech, no matter how short or long); how to count events on the monthly calendar that appeared daily, such as an art exhibit that lasted a month (counted as once, not thirty times a month, which would have exaggerated its presence on campus); whether to count labs, independent studies, instrumental music, and sports courses (no); how far to peruse the web sites (two clicks in every direction from the homepage, and then up to six clicks when diversity-related material continued to show up in a particular direction).

Because of space constraints, I cannot include here all of the decisions that guided the content analyses. I would be happy to discuss them with researchers who are interested in doing similar content analyses of documents and texts at other universities.

As reported in chapter 3, I also did qualitative content analyses of CU's student newspaper and student government minutes. These cover only the academic year in the mid-2000s during which I did the interviews. I pulled out all of the newspaper items that had been coded for explicit diversity content. As I reread these articles, letters, and opinion pieces, I noticed which issues and events got the most play, which ones were the most contentious, the range of views and perspectives expressed about them, and the tone of each item (neutral reporting, argumentative, educational). I did the same with the student government talk that had been coded for explicit diversity content. I am lucky that CU's student government minutes for that year are extensive. Of course the minutes are already an interpretation of "what happened and what got said," but they proved to be a goldmine nonetheless. As the excerpts in chapters 2 and 3 show, the minute-taker seemed to be trying to take verbatim notes of everything that was said. While the extensiveness of those minutes gave me exceptionally strong *qualitative* data, it did not skew the *quantitative* results. Whether a speaker's talk took up one line or a full page, it was treated as one speech.

# Notes

## Introduction

1. Adia Harvey Wingfield, "The Modern Mammy and the Angry Black Man: African American Professionals' Experiences with Gendered Racism in the Workplace," *Race, Class, and Gender* 14 (2007): 196–212; Kristen Myers, *Racetalk: Racism Hiding in Plain Sight* (Lanham, MD: Rowman and Littlefield, 2005); Sara Ahmed, "Embodying Diversity: Problems and Paradoxes for Black Feminists," *Race, Ethnicity, and Education* 12 (2009): 41–52; Tiffany Taylor, "Anger Privilege: Deconstructing the Controlling Image of the 'Angry Black Woman,'" Paper presented at the meetings of the American Sociological Association, 2004.

2. Patricia Hill Collins, *Black Sexual Politics: African Americans, Gender, and the New Racism* (New York: Routledge, 2004), 350.

3. Mark Chesler, Amanda Lewis, and James Crowfoot, *Challenging Racism in Higher Education: Promoting Justice* (Lanham, MD: Rowman and Littlefield, 2005); Julia Lesage, Abby L. Ferber, Debbie Storrs, and Donna Wong, *Making a Difference: University Students of Color Speak Out* (Lanham, MD: Rowman and Littlefield, 2002); Joe R. Feagin, Hernan Vera, and Nikitah Imani, *The Agony of Education: Black Students at White Colleges and Universities* (New York: Routledge, 1996); William G. Bowen and Derek Bok, *The Shape of the River: Long-term Consequences of Considering Race in College and University Admissions* (Princeton, NJ: Princeton University Press, 2000); Eduardo Bonilla-Silva, *Racism without Racists: Color-Blind Racism and the Persistence of Racial Inequality in the United States* (Lanham, MD: Rowman and Littlefield, 2003); Sarah Susannah Willie, *Acting Black: College, Identity, and the Performance of Race* (New York: Routledge, 2003); Ruth Sidel, *Battling Bias: The Struggle for Identity and Community on College Campuses* (New York: Viking, 1994).

4. These theoretical traditions include ethnomethodology, symbolic interaction, and social constructionism. See Peter L. Berger and Thomas Luckmann, *The Social Construction of Reality: A Treatise on the Sociology of Knowledge* (New York: Anchor, 1967); Darin Weinberg, "The Philosophical Foundations of Constructionist Research," in *Handbook of Constructionist Research*, ed. James A. Holstein and Jaber F. Gubrium (New York: Guilford, 2008), 13–39; Joel Best, "Historical Development and Defining Issues of Constructionist Inquiry," in *Handbook of Constructionist Research*, 41–64; Alan Blum and Peter McHugh, *Self-Reflection in the Arts and Sciences* (Atlantic Highlands, NJ: Humanities Press, 1984); Harold Garfinkel, *Studies in Ethnomethodology* (Englewood Cliffs, NJ: Prentice Hall, 1967); Hans-Georg Gadamer, *Truth and Method* (New York: Seabury Press, 1975); Kenneth Burke, *Language as Symbolic Action: Essays on Life, Literature, and Method* (Berkeley: University of California Press, 1966); and C. Wright Mills, "Situated Actions and Vocabularies of Motive," *American Sociological Review* 5 (1940): 904–13.

5. Jaber F. Gubrium and James A. Holstein, *Analyzing Narrative Reality* (Thousand Oaks, CA: Sage, 2009). Gubrium and Holstein also developed the other concepts I describe here: "narrative practice," "narrative environment," and the "reflexive interplay" between them. For different takes on narrative inquiry (which have also influenced my work), see Catherine Kohler Riessman, *Narrative Methods for the Human Sciences* (Thousand Oaks, CA: Sage, 2008); Mary Jo Maynes, Jennifer L. Pierce, and Barbara Laslett, *Telling Stories: The Use of Personal Narratives in the Social Sciences and History* (Ithaca: Cornell University Press, 2008); D. Jean Clandinin, ed., *Handbook of Narrative Inquiry: Mapping a Methodology* (Thousand Oaks, CA: Sage, 2007); and Dan P. McAdams, Ruthellen Josselson, and Amia Lieblich, eds., *Identity and Story: Creating Self in Narrative* (Washington, DC: American Psychological Association, 2006).

6. Gubrium and Holstein, *Analyzing Narrative Reality,* xviii.

7. Alfred Schutz, *Collected Papers I: The Problem of Social Reality,* edited and introduced by Maurice Natanson (The Hague: Martinus Nijhoff, 1967); Garfinkel, *Studies in Ethnomethodology;* Peter McHugh, *Defining the Situation: The Organization of Meaning in Social Interaction* (New York: Bobbs-Merrill, 1968).

8. For example, silent protests were used by women suffragists during the early 1900s and by civil rights activists during the 1960s. Silence is currently used to protest violence against GLBT people during the annual National Day of Silence. Students on campuses across the United States and activists across the globe use silence to bring attention to their causes.

9. Bonilla-Silva, *Racism without Racists;* Myers, *Racetalk;* Melanie E. L. Bush, *Breaking the Code of Good Intentions: Everyday Forms of Whiteness* (Lanham, MD: Rowman and Littlefield, 2004); Barbara Trepagnier, *Silent Racism: How Well-Meaning White People Perpetuate the Racial Divide* (Boulder, CO: Paradigm, 2006); Harry van den Berg, Margaret Wetherell, and Hanneke Houtkoop-Steenstra, eds., *Analyzing Race Talk: Multidisciplinary Perspectives on the Research Interview* (New York: Cambridge University Press, 2003); Karyn D. McKinney, *Being White: Stories of Race and Racism* (New York: Routledge, 2005).

10. Some research on racial discourses does attend to local contexts, for example, Leslie Houts Picca and Joe R. Feagin, *Two-Faced Racism: Whites in the Backstage and Frontstage* (New York: Routledge, 2007).

11. See Mitch Berbrier, "The Diverse Construction of Race and Ethnicity," in *Handbook of Constructionist Research,* 567–91.

12. For example, the European Union designated 2008 the European Year of Intercultural Dialogue (http://ec.europa.eu/culture/portal/action/dialogue/dial_en.htm).

13. Susan E. Bell uses the same phrase, "Turning Talk into Text," to describe how she created transcripts for *DES Daughters: Embodied Knowledge and the Transformation of Women's Health Politics* (Philadelphia: Temple University Press, 2009).

14. Riessman, *Narrative Methods.* See also, Elliot G. Mishler, "Representing Discourse: The Rhetoric of Transcription," *Journal of Narrative and Life History* 1 (1991): 255–80; and James Paul Gee, "A Linguistic Approach to Narrative," *Journal of Narrative and Life History* 1 (1991): 15–39.

15. Mishler, "Representing Discourse," and Riessman, *Narrative Methods,* 50.

16. Other studies that use line breaks in this way include Bell, *DES Daughters;* Riessman, *Narrative Methods;* Elliot G. Mishler, *Storylines: Craftartists' Narratives of Identity* (Cambridge: Harvard University Press, 1999); Catherine Kohler Riessman, *Divorce Talk: Women and Men Make Sense of Personal Relationships* (New Brunswick, NJ: Rutgers University Press, 1990); and Susan E. Chase, *Ambiguous Empowerment: The Work Narratives of Women School Superintendents* (Amherst: University of Massachusetts Press, 1995).

17. Richard Buttny, *Talking Problems: Studies of Discursive Construction* (Albany: State University of New York Press, 2004), 119.

## Chapter 1. Diversity at City University

1. Robert A. Rhoads compares student activism in the 1960s and 1990s, in *Freedom's Web: Student Activism in an Age of Cultural Diversity* (Baltimore: The Johns Hopkins University Press, 1998).

2. To my knowledge, institutional theorists in sociology have not explored in any depth the institutionalization of diversity in higher education. Nonetheless, as I read the literature about the history of diversity in higher education, it struck me that the general direction of change described (toward greater diversity and equity) could be understood through the concept of institutionalization. Institutional theorists argue that despite "enormous variation in social, cultural, and economic conditions within countries and (even more) across the world," colleges and universities are "remarkably similar around the world, and increasingly so over time" (John W. Meyer et al., "Higher Education as an Institution," in *Sociology of Higher Education: Contributions and Their Contexts,* ed. Patricia J. Gumport [Baltimore: The Johns Hopkins University Press, 2007], 193). Such similarities include universities' claims to cosmopolitanism; patterns of expansion and enrollment growth, especially since World War II; types of degrees and credentials conferred; systems for accrediting and ranking universities; the meaning of "student" and "professor"; and the curriculum. Meyer et al. explain these and other similarities in terms of the nature of the university as an institution: the university has been the central cultural institution in Western societies for centuries and more recently in non-Western societies as well. More so than other structures, the university operates according to "cultural scripts and organizational rules built into the wider national and world environments" (Ibid., 190–91, quote on 188). Furthermore, during the second-half of the twentieth century, the worldwide cultural script of optimism and progress generated the idea that higher education is an individual and collective good. The more education the better, for both individuals and societies: more education for the individual and the collective will lead to social progress and more just societies (Ibid., 202).

Together these concepts led me to speculate that an important similarity across predominantly white universities in the United States is the institutionalization of attention to diversity. If for no other reason than getting reaccredited or avoiding lawsuits, predominantly white universities must, at the very least, develop an institutional narrative of commitment to diversity.

3. In 1973, U.S. students of color composed less than 10% of all undergraduates. By 1980, they composed 17% (Anthony Lising Antonio and Marcela M. Muñiz, "The Sociology of Diversity," in *Sociology of Higher Education,* 266). By 1993, they composed 23%, and in 2003, 29% (Bryan J. Cook and Diana I. Córdova, *Minorities in Higher Education: Twenty-second Annual Status Report* [Washington, DC: American Council on Education, 2006], table 7, p. 46). These figures include undergraduates in all types of institutions—public, private not-for-profit, private for-profit, two-year, four-year, predominantly white institutions, Historically Black Colleges and Universities, and so on. In 1993–1994, students of color earned 16.4% of bachelor's degrees and in 2003–2004, 22% (Ibid., table 15, in the Errata Section). Despite these significant increases, African American and Hispanic people age 18 to 24 who have high school degrees are still less likely than their white peers to be enrolled in college; they are more likely than white students to be enrolled at two-year institutions than at four-year institutions; they appear even less among "high achieving" undergraduates at selective colleges and universities; and they have lower retention rates than white students (Ibid., figure 2, p. 3; table 4, p. 43; figure 5b, p. 14; and L. Scott Miller, Mehmet Dali Ozturk, and Lisa Chavez, "Increasing African American, Latino, and Native American Representation among High Achieving Undergraduates at Selective Colleges and Universities," UC Berkeley: Institute for the Study of Social Change. September 1, 2005. http://escholarship.org/uc/item/10s3p1xt).

4. In the United States, full-time faculty of color increased from 11.9% in 1993 to 15.6% in 2003, but Asian American faculty experienced a greater increase than other racial-ethnic groups. Over that decade, Asian American faculty increased from 4.6% to 6.6%, African American faculty from 4.7% to 5.3%; Hispanic faculty from 2.2% to 3.2%, and American Indian faculty from 0.4% to 0.5% (Cook and Córdova, *Minorities,* table 26, p. 79). A closer look shows that faculty of color have greater representation at the lower ranks (Ibid., table 27, pp. 80–81). Many factors affect the low representation of people of color among faculty, including low rates among people earning Ph.D.'s (in 2004, 14.4% of Ph.D. degrees were earned by people of color [Ibid., table 18, in Errata section]); low tenure rates among faculty of color; individual and institutional racism embedded in recruitment and promotion processes; and unwelcoming departmental climates (Antonio and Muñiz, "The Sociology of Diversity," 281). See also Caroline Sotello Viernes Turner and Samuel L. Myers Jr., *Faculty of Color in Academe:*

*Bittersweet Success* (Boston: Allyn and Bacon, 2000), and JoAnn Moody, *Faculty Diversity: Problems and Solutions* (New York: RoutlegeFalmer, 2004).

5. For legal history regarding affirmative action in admissions in higher education, see Chesler et al., *Challenging Racism,* 42–46. Regarding gender discrimination, see Susan Ware, *Title IX: A Brief History with Documents* (Boston: Bedford/St. Martins, 2007).

6. The first African American studies program was created in 1968; about 120 institutions now offer degrees in African American studies and another 100 offer a minor or certificate (Fabio Rojas, "Social Movement Tactics, Organizational Change, and the Spread of African American Studies," *Social Forces* 84 [2006], 2151). See also Susan Olzak and Nicole Kangas, "Ethnic, Women's, and African American Studies Majors in U.S. Institutions of Higher Education," *Sociology of Education* 81 (2008), 163–88. The first women's and gender studies programs were created around 1970; there are now about 650 programs and about 44% of them offer an undergraduate major (*A National Census of Women's and Gender Studies Programs in U.S. Institutions of Higher Education,* December 26, 2007, 3, 11. http://www.nwsa.org/research/programadmin/database/downloads/NWSA_Data_Report_08.pdf). Six universities offer a major in LGBTQ studies with numerous others offering minors or certificates (http://people.ku.edu/~jyounger/lgbtqprogs.html).

7. Clarence G. Williams, "The MIT Experience: Personal Perspectives on Race in a Predominantly White University," in *What Makes Racial Diversity Work in Higher Education: Academic Leaders Present Successful Policies and Strategies,* ed. Frank W. Hale Jr. (Sterling, VA: Stylus, 2004), 88.

8. Chesler et al., *Challenging Racism,* 269.

9. The historical material and institutional descriptions in this section are drawn from several sources I cannot cite because doing so would reveal CU's identity. I also draw on information I gathered from faculty and administrators who had been at the university for thirty years. I describe dates and academic programs in general terms as another way of protecting CU's identity.

10. Donna Wong describes similar attempts to alter a multicultural curriculum requirement at the University of Oregon ("A Historical Look at Students of Color at the University of Oregon," in *Making a Difference,* 145–47).

11. Williams, "The MIT Experience," 92.

12. Other institutions have similar residential options. The University of Oregon, for example, offers a multicultural dormitory (Lesage et al., *Making a Difference*).

13. Gubrium and Holstein, *Analyzing Narrative Reality,* xvii.

14. Ibid., 173.

15. Martha C. Nussbaum, *Cultivating Humanity: A Classical Defense of Reform in Liberal Education* (Cambridge: Harvard University Press, 1997).

16. Ronald L. Jepperson and Ann Swidler, "What Properties of Culture Should We Measure?" *Poetics* 22 (1994): 359–71.

17. Gubrium and Holstein, *Analyzing Narrative Reality;* Riessman, *Narrative Methods.*

18. Meyer et al., "Higher Education as an Institution," 208.

19. Gubrium and Holstein, *Analyzing Narrative Reality,* 173.

20. In his discussion of Frank Donoghue's book, *The Last Professors: The Corporate University and the Fate of the Humanities* (Bronx, NY: Fordham University Press, 2008), Stanley Fish presents Donoghue's conclusion that current conditions in higher education strongly discourage the ethic of the liberal arts—inquiry for its own sake. Instead higher education has become dominated by marketplace ideas, both in its attempt to give students marketable skills and the pressure universities face to reduce costs by hiring adjuncts (Fish, "The Last Professor," *New York Times* blog, January 18, 2009 [http://fish.blogs.nytimes.com/2009/01/18/the-last-professor/]).

21. Gubrium and Holstein, *Analyzing Narrative Reality,* 173.

22. Ibid., 124, and chapter 14. Margaret Wetherell uses the term "big discourse" in the same way, in "Racism and the Analysis of Cultural Resources in Interviews," in *Analyzing Race Talk,* 12.

## Chapter 2. Conflicting Discourses

1. That lunch table also included a white male philosophy professor, a white male student who was president of CU's Conservative Students, and a Native American woman who was a student government representative.

2. As Wetherell states, "Interviews [and other forms of discourse] tell us about the cultural resources people have available for telling their patch of the world. . . . Such resources are both independent of local talk in a limited sense and need to be continually instantiated through that talk" ("Racism and the Analysis of Cultural Resources," 13).

3. Paula S. Rothenberg, ed., *White Privilege: Essential Readings on the Other Side of Racism* (New York: Worth, 2002).

4. Jo Freeman and Victoria Johnson, eds., *Waves of Protest: Social Movements Since the Sixties* (Lanham, MD: Rowman and Littlefield, 1999).

5. Gubrium and Holstein use the term *intertextuality* to describe this intermingling of resources from different narrative environments (*Analyzing Narrative Reality,* chapter 15).

6. I took these descriptions of the Institutes at the 2008 White Privilege Conference from an e-mail Abby Ferber circulated to Sociologists for Women in Society. Jorge Zellabos, Robin Parker, and Pamela Smith Chambers led the first Institute and Frances Kendall led the second one. I assume the Institute leaders wrote the descriptions. For information about the annual White Privilege Conference, see http://www.uccs.edu/~wpc/.

7. Frances E. Kendall, *Understanding White Privilege: Creating Pathways to Authentic Relationships across Race* (New York: Routledge, 2006), 41.

8. Nussbaum, *Cultivating Humanity,* 10.

9. Ibid., 10–11.

10. Chesler et al., *Challenging Racism,* 14–15.

11. Bonilla-Silva, *Racism without Racists,* 15. See also, Michael K. Brown et al., *Whitewashing Race: The Myth of a Color-blind Society* (Berkeley: University of California Press, 2005); and Ashley W. Doane and Eduardo Bonilla-Silva, eds., *White Out: The Continuing Significance of Racism* (New York: Routledge, 2003).

12. Thanks to Joli Jensen for reminding me of "the united colors of Benetton." The fact that Barack Obama's "race speech" during the 2008 presidential campaign was seen by some in the media as radical reflects the unusualness of social justice discourse in the political arena. For a transcript of the speech, see *New York Times,* March 18, 2008. http://www.nytimes.com/2008/03/18/us/politics/18text-obama.html.

13. In *Racism without Racists,* Bonilla-Silva argues that the foundation of the ideology of color-blind racism is "abstract liberalism" (26, 28, 30). "The frame of *abstract liberalism* involves using ideas associated with political liberalism (e.g., 'equal opportunity,' the idea that force should not be used to achieve social policy) and economic liberalism (e.g., choice, individualism) in an *abstract* manner to explain racial matters. By framing race-related issues in the language of liberalism, whites can appear 'reasonable,' and even 'moral,' while opposing almost all practical approaches to deal with de facto racial inequality" (28). Bonilla-Silva's analysis gave me the idea for the label, "abstract inclusion," for the second discourse described in this chapter.

14. These students also told me that CU administrators were concerned about liability issues that could arise from student use of firearms, even off campus, if their activities were funded by the student government. An administrator confirmed that concern and told me about meeting with SFSR to clarify their activities.

15. Bonilla-Silva, *Racism without Racists,* 60–62.

16. Ibid., 63–66.

17. A program director in the Office of Student Affairs made a comment that reflected a different way of perceiving what Kane and other students experienced as an oversaturation of diversity talk: "It's sort of like you [students] absorb it whether or not you're really engaged because you hear the language [of diversity], you hear students talking about it, whether in student government, or in a classroom, or during programs. Even someone who's not really engaged [with diversity issues] on campus—it would be hard for them not to notice that there's a little more going on here at CU than at other universities."

18. Paul Berman, ed., *Debating P.C.: The Controversy over Political Correctness on College Campuses* (New York: Dell, 1992).

19. David Horowitz, *Indoctrination U: The Left's War Against Academic Freedom* (New York: Encounter Books, 2007), xiv.

20. Ibid., xiv.

21. Ibid., xiv. Horowitz created the organization, Students for Academic Freedom. http://www .studentsforacademicfreedom.org. In June 2008, the website listed 213 colleges and universities in the United States as having chapters.

22. Horowitz documents that controversy in *Indoctrination U*. For other points of view, see Melanie E. L. Bush, "The Movement for an 'Academic Bill of Rights': A New Assault on Academic Freedom," *North American Dialogue: Newsletter of the Society for the Anthropology of North America* 8 (April 2005): 16–19; Paul Krugman, "An Academic Question," *New York Times*, April 5, 2005, A23; and Yilu Zhao, "Taking the Liberalism Out of Liberal Arts," *New York Times*, April 3, 2004, B9.

23. See also Lesage et al., *Making a Difference*.

24. As I worked on this section, I was confused about the inclusion of "political affiliation" in the list of statuses that could qualify a student group as an advocacy organization. So I asked one of the administrators who advises the student government for clarification. My statements in the text are based on the adviser's explanations. The adviser also told me that a group of students organized around political freedom in Tibet *is* deemed an advocacy organization based on political affiliation.

25. Mitch Berbrier shows how activists in dissimilar social movements (gays; deaf people; white supremacists) aim "to replace a stigmatized status with a valued one by portraying their groups as resembling established minorities . . . and as differing from groups stigmatized as deviant. . . . Tactically, these minority status claims exploit both the resonance of cultural pluralism and state recognition of minorities" ("Making Minorities: Cultural Space, Stigma Transformation Frames, and the Categorical Status Claims of Deaf, Gay, and White Supremacist Activists in Late Twentieth Century America," *Sociological Forum* 17 [2002]: 553).

26. Horowitz, *Indoctrination U*.

27. Bonilla-Silva, *Racism without Racists,* 71.

28. Joli Jensen discusses the new humanism of the 1920s and the mass culture debates of the 1940s and 1950s as earlier forms of these political battles in which the nature of the university is on trial (*Is Art Good for Us? Beliefs about High Culture in American Life* [Lanham, MD: Rowman and Littlefield, 2002]). See also Donoghue, *The Last Professors*.

29. Antonio and Muñiz, "The Sociology of Diversity," 279. See also, Berman, ed., *Debating P.C.*

## Chapter 3. Race in CU's Narrative Landscape

1. Http://www.umich.edu/news/Releases/2003/Juno3/supremecourt.html.

2. Antonio and Muñiz, "The Sociology of Diversity." See also, Patricia Gurin, Eric L. Dey, Sylvia Hurtado, and Gerald Gurin, "Diversity and Higher Education: Theory and Impact on Educational Outcomes," *Harvard Educational Review* 72 (2002): 330–66.

3. Raymond A. Winbush, "A Brief Meditation on Diversity and 'Duhversity,'" in *What Makes Racial Diversity Work*, 33. Winbush argues that a linguistic shift from talking about "race" to talking about "diversity" has helped push affirmative action efforts off center stage. I suspect that this shift also makes it possible for "diversity" to be treated as matters of abstract inclusion and political difference.

4. David Schuman, *Diversity on Campus* (Dubuque, IA: Kendall/Hunt, 2004).

5. William Labov, *Language in the Inner City: Studies in the Black English Vernacular* (Philadelphia: University of Pennsylvania Press, 1972), 363.

6. After my research at CU in the mid-2000s, I wrote a report for CU administrators that focused on students' perceptions of whether and where productive dialogue about diversity takes place at CU. Systematic analysis of my data made clear that students perceive RC as the most productive site of diversity dialogue on campus.

7. When my manuscript was being reviewed for publication, one reviewer asked whether other researchers on diversity in higher education have found a similar process on other campuses. I am not aware of any such research, but I wouldn't be surprised if similar processes do occur elsewhere.

8. Bonnie Thornton Dill, "Race, Class, and Gender: Prospects for an Inclusive Sisterhood," *Feminist Studies* 9 (1983): 131–50; Patricia Hill Collins, *Black Feminist Thought: Knowledge, Consciousness, and the Politics of Empowerment* (Boston: Unwin Hyman, 1990); Collins, *Black Sexual Politics*.

9. A faculty member who has served on the RC planning committee gave me this breakdown for one RC: of 46 students, 43 identified their race: 10 Asian Americans, 6 African Americans; 1 Latino; 6 biracial/multiracial; 20 white. Twenty-seven were attending for the first time; 9 for the second time; 6 for the third time, and 2 for the fourth time. Student facilitators were among those attending for the third and fourth times.

10. Charmaine L. Wijeyesinghe and Bailey W. Jackson III, eds., *New Perspectives on Racial Identity Development: A Theoretical and Practical Anthology* (New York: New York University Press, 2001); Vasti Torres, Mary F. Howard-Hamilton, and Diane L. Cooper, *Identity Development of Diverse Populations: Implications for Teaching and Administration in Higher Education* (San Francisco: Jossey-Bass, 2003).

11. Bonilla-Silva supports this idea in *Racism without Racists*, 71.

12. In *Two-Faced Racism,* Picca and Feagin discuss how white people internalize racist images, 245–46. In *Racetalk,* Myers discusses the racist image of black men as sexual predators of white women, 95–96, 115–17. In *Black Sexual Politics,* Collins discusses the history of this controlling image of black men, 63–64, 102–3, 152–53, 221–22.

13. This all-day conference was attended primarily by CU staff and some students. CU requires staff to participate in ongoing diversity education.

14. Meyer et al., "Higher Education as an Institution," 211.

15. My description of this critique also draws on a white student's honors thesis in the mid-2000s. Her thesis focused on the history of CU's cultural diversity requirement and the mostly unsuccessful attempts to revise it since its creation in the late 1980s.

16. Bonilla-Silva points out that the ideology of color blindness allows people to claim they are not racist while rejecting practical efforts to redress the effects of long-term institutional racism (*Racism without Racists,* 28).

17. I only coded the student government's regular meeting minutes. I had access to some committee meeting minutes, such as these, but I did not code them since they were not kept as consistently as the minutes for the regular weekly meetings of the entire student government.

18. Faculty and staff also constructed race as the most prominent diversity category, but they tended to do so more indirectly than students. When I asked faculty and staff what diversity means at CU, they usually offered a list first, and then spoke more about race.

## Chapter 4. Learning to Speak

1. The two students who didn't bring up diversity issues spontaneously were struggling with serious personal problems, which dominated their narratives.

2. David A. Karp, Lynda Lytle Holmstrom, and Paul S. Gray, "Leaving Home for College: Expectations for Selective Reconstruction of Self," *Symbolic Interaction* 21 (1998): 265.

3. Peter Kaufman and Kenneth A. Feldman, "Forming Identities in College: A Sociological Approach," *Research in Higher Education* 45 (2004): 463–96.

4. In this chapter I use the term *personal narrative* to refer to a first-person account where the speaker is a protagonist in the action, either as actor or interested observer.

5. Gubrium and Holstein, *Analyzing Narrative Reality;* Riessman, *Narrative Methods.*

6. Melanie Walker makes a similar argument in "Rainbow Nation or New Racism? Theorizing Race and Identity Formation in South African Higher Education," *Race, Ethnicity, and Education* 8 (2005): 129–46.

7. Riessman, *Narrative Methods.*

8. It is not unusual for Asian American college students to narrate struggles with their racial

identities in childhood, adolescence, and in college. See Andrew Garrod and Robert Kilkenny, eds., *Balancing Two Worlds: Asian American College Students Tell Their Life Stories* (Ithaca: Cornell University Press, 2007).

9. Jean Kim, "Asian American Identity Development Theory," in *New Perspectives on Racial Identity Development*, 74–75.

10. Upward Bound's website is http://www.ed.gov/programs/trioupbound/index.html.

11. In *Women without Class: Girls, Race, and Identity* (Berkeley: University of California Press, 2003), Julie Bettie writes about working-class Mexican American girls who lack middle-class cultural capital and get tracked into expensive and useless business school after high school. She offers tentative explanations of those few girls who make it to the college track: some have helpful older siblings and some are exceptionally motivated because they have watched their older brothers cause their parents grief. Kia mentions aunts who are only a few years older than herself and who managed to make it to college, but they barely figure in her narrative.

12. Laurel Richardson defines "collective stories" as those that connect an individual's story to the broader story of a marginalized social group ("Narrative and Sociology," *Journal of Contemporary Ethnography* 19 [1990]: 116–35). See also Lillian Faderman (with Ghia Xiong), *I Begin My Life All Over: The Hmong and the American Immigrant Experience* (Boston: Beacon, 1998).

13. A Better Chance's website is http://www.abetterchance.org/.

14. Chesler et al., *Challenging Racism;* Lesage et al., *Making a Difference,* 73–78.

15. Having to educate white students (and professors), over and over, about the same racial issues, is a theme in studies of students of colors' experiences on campus. See David Stark and Jerlena D. Griffin, eds., *Facing You, Facing Me: Race, Class, and Gender among U.C. Berkeley Student Leaders* (Berkeley: Stiles Hall, 2001); Lesage et al., *Making a Difference;* Chesler et al., *Challenging Racism;* Helen Fox, *"When Race Breaks Out": Conversations about Race and Racism in College Classrooms* (New York: Peter Lang, 2007).

16. When a participant in the fishbowl feels they need a break, they can signal that they are ready to be replaced by someone in the larger circle outside the fishbowl. Those in the larger circle listen silently to the dialogue in the fishbowl.

17. Myers analyzes this stereotype as an updated version of "the black matriarch." In the contemporary version, the black woman is viewed as "loud, obnoxious, disrespectful, and ungrateful for all that she is given. She is an uppity black woman with an attitude" (*Racetalk,* 105). See also, Ahmed, "Embodying Diversity"; and Taylor, "Anger Privilege."

18. Collins, *Black Sexual Politics,* 350.

19. Lesage et al., *Making a Difference,* 205.

20. Cheryl Townsend Gilkes, "Going Up for the Oppressed: The Career Mobility of Black Women Community Workers," *Journal of Social Issues* 39 (1983): 115–39; Collins, *Black Feminist Thought,* 156–60.

21. On the erasure of discourse about class, see Bettie, *Women Without Class;* Correspondents of the *New York Times,* intro by Bill Keller, *Class Matters* (New York: Henry Holt, 2005); and Kris Paap, *Working Construction: Why White Working-Class Men Put Themselves—and the Labor Movement—in Harm's Way* (Ithaca: Cornell University Press, 2006).

22. Collins, *Black Feminist Thought;* Patricia Hill Collins, *Fighting Words: Black Women and the Search for Justice* (Minneapolis: University of Minnesota Press, 1998).

23. During my group interview with the Southeast Asian Association, Kia and May told me about a panel discussion they had recently participated in (with other SAA members) at the Hmong National Development conference. Their contribution was about the continued persecution of Hmong people in Southeast Asia, and they told me that two hundred people were at their session. This national conference, then, is another context in which Kia has taken up the opportunity to speak publicly and authoritatively about social justice issues.

24. Ernest T. Pascarella and Patrick T. Terenzini, *How College Affects Students. Vol. 2, A Third Decade of Research* (San Francisco: John Wiley and Sons, 2005), 187–98.

## Chapter 5. Learning to Listen

1. Hannah is talking about racism as nonconscious prejudice. This is an example of the type of attitude studied by Project Implicit, an ongoing investigation by researchers at Harvard University, University of Virginia, and University of Washington. See https://implicit.harvard .edu/implicit/.

2. Steven is one of the diverse group of fourteen men who published an article in the student newspaper inviting others to join their informal group, Men Against Sexism (see chapter 3).

3. Mark Freeman, "Narrative and Relation: The Place of the Other in the Story of the Self," in *The Meaning of Others: Narrative Studies of Relationships*, ed. Ruthellen Josselson, Amia Lieblich, and Dan P. McAdams (Washington, DC: American Psychological Association, 2007), 11.

4. My finding supports George Yancey's argument that contact in itself doesn't necessarily affect white people's attitudes toward people of color. He states, "Contact that is egalitarian, intimate, voluntary, and cooperative and is supported by relevant authority figures is most likely to produce alterations in a person's racial attitudes" (*Interracial Contact and Social Change* [Boulder, CO: Lynne Rienner, 2007], 25). In a similar but more general vein, Pascarella and Terenzini write, "The student-peer contacts that matter most appear to be those that expose the student to diverse racial, cultural, social, value, and intellectual perspectives. That is, students derive the greatest developmental benefits from engagement in *peer networks* that expose them to individuals different from themselves. Net of confounding influences, interactions with diverse peers have modest but consistently positive impacts on knowledge acquisition, dimensions of cognitive development such as critical thinking and complexity of thought, principled moral reasoning, and self-rated job skills after college" (*How College Affects Students,* 615, emphasis added).

5. McKinney also tells of white students learning from students of color's stories (*Being White,* 200).

6. Gubrium and Holstein write, "Researchers should bear in mind that storytelling is a complex process that responds to multiple layers of resources and varied forms of narrative influence, contest, struggle, and control. . . . As important as they are in setting the narrative stage, narrative environments do not fully dictate narrative practice" (*Analyzing Narrative Reality,* 183).

## Chapter 6. Creating a Voice of Protest

1. I did not interview Professor Thomas. I read his account of events in the student newspaper.

2. Fox, "*When Race Breaks Out*"; Stark and Griffin, eds., *Facing You;* Chesler et al., *Challenging Racism;* Lesage et al., *Making a Difference;* Willie, *Acting Black;* Rhoads, *Freedom's Web;* Beverly Daniel Tatum, *Can We Talk about Race?* (Boston: Beacon, 2007).

3. Chesler et al. describe a continuum of strategies for achieving organizational change. The silent rally lies toward the end of the continuum they call "pressure strategies." The other end of the continuum consists of "persuasive strategies," which include educational events such as those sponsored by CU's student of color organizations. The Activists' official document lies in the middle as a "mixed strategy," as a combination of the "presentation of grievances" and "proposed solutions" (*Challenging Racism,* 177).

4. Similarly, Wong discusses a coalition of five groups of students of color—Students of Color Building Bridges—at the University of Oregon ("A Historical Look," 146).

5. Through an innovative seminar on interracial dialogue at U.C. Berkeley, students of color have experienced a similar realization that despite their racial differences they are all fighting unjust stereotypes (Stark and Griffin, eds., *Facing You,* 5–6).

6. Collins analyzes the racist and sexist implications of the term *black bitch* (*Black Sexual Politics,* 130).

7. In *The Racial Middle: Latinos and Asian Americans Living Beyond the Racial Divide*

(New York: New York University Press, 2008), Eileen O'Brien shows that whether and how people of color make connections across racial lines depends on various circumstances.

8. This need is well-recognized in the literature on diversity issues in higher education. See Tatum, *Can We Talk About Race?* 114–17; and Frank W. Hale, Jr., "Appendix: Hale's Inventory for Assessing an Institution's Commitment to Multicultural Programming," in *What Makes Racial Diversity Work,* 308.

9. Buttny found that African American students' demand for respect was a major theme in their accounts of what goes wrong in interracial relations, especially in public settings such as shops and stores. The students in his study distinguished being respected from being liked (*Talking Problems,* 147). This distinction, although not made explicit by the Black Collegians, resonates in their talk.

10. The idea that white people benefit from education about race and racism is a theme in studies of white privilege. Kendall, *Understanding White Privilege;* Tim Wise, *White Like Me: Reflections on Race from a Privileged Son* (Brooklyn, NY: Soft Skull Press, 2008); Diane J. Goodman, *Promoting Diversity and Social Justice: Educating People from Privileged Groups* (Thousand Oaks, CA: Sage, 2001). Similarly, in *Cultivating Humanity,* Nussbaum argues that racial and ethnic studies, women's studies, and sexuality studies are for *all* students.

11. In the following, Peter Lyman is writing about the role of anger in political dialogue in general, but he could just as easily be talking about diversity dialogue on campus: "The anger of the powerless is an essential voice in politics, not least because angry speech contains a claim that an injustice has been committed. When anger is taken seriously as a communication, rather than as psychological disorder or uncivil behavior, a spirited but ultimately constructive public dialogue about the justice of the dominant political order is possible" ("The Domestication of Anger: The Use and Abuse of Anger in Politics," *European Journal of Social Theory* 7 [2004]: 133).

12. Antonio and Muñiz, "The Sociology of Diversity," 284.

13. In an effort to pressure the administration to improve campus conditions for minority students, students of color at the University of Oregon threatened to withdraw their assistance in recruiting new students and threatened to discourage alumni donations (Wong, "A Historical Look," 146).

14. Willie reports that black students at Northwestern University expressed a similar sense of "two worlds" (*Acting Black,* 46). This metaphor may be interpreted as an extreme statement that others are meant to take seriously (see Charles Antaki, "The Uses of Absurdity," in *Analyzing Race Talk,* 92). Scholars have used similar metaphors to describe race relations more generally; for example, Andrew Hacker, *Two Nations: Black and White, Separate, Hostile, Unequal* (New York: Scribner, 1992).

15. At the cultural diversity forum statements such as the following were made: the cultural diversity requirement can be fulfilled without taking any course that specifically addresses race; the requirement fails to live up to CU's cultural diversity policy (which states that the university is committed to educating everyone on campus about sexism, racism, and heterosexism); courses that fulfill the requirement do not always do what they promise to do; the process by which courses get included in the cultural diversity list needs to be examined; cultural diversity courses need to be evaluated in specific ways; the low student response rate on course evaluations is a problem; tenured faculty can choose not to have their courses evaluated; when faculty don't address diversity issues in classes, the burden falls to students of color; professors are educated in their fields but not about how to teach; and very few faculty attend student of color events. And many questions got raised: what kind of professional development is available to faculty? Are faculty expected to engage in professional development regarding diversity? How are faculty held accountable for their teaching? What role do students play in holding faculty accountable? What incentives, resources, and support are given to the faculty for diversifying their courses? What is the relationship between academic freedom and the need for diversification of the curriculum? Why is the staff required to undergo diversity education while the faculty is not?

16. Chesler et al., *Challenging Racism,* 115; Buttny, *Talking Problems,* 114.

17. Before the end of the semester, the Faculty Diversity Group responded to Dr. Miller's

memo with an ambitious three-year faculty development plan, with a price tag of more than $200,000. The plan included ideas for addressing diversity-related topics at the annual faculty retreat; creating new faculty and staff reading groups on diversity issues; creating an annual summer institute for faculty development on diversity that would serve faculty at CU as well as other institutions; and getting the development office to find a grant to fund all of the above.

## Chapter 7. Walking on Eggshells

1. Antaki, "The Uses of Absurdity," 94.

2. Collins, *Black Sexual Politics*, 350.

3. As Mr. Robert continued here, he said this demonization of black people, under certain circumstances, can get extended to white people as well. "When I develop a relationship with white students to the point where we can joke about their place in racial justice work, I tell them, 'You're going to be treated like a black person.' In fact there was a young white man that I had that conversation with about three months ago. 'So now that you're at this spot and now that you're taking this opportunity and now that you're challenging other white people, you're going to be treated as if you're black.' And he sort of laughed it off, but I think he got it. That again, black people are demonized and that gets extended to others who make us uncomfortable." Interestingly, in *The Racial Middle*, O'Brien shows that in some contexts Latinos and Asian Americans get treated as if they are more black than white, and in some contexts, more white than black. And sometimes they resist this binary racial divide.

4. Antaki, "The Uses of Absurdity," 90–93.

5. I was not able to get the student government budget for the year that Dan is talking about—but I do have the budget for the next year. Thirty-nine percent of student organizations receiving student government funds that year were diversity-related (student of color organizations, the GLBT Organization, Women's Collective, Students for Disability Rights, etc). Those 39% of student organizations received 43% of student government funds. A closer look shows that 15% of organizations receiving funds were *race*-related and that *their* share of the budget was 22%. That certainly looks like a disproportionate share for student of color groups, but an even closer look shows that the disproportion is totally accounted for by one student of color group which had a very high budget for conference travel that year. That group was not the Black Collegians.

6. Ashley W. Doane argues that "white defensiveness can take the form of either overt expressions of white supremacy (as has occurred among the far right) or, more frequently, the subtle or even transparent (in terms of lack of awareness) use of whiteness as the 'mainstream' or unexamined center" ("Rethinking Whiteness Studies," in *White Out*, 15–16).

7. Myers found this racist discourse embedded in white people's everyday talk in private (that is, monoracial) settings (*Racetalk*, 106–8). See also, Michael K. Brown et al., *Whitewashing Race*.

8. As I worked on this chapter, I was surprised to find that little research has been published on how college newspapers deal with diversity issues. Examples from that sparse literature include Chiung Hwang Chen, "Internationalization of a College Newspaper: The Case of Ke Alaka'i," *Journalism and Mass Communication Educator* 59 (2004): 143–55; and Kathleen Woodruff Wickham, "An Examination of Diversity Issues in SE Journalism College Newspapers," *Newspaper Research Journal* 25 (2004): 103–9. When I asked Professor Collins about this, he concurred that the literature on diversity and college newspapers is sparse.

9. See Kathleen Woodruff Wickham, "Diversity Also Important for Campus Media," *Quill Magazine* 91 (August 2003): 30–31.

10. Bush, *Breaking the Code*; Trepagnier, *Silent Racism*.

11. My description of the Activists' complaints about the student newspaper comes from their official document, their conversations with me, and the journalists' conversation with me.

12. Professor Collins's accounts suggest that he is very involved with the student newspaper staff. He told me that as the paper's faculty adviser, he does not tell students what to write and he does not read and comment on each issue of the paper in its entirety before it is published. In chapter 6 we heard Mr. Davis, a senior administrator, comment on the independence of the

student newspaper and student government. He said that as a result of the Activists' protest, the question of how these organizations should be advised was now on the table.

13. Connie, a white student who was present at the meeting between the Activists and the journalists, said to me, "You may have seen the changes in the student newspaper—it's all because of our meeting, which is very exciting."

14. Chase, *Ambiguous Empowerment*, 51, 53, 55, 80–84.

15. Speakers typically listen to themselves through their audience's perspective, but sometimes we can *hear* a speaker taking into account what another might say in response. Following Mikhail Bakhtin, Jane H. Hill calls this "discourse with a sideward glance at the word of another" ("Review: The Refiguration of the Anthropology of Language," *Cultural Anthropology* 1 [1986]: 97).

16. Buttny, "Multiple Voices in Talking Race: Pakeha Reported Speech in the Discursive Construction of the Racial Other," in *Analyzing Race Talk*, 116.

17. Wetherell, "Racism and the Analysis of Cultural Resources," 19–21.

18. McKinney also finds these themes in the narratives of some white college students (*Being White*, 194, 200).

19. James A. Holstein and Jaber F. Gubrium, *The Self We Live By: Narrative Identity in a Postmodern World* (New York: Oxford University Press, 2000).

20. The Conservative Students' account provides a nice example of what Gubrium and Holstein call "intertextuality," the intersections between various narrative environments that get expressed in people's accounts (*Analyzing Narrative Reality*, chapter 15).

## Chapter 8. Doing the Work of Allies

1. Peggy McIntosh, "White Privilege: Unpacking the Invisible Knapsack," in *Race, Class, and Gender: An Anthology,* ed. Margaret L. Andersen and Patricia Hill Collins, 5th ed. (Belmont, CA: Thompson/Wadsworth, 2004), 103–8.

2. Kendall, *Understanding White Privilege,* 128.

3. Myers makes a similar point in *Racetalk,* 4.

4. Kendall, *Understanding White Privilege,* 128. See also, Bush, *Breaking the Code.*

5. Bailey W. Jackson III, "Black Identity Development: Further Analysis and Elaboration," in *New Perspectives on Racial Identity Development,* 22. Similarly, in "Asian American Identity Development Theory," Jean Kim describes stage three, "awakening to social political consciousness," as a time when "White people become the antireferent group, people they don't want to be like" (in *New Perspectives on Racial Identity Development,* 77).

6. See McKinney, *Being White,* chapter 5.

7. Chesler et al., *Challenging Racism,* 177.

8. As in chapter 5, we see "relational thinking" in these students' narratives (Freeman, "Narrative and Relation," 11–19).

9. McKinney, *Being White,* 212. See also Paul Kivel, *Uprooting Racism: How White People Can Work for Racial Justice* (Gabriola Island, B.C.: New Society, 2002). For a discussion of white racial identities see Rita Hardiman, "Reflections on White Identity Development Theory," in *New Perspectives on Racial Identity Development,* 108–28.

10. The way these white students draw on narrative resources provided by CU's interconnected group, NCORE, and antiracism groups in the city provides another example of "intertextuality" (Gubrium and Holstein, *Analyzing Narrative Reality,* chapter 15).

## Reflections

1. Pascarella and Terenzini, *How College Affects Students,* 608–18.

2. Fox, "*When Race Breaks Out*"; Bonnie Tusmith and Maureen T. Reddy, eds., *Race in the College Classroom: Pedagogy and Politics* (New Brunswick, NJ: Rutgers University Press, 2002); Mathew L. Ouellett, ed., *Teaching Inclusively: Resources for Course, Department, and Institutional Change in Higher Education* (Stillwater, OK: New Forums Press, 2005). Some

books include both under one cover, but not in the same chapter (Hale, Jr., ed., *What Makes Racial Diversity Work;* Chesler et al., *Challenging Racism*).

3. Bush, *Breaking the Code,* 245.

4. Wong, "A Historical Look at Students of Color at the University of Oregon, in *Making a Difference,* 149.

5. Leonard A. Valverde and Louis A. Castenell, Jr., eds., *The Multicultural Campus: Strategies for Transforming Higher Education* (Walnut Creek, CA: AltaMira, 2000). Also, Abby L. Ferber and Donna Wong, "Conclusion: This is Only the Beginning," in *Making a Difference,* 178–79.

6. Chesler et al., *Challenging Racism,* 255.

7. Pascarella and Terenzini, *How College Affects Students,* 647.

8. Lesage et al., *Making a Difference,* xi. The film is *In Plain English.*

9. Stark and Griffin, eds., *Facing You;* Garrod and Kilkenny, eds., *Balancing Two Worlds;* Lesage et al., *Making a Difference;* Greg Tanaka, *The Intercultural Campus: Transcending Culture and Power in American Higher Education* (New York: Peter Lang, 2003); Andrew Garrod, Robert Kilkenny, and Christina Gómez, eds., *Mi Voz, Mi Vida: Latino College Students Tell Their Life Stories* (Ithaca: Cornell University Press, 2007). Films include *Skin Deep* and *What's Race Got to Do With It?*

10. Nussbaum, *Cultivating Humanity,* 10–11. In 1999, the Association for American Colleges and Universities gave this book the Frederic W. Ness Book Award, for the Most Significant Contribution to Studies on Liberal Education. *Cultivating Humanity* has been described as both a "dispassionate defense of Socratic education and citizenship," and "a passionate, closely argued and classical defense of multiculturalism." http://www.hup.harvard.edu/catalog/NUSCUL.html?show=reviews.

11. Nussbaum, *Cultivating Humanity,* 9.

12. Lynn Weber Cannon, "Fostering Positive Race, Class, and Gender Dynamics in the Classroom," *Women's Studies Quarterly* 18 (1990): 126–34; Beverly Daniel Tatum, "Talking about Race, Learning about Racism: The Application of Racial Identity Development Theory in the Classroom," *Harvard Educational Review* 62 (1992): 1–24; Alison Roberts and Keri Iyall Smith, "Managing Emotions in the College Classroom: The Cultural Diversity Course as an Example," *Teaching Sociology* 30 (2002): 291–301.

13. Tatum, *Can We Talk about Race?,* 114–17; quote on 115.

14. Frank W. Hale, Jr., "Appendix: Hale's Inventory for Assessing an Institution's Commitment to Multicultural Programming," in *What Makes Racial Diversity Work,* 308.

15. Leah Wing and Janet Rifkin "Racial Identity Development and the Mediation of Conflicts," in *New Perspectives on Racial Identity Development,* 183.

16. Yancey, *Interracial Contact,* 25. Similarly, Shaun R. Harper and Stephen John Quaye emphasize "the importance of shifting the onus for engagement from students to educators and administrators" (*Student Engagement in Higher Education: Theoretical Perspectives and Practical Approaches for Diverse Populations* [New York: Routledge, 2009], 2).

17. Nicholas Sorensen, Biren Nagda, Patricia Gurin, and Kelly E. Maxwell present results of multi-university research that support the value of a model of intergroup dialogue for intergroup relationships, understanding, and collaboration ("Taking a 'Hands On' Approach to Diversity in Higher Education: A Critical-Dialogic Model for Effective Intergroup Interaction, *Analyses of Social Issues and Public Policy* 9 [2009]: 3–35).

18. Elizabeth Aries's study of first-year students at Amherst College looks at students' perspectives through both racial and class lenses (*Race and Class Matters at an Elite College* [Philadelphia: Temple University Press, 2008]). See also, Kathleen Cushman, *First in the Family: Advice about College from First-Generation Students* (Providence, RI: Next Generation Press, 2005). For a summary of research on low-income, first generation college students see Harper and Quaye, eds., *Student Engagement in Higher Education,* chapters 13 and 14.

19. For much of the twentieth century, labor unions, colleges, and universities developed special educational programs for workers (as distinct from traditional-age college students from working-class backgrounds). These programs were quite separate from the higher education offered to middle-class, upper-middle class, and wealthy students. See, for example, Joyce L. Korn-

bluh and Mary Frederickson, eds., *Sisterhood and Solidarity: Workers' Education for Women, 1914–1984* (Philadelphia: Temple University Press, 1984).

20. Dana Jennings, "A Second Home for First-Gens," *New York Times,* July 26, 2009, Education Life, 14. Thanks to Joli Jensen for drawing my attention to this article.

21. Ibid., 32.

## Appendixes

1. Riessman, *Narrative Methods,* chapter 2; Gubrium and Holstein, *Analyzing Narrative Reality,* chapter 8.

2. Susan E. Chase, "Narrative Inquiry: Multiple Lenses, Approaches, Voices," in *Handbook of Qualitative Research,* 3rd ed., ed. Norman K. Denzin and Yvonna S. Lincoln (Thousand Oaks, CA: Sage, 2005), 660–62.

# Selected References

Ahmed, Sara. "Embodying Diversity: Problems and Paradoxes for Black Feminists." *Race, Ethnicity, and Education* 12 (2009): 41–52.

Antaki, Charles. "The Uses of Absurdity." In *Analyzing Race Talk: Multidisciplinary Perspectives on the Research Interview,* edited by Harry van den Berg, Margaret Wetherell, and Hanneke Houtkoop-Steenstra, 85–102. New York: Cambridge University Press, 2003.

Antonio, Anthony Lising, and Marcela M. Muñiz. "The Sociology of Diversity." In *Sociology of Higher Education: Contributions and Their Contexts,* edited by Patricia J. Gumport, 266–94. Baltimore: The Johns Hopkins University Press, 2007.

Aries, Elizabeth. *Race and Class Matters at an Elite College.* Philadelphia: Temple University Press, 2008.

Bell, Susan E. *DES Daughters: Embodied Knowledge and the Transformation of Women's Health Politics.* Philadelphia: Temple University Press, 2009.

Berbrier, Mitch. "Making Minorities: Cultural Space, Stigma Transformation Frames, and the Categorical Status Claims of Deaf, Gay, and White Supremacist Activists in Late Twentieth Century America." *Sociological Forum* 17 (2002): 553–91.

——. "The Diverse Construction of Race and Ethnicity." In *Handbook of Constructionist Research,* edited by James A. Holstein and Jaber F. Gubrium, 567–91. New York: Guilford, 2008.

Berger, Peter L., and Thomas Luckmann. *The Social Construction of Reality: A Treatise in the Sociology of Knowledge.* New York: Anchor, 1967.

Berman, Paul, ed. *Debating PC: The Controversy over Political Correctness on College Campuses.* New York: Dell, 1992.

Best, Joel. "Historical Development and Defining Issues of Constructionist Inquiry." In *Handbook of Constructionist Research,* edited by James A. Holstein and Jaber F. Gubrium, 41–64. New York: Guilford, 2008.

Bettie, Julie. *Women without Class: Girls, Race, and Identity.* Berkeley: University of California Press, 2003.

Blum, Alan, and Peter McHugh. *Self-Reflection in the Arts and Sciences*. Atlantic Highlands, NJ: Humanities Press, 1984.

Bonilla-Silva, Eduardo. *Racism without Racists: Color-Blind Racism and the Persistence of Racial Inequality in the United States*. Lanham, MD: Rowman and Littlefield, 2003.

Bowen, William G., and Derek Bok. *The Shape of the River: Long-term Consequences of Considering Race in College and University Admissions*. Princeton: Princeton University Press, 2000.

Brown, Michael K., et al. *Whitewashing Race: The Myth of a Color-blind Society*. Berkeley: University of California Press, 2005.

Burke, Kenneth. *Language as Symbolic Action: Essays on Life, Literature, and Method*. Berkeley: University of California Press, 1966.

Bush, Melanie E. L. *Breaking the Code of Good Intentions: Everyday Forms of Whiteness*. Lanham, MD: Rowman and Littlefield, 2004.

Buttny, Richard. "Multiple Voices in Talking Race: Pakeha Reported Speech in the Discursive Construction of the Racial Other." In *Analyzing Race Talk: Multidisciplinary Perspectives on the Research Interview,* edited by Harry van den Berg, Margaret Wetherell, and Hanneke Houtkoop-Steenstra, 103–18. New York: Cambridge University Press, 2003.

——. *Talking Problems: Studies of Discursive Construction*. Albany: State University of New York Press, 2004.

Chase, Susan E. *Ambiguous Empowerment: The Work Narratives of Women School Superintendents*. Amherst: University of Massachusetts Press, 1995.

——. "Narrative Inquiry: Multiple Lenses, Approaches, Voices." In *Handbook of Qualitative Research,* 3rd ed., edited by Norman K. Denzin and Yvonna S. Lincoln, 651–79. Thousand Oaks, CA: Sage, 2005.

Chesler, Mark, Amanda Lewis, and James Crowfoot. *Challenging Racism in Higher Education: Promoting Justice*. Lanham, MD: Rowman and Littlefield, 2005.

Clandinin, D. Jean, ed. *Handbook of Narrative Inquiry: Mapping a Methodology*. Thousand Oaks, CA: Sage, 2007.

Collins, Patricia Hill. *Black Feminist Thought: Knowledge, Consciousness, and the Politics of Empowerment*. Boston: Unwin Hyman, 1990.

——. *Black Sexual Politics: African Americans, Gender, and the New Racism*. New York: Routledge, 2004.

Cook, Bryan J., and Diana I. Córdova. *Minorities in Higher Education: Twenty-second Annual Status Report*. Washington, DC: American Council on Education, 2006.

Dill, Bonnie Thornton. "Race, Class, and Gender: Prospects for an Inclusive Sisterhood." *Feminist Studies* 9 (1983): 131–50.

Doane, Ashley W., and Eduardo Bonilla-Silva, eds. *White Out: The Continuing Significance of Racism*. New York: Routledge, 2003.

Donoghue, Frank. *The Last Professors: The Corporate University and the Fate of the Humanities*. Bronx, NY: Fordham University Press, 2008.

Feagin, Joe R., Hernan Vera, and Nikitah Imani. *The Agony of Education: Black Students at White Colleges and Universities*. New York: Routledge, 1996.

Ferber, Abby L., and Donna Wong. "Conclusion: This is Only the Beginning." In

*Making a Difference: University Students of Color Speak Out,* edited by Julia Lesage et al., 176–202. Lanham, MD: Rowman and Littlefield, 2002.

Fish, Stanley. "The Last Professor." *New York Times* blog, January 18, 2009. http://fish.blogs.nytimes.com/2009/01/18/the-last-professor/.

Fox, Helen. *"When Race Breaks Out": Conversations about Race and Racism in College Classrooms.* New York: Peter Lang, 2007.

Freeman, Jo, and Victoria Johnson, eds. *Waves of Protest: Social Movements since the Sixties.* Lanham, MD: Rowman and Littlefield, 1999.

Freeman, Mark. "Narrative and Relation: The Place of the Other in the Story of the Self." In *The Meaning of Others: Narrative Studies of Relationships,* edited by Ruthellen Josselson, Amia Lieblich, and Dan P. McAdams, 11–19. Washington, DC: American Psychological Association, 2007.

Garfinkel, Harold. *Studies in Ethnomethodology.* Englewood Cliffs, NJ: Prentice Hall, 1967.

Garrod, Andrew, and Robert Kilkenny, eds. *Balancing Two Worlds: Asian American College Students Tell Their Life Stories.* Ithaca: Cornell University Press, 2007.

Garrod, Andrew, Robert Kilkenny, and Christina Gómez, eds. *Mi Voz, Mi Vida: Latino College Students Tell Their Life Stories.* Ithaca: Cornell University Press, 2007.

Gubrium, Jaber F., and James A. Holstein. *Analyzing Narrative Reality.* Thousand Oaks, CA: Sage, 2009.

Gurin, Patricia, Eric L. Dey, Sylvia Hurtado, and Gerald Gurin. "Diversity and Higher Education: Theory and Impact on Educational Outcomes." *Harvard Educational Review* 72 (2002): 330–66.

Hale, Jr., Frank W., ed. *What Makes Racial Diversity Work in Higher Education: Academic Leaders Present Successful Policies and Strategies.* Sterling, VA: Stylus, 2004.

Hardiman, Rita. "Reflections on White Identity Development Theory." In *New Perspectives on Racial Identity Development,* edited by Charmaine L. Wijeyesinghe and Bailey W. Jackson III, 108–28. New York: New York University Press, 2001.

Harper, Shaun R., and Stephen John Quaye, eds. *Student Engagement in Higher Education: Theoretical Perspectives and Practical Approaches for Diverse Populations.* New York: Routledge, 2009.

Holstein, James A., and Jaber F. Gubrium. *The Self We Live By: Narrative Identity in a Postmodern World.* New York: Oxford University Press, 2000.

Horowitz, David, *Indoctrination U: The Left's War Against Academic Freedom.* New York: Encounter Books, 2007.

Jackson III, Bailey W. "Black Identity Development: Further Analysis and Elaboration." In *New Perspectives on Racial Identity Development: A Theoretical and Practical Anthology,* edited by Charmaine L. Wijeyesinghe and Bailey W. Jackson III, 8–31. New York: New York University Press, 2001.

Jensen, Joli. *Is Art Good For Us? Beliefs about High Culture in American Life.* Lanham, MD: Rowman and Littlefield, 2002.

Jepperson, Ronald L., and Ann Swidler. "What Properties of Culture Should We Measure?" *Poetics* 22 (1994): 359–71.

Karp, David A., Lynda Lytle Holmstrom, and Paul S. Gray. "Leaving Home for College: Expectations for Selective Reconstruction of Self." *Symbolic Interaction* 21 (1998): 253–76.

Kaufman, Peter, and Kenneth A. Feldman. "Forming Identities in College: A Sociological Approach." *Research in Higher Education* 45 (2004): 463–96.

Kendall, Frances E. *Understanding White Privilege: Creating Pathways to Authentic Relationships across Race.* New York: Routledge, 2006.

Kim, Jean. "Asian American Identity Development Theory." In *New Perspectives on Racial Identity Development: A Theoretical and Practical Anthology,* edited by Charmaine L. Wijeyesinghe and Bailey W. Jackson III, 67–90. New York: New York University Press, 2001.

Lesage, Julia, Abby L. Ferber, Debbie Storrs, and Donna Wong. *Making a Difference: University Students of Color Speak Out.* Lanham, MD: Rowman and Littlefield, 2002.

Maynes, Mary Jo, Jennifer L. Pierce, and Barbara Laslett. *Telling Stories: The Use of Personal Narratives in the Social Sciences and History.* Ithaca: Cornell University Press, 2008.

McAdams, Dan P., Ruthellen Josselson, and Amia Lieblich, eds. *Identity and Story: Creating Self in Narrative.* Washington, DC: American Psychological Association, 2006.

McKinney, Karyn D. *Being White: Stories of Race and Racism.* New York: Routledge, 2005.

Meyer, John W., Francisco O. Ramirez, David John Frank, and Evan Schofer. "Higher Education as an Institution." In *Sociology of Higher Education: Contributions and Their Contexts,* edited by Patricia J. Gumport, 187–221. Baltimore: The Johns Hopkins University Press, 2007.

Mishler, Elliot G. "Representing Discourse: The Rhetoric of Transcription." *Journal of Narrative and Life History* 1 (1991): 255–80.

Myers, Kristen. *Racetalk: Racism Hiding in Plain Sight.* Lanham, MD: Rowman and Littlefield, 2005.

Nussbaum, Martha C. *Cultivating Humanity: A Classical Defense of Reform in Liberal Education.* Cambridge: Harvard University Press, 1997.

O'Brien, Eileen. *The Racial Middle: Latinos and Asian Americans Living Beyond the Racial Divide.* New York: New York University Press, 2008.

Olzak, Susan, and Nicole Kangas. "Ethnic, Women's, and African American Studies Majors in U.S. Institutions of Higher Education." *Sociology of Education* 81 (2008): 163–88.

Ouellett, Mathew L., ed. *Teaching Inclusively: Resources for Course, Department, and Institutional Change in Higher Education.* Stillwater, OK: New Forums Press, 2005.

Paap, Kris. *Working Construction: Why White Working-Class Men Put Themselves—and the Labor Movement—in Harm's Way.* Ithaca: Cornell University Press, 2006.

Pascarella, Ernest T., and Patrick T. Terenzini. *How College Affects Students. Vol. 2. A Third Decade of Research.* San Francisco: John Wiley and Sons, 2005.

Picca, Leslie Houts, and Joe R. Feagin. *Two-Faced Racism: Whites in the Backstage and Frontstage.* New York: Routledge, 2007.

Rhoads, Robert A. *Freedom's Web: Student Activism in an Age of Cultural Diversity.* Baltimore: The Johns Hopkins University Press, 1998.

Richardson, Laurel. "Narrative and Sociology." *Journal of Contemporary Ethnography* 19 (1990): 116–35.

Riessman, Catherine Kohler. *Narrative Methods for the Human Sciences.* Thousand Oaks, CA: Sage, 2008.

Roberts, Alison, and Keri Iyall Smith. "Managing Emotions in the College Classroom: The Cultural Diversity Course as an Example." *Teaching Sociology* 30 (2002): 291–301.

Rojas, Fabio. "Social Movement Tactics, Organizational Change, and the Spread of African American Studies." *Social Forces* 84 (2006): 2147–66.

Rothenberg, Paula S., ed. *White Privilege: Essential Readings on the Other Side of Racism.* New York: Worth, 2002.

Schuman, David. *Diversity on Campus.* Dubuque, IA: Kendall/Hunt, 2004.

Schutz, Alfred. *Collected Papers I: The Problem of Social Reality,* edited and introduced by Maurice Natanson. The Hague: Martinus Nijhoff, 1967.

Sorensen, Nicholas, Biren Nagda, Patricia Gurin, and Kelly A. Maxwell. "Taking a 'Hands On' Approach to Diversity in Higher Education: A Critical-Dialogic Model for Effective Intergroup Interaction." *Analyses of Social Issues and Public Policy* 9 (2009): 3–35.

Stark, David, and Jerlena D. Griffin, eds. *Facing You, Facing Me: Race, Class, and Gender among U.C. Berkeley Student Leaders.* Berkeley: Stiles Hall, 2001.

Tanaka, Greg. *The Intercultural Campus: Transcending Culture and Power in American Higher Education.* New York: Peter Lang, 2003.

Tatum, Beverly Daniel. "Talking about Race, Learning about Racism: The Application of Racial Identity Development Theory in the Classroom." *Harvard Educational Review* 62 (1992): 1–24.

——. *Can We Talk about Race? And Other Conversations in an Era of School Resegregation.* Boston: Beacon, 2007.

Taylor, Tiffany. "Anger Privilege: Deconstructing the Controlling Image of the 'Angry Black Woman.'" Paper presented at the meetings of the American Sociological Association, 2004.

Trepagnier, Barbara. *Silent Racism: How Well-Meaning White People Perpetuate the Racial Divide.* Boulder, CO: Paradigm, 2006.

Tusmith, Bonnie, and Maureen T. Reddy, eds. *Race in the College Classroom: Pedagogy and Politics.* New Brunswick, NJ: Rutgers University Press, 2002.

Valverde, Leonard A., and Louis A. Castenell, Jr., eds. *The Multicultural Campus: Strategies for Transforming Higher Education.* Walnut Creek, CA: AltaMira, 2000.

Van den Berg, Harry, Margaret Wetherell, and Hanneke Houtkoop-Steenstra, eds. *Analyzing Race Talk: Multidisciplinary Perspectives on the Research Interview.* New York: Cambridge University Press, 2003.

Walker, Melanie. "Rainbow Nation or New Racism? Theorizing Race and Identity Formation in South African Higher Education." *Race, Ethnicity, and Education* 8 (2005): 129–46.

Weinberg, Darin. "The Philosophical Foundations of Constructionist Research." In *Handbook of Constructionist Research,* edited by James A. Holstein and Jaber F. Gubrium, 13–39. New York: Guilford, 2008.

Wetherell, Margaret. "Racism and the Analysis of Cultural Resources in Interviews." In *Analyzing Race Talk,* edited by Harry van den Berg, Margaret Wetherell, and Hanneke Houtkoop-Steenstra, 11–30. New York: Cambridge University Press, 2003.

Wijeyesinghe, Charmaine L., and Bailey W. Jackson III, eds. *New Perspectives on Racial Identity Development: A Theoretical and Practical Anthology.* New York: New York University Press, 2001.

Williams, Clarence G. "The MIT Experience: Personal Perspectives on Race in a Predominantly White University." In *What Makes Racial Diversity Work,* edited by Frank W. Hale, Jr., 74–92. Sterling, VA: Stylus, 2004.

Willie, Sarah Susannah. *Acting Black: College, Identity, and the Performance of Race.* New York: Routledge, 2003.

Winbush, Raymond A. "A Brief Meditation on Diversity and 'Duhversity.'" In *What Makes Racial Diversity Work,* edited by Frank W. Hale, Jr., 32–37. Sterling, VA: Stylus, 2004.

Wingfield, Adia Harvey. "The Modern Mammy and the Angry Black Man: African American Professionals' Experiences with Gendered Racism in the Workplace." *Race, Class, and Gender* 14 (2007): 196–212.

Wing, Leah, and Janet Rifkin. "Racial Identity Development and the Mediation of Conflicts." In *New Perspectives on Racial Identity Development,* edited by Charmaine L. Wijeyesinghe and Bailey W. Jackson III, 182–208. New York: New York University Press, 2001.

Wise, Tim. *White Like Me: Reflections on Race from a Privileged Son.* Brooklyn, NY: Soft Skull Press, 2008.

Wong, Donna. "A Historical Look at Students of Color at the University of Oregon." In *Making a Difference,* edited by Julia Lesage et al., 133–52. Lanham, MD: Rowman and Littlefield, 2002.

Yancey, George. *Interracial Contact and Social Change.* Boulder, CO: Lynne Rienner, 2007.

# Index

abstract inclusion discourse: conservative use of, 174, 177; cultural embeddedness of, 41, 65; defined, 33; reverse racism and, 213; social justice discourse critiqued through, 46–48; tensions with other discourses, 54–56; "we are all diverse" version, 43–46; "we are all people" version, 41–43, 107–8. *See also* color blindness

abstract liberalism, 265n13

Academic Bill of Rights, 50, 53–54, 56

academic freedom, 161–62, 164, 266n22

accessibility, 70–71, 77–78, 234, 258

"Active White Identification," 89

Activists (student protest group): anger of, 185, 190–92; black students conflated with, 171–72; critical self-examination by, 229; formation of, 1, 8, 139–41, 165–66, 198; listening to, 206; meetings conducted by, 206; membership of, 139; white students involved in, 3–4, 203–4, 211; white students' racial education and, 151

Activists' protest: administrative response to, 155–56, 162–64, 179, 202–3; community of color behind, 145–49, 154–55, 269nn4–5 (Ch. 6); CU cultural diversity requirement and, 21, 74, 139–41, 143, 171, 172; CU narrative environment and, 165–66; demands made in, 1, 2–3, 182, 184; divergent voice strategies used in, 144–45, 269n3 (Ch. 6); faculty response to, 156–62; GLBT rally compared to, 81–82; official protest document, 9, 142–44, 153, 155–56, 201–2, 269n3 (Ch. 6); public disappearance following, 187–90; silent rally, 1–2, 81–

82, 141–42, 181–82; student newspaper and, 181–82, 186–87; as voice, 141–45, 165–66, 183. *See also* silent rally, the Activists'

Activists' protest—white students' reactions: ambivalence, 179–94, 195–96; author's interviews about, 167; CU narrative environment and, 194–96; dismissal, 167–69, 194; hostility, 169–79, 194–96; wide range of, 167; WSRR and, 220

advocacy organizations: budgets of, 271n5; cultural diversity policy and, 52–53; defined, 24, 53; educational events required of, 151; interconnections of, 223; narratives of students involved in, 88; "political affiliation" as status qualification for, 266n24; social justice discourse and, 53, 54–55. *See also specific organization*

affirmative action, 19, 266n3

African American men, 117–18

African American students, 171, 172, 208–9, 226, 263n3, 270n9, 271n3

African American studies, 264n6. *See also* racial-ethnic studies

African American women, 147, 269n6 (Ch. 6)

African Student Association, 24, 76

Alan (GLBT student/resident adviser), 62, 167–69, 194

alcohol, 87–88

Amherst College, 273n18

Amnesty International, 45, 76

anger: of the Activists, 2–3, 141–42, 183–84, 187, 189–91; of black women, 105–8; in diversity dialogue, 71–72, 150–51,

detriment to, 170; student fees of, as supporting black programs, 174–76; student of color distrust of, 211–14; student of color interaction with, 210–11; students of color educational events unattended by, 108, 210–11; WSRR and education of, 199. *See also* Activists' protest—white students' reactions

White Students Resisting Racism (WSRR), 3–4, 62; antiracism work of, as allies, 203–18; author's meetings with, 10, 64–66, 197, 199; conceptual/emotional shifts made by, 203–6, 207–8, 212, 214–18; conservative students' view of, as "elitist," 220–21; CU narrative environment and, 218–21; educational role of, 199, 209–10; formation of, 197; goals of, 214–15; interconnections of, 197, 215; intertextuality in accounts of, 272n10; listening by, 197–98; Melanie joins, 127, 129; race self-education of, 215; RC attendance of, 208–10; as safe environment for race discussions, 207–8; student of color events attended by, 206–7; student of color trust of, 211–14; as support, 230; supportive public actions of, 198–203; as unchartered student organization, 25, 64; "voice" theme of, 204–5; "work" theme of, 205–6; zine published by, 9, 199, 201–2, 206, 217, 220–21

white supremacy, 175, 218, 271n6
Williams, Clarence G., 19
Willie, Sarah Susannah, 270n14
Wilson (CU professor), 158–59, 164
Winbush, Raymond A., 266n 3
Wing, Leah, 231
women: in CU diversity goals, 20; as oppressed group, 34
Women's Coalition, 111; author's meetings with, 10, 58–60, 117; budget of, 271n5; as chartered student organization, 24, 58; creation of, 21; CU support of, 233–34; events organized by, 24, 59; further diversity measures desired by, 234; interconnections of, 26; race as diversity issue for, 59–60
Women's History Month, 25, 59
women's movement, 19
women's studies, 19, 35, 111, 117, 264n6
women's suffrage movement, 262n8
Wong, Donna, 225, 264n10, 269n4 (Ch. 6)
"work, the," 36–39, 92, 106, 109, 110, 205–6
workers, special educational programs for, 273–74n19
working-class students, 90, 178, 234–35
World Aids Month, 76

Yancey, George, 231, 269n4 (Ch. 5)
Young (CU professor), 29, 160–61, 165